Jean Toomer and the Harlem Renaissance

Edited by
GENEVIÈVE FABRE
MICHEL FEITH

RUTGERS UNIVERSITY PRESS
New Brunswick, New Jersey, and London

Library of Congress Cataloging-in-Publication Data

Jean Toomer and the Harlem Renaissance / edited by Geneviève Fabre and Michel Feith.
p. cm.
Includes bibliographical references and index.
ISBN 0-8135-2845-3 (alk. paper) — ISBN 0-8135-2846-1 (pbk. : alk. paper)
1. Toomer, Jean, 1894–1967—Criticism and interpretation. 2. Toomer, Jean, 1894–1967. Cane. 3. Afro-Americans in literature. 4. Harlem Renaissance. I. Fabre, Geneviève. II. Feith, Michel, 1966–

PS3539.O478 Z685 2000
813'.52—dc21 00-025193

British Cataloging-in-Publication data for this book is available from the British Library

Manufactured in the United States of America

Contents

Acknowledgments

This book exists mainly thanks to the persons and institutions that helped us organize an international conference on the Harlem Renaissance in Paris in January 1998, thanks to the participants of the conference, all of whom are unfortunately not present in this collection, and thanks to the editors of the press, who have put great care in the preparation of this publication. We wish to express our gratitude to the University of Paris VII Denis Diderot, to staff, colleagues, and graduate students from our research laboratory and from many other French, European, and American universities, to the Centre d'Etudes Africaines-Américaines (CEAA), to the Florence Gould Foundation, to the Cultural Services of the U.S. Embassy in Paris, to the Rectorate of the University of Paris, and to the Institute of African Affairs of New York University.

Reference librarians of the National Humanities Center have provided us with documents at the initial stage of this project, and we also want to acknowledge the valuable contributions of librarians, archivists, and directors of collections who have given individual assistance to each contributor. It is not possible to name the many scholars and friends who have aided us. Our sincere thanks to all.

We have appreciated the suggestions and sustained support of Arnold Rampersad, Myra Jehlen, Manthia Diawara, and Werner Sollors in turning this project into a book and the careful attention each author has given to our queries and editorial remarks. We are also endebted to several persons for the practical help they gave us: Jeanine Lecourt for her careful handling of multiform administrative tasks regarding the Center for African American Research, Bénédicte Alliot for her helpful hints and support, Fatiha El Ghorri for her efficient use of web sites, Michel Fabre, Hélène Chabaille, and Giani Candusso for their contribution in typing the bibliography and formatting the text, and the staff of the Institut Charles V for the final printed version of the essays. We also would like to thank the staff at Rutgers University Press, especially Leslie Mitchner, our acquiring editor, and Ingrid Muller for skillful copyediting.

Chronology

1894 Nathan Pinchback Toomer (Jean Toomer) is born in Washington, D.C., the son of Nathan Toomer, a Georgian planter, and Nina Pinchback, daughter of Pinkney Benton Stewart Pinchback, a prominent Louisiana politician during Reconstruction.

1896 Nathan Toomer leaves his wife and child. Nina moves back to P.B.S. Pinchback's house in Washington. The boy is then named Eugene Pinchback by his grandparents.

1906 His mother remarries and moves first to Brooklyn, then to New Rochelle, where Eugene starts reading widely and discovers the literature of chivalry.

1909 Nina Pinchback dies. Her son returns to Washington to live with his grandparents, who, because of economic difficulties, are soon forced to leave their upper-middle-class white neighborhood for an interracial section of the city.

1910 The child goes to M Street (later called Paul Laurence Dunbar) High School. Reads Dickens and Shakespeare.

1914–1919 Graduates. 1914: Enrolls at the University of Wisconsin to study agriculture. Leaves a few months later. College years at different institutions. 1915: Massachusetts College of Agriculture, Amherst. 1916:

Lives in Chicago and enters the American College of Physical Training. Interest in social and political thought, socialism, and literature. Reads Shaw, Ibsen, Whitman, and Goethe. 1917: New York University. Enrolls at City College in 1918 to study law.

1919–1920 Reads widely, begins writing, and changes his name to Jean Toomer. Lives in New York, Greenwich Village; meets writers and critics Van Wyck Brooks, Witter Bynner, and Edwin Arlington Robinson; is interested in world religions, especially Buddhism. Reads French and Russian authors, but also Frost, Lewis, and Dreiser and publications like the *Nation* and the *New Republic*. Meets Waldo Frank through Lola Ridge, editor of *Broom*. Gets acquainted with Sherwood Anderson's work.

1921 For financial reasons, he goes back to Washington. Receives a small allowance for taking care of his grandparents. Starts working on a long poem, "The First American."

1921 (fall) Leaves his grandparents to take a temporary teaching position in Sparta, Georgia, at an agricultural and industrial institute. Sends a poem, "Georgia Dusk," to the *Liberator* and continues writing. Returns to Washington in November and almost completes the first part of *Cane*. Death of his grandfather in December, when he is finishing "Kabnis." Takes his grandfather's body back to Louisiana.

1922 Writes two plays, *Balo* and *Natalie Mann*. Returns to the South with Waldo Frank. Completes *Cane* in December. Publishes "Song of the Son" in *Crisis*, "Fern" in *Little Review*, "Storm Ending," "Nora," and "Harvest Song" in *Double Dealer*, and "Karintha" in *Broom*. Is introduced to New York literary circles. Meets Sherwood Anderson and Gorham Munson, then editor of *Secession*. Frank encourages him to collect his writings in a book and introduces him to his publishers, Boni and Liveright.

1923 In January, Boni and Liveright accept *Cane* for publication. *Balo* is produced by the Howard University Repertory Company. "Seventh Street" and "Kabnis" appear in *Broom*, "November Cotton Flower" is published in *Nomad*, and "Gum" appears in the *Chapbook*. *Cane* appears in October with a foreword by Waldo Frank and Toomer joins an informal brotherhood of writers, intellectuals, and critics, including Waldo Frank, Gorham Munson, Alfred Kreymborg, Allen Tate, Van Wyck Brooks, Matthew Josephson, and Kenneth Burke. He serves with Munson on the editorial board of *S3N*. Toomer becomes more involved with the teachings of Gurdjieff and decides to join his adepts.

1924 Spends the summer at Gurdjieff's Institute for the Harmonious Development of Man in Fontainebleau, near Paris, in France.

1925–1933 Works with the Gurdjieff Institute; leads workshops in New York, Chicago, and Portage, Wisconsin, where he conducts the Cottage Experiment from 1931 to 1932. Marries in October 1931 the novelist Margery Latimer; lives in Carmel, California, then Chicago. Visits Taos. His wife, Margery, dies a few days after the birth of their daughter, Margery. In September 1934 he marries Marjorie Content. They live in New York and soon move to Doylestown, Pennsylvania.

Toomer publishes "Easter" in *Little Review* (1925) and writes a response to Munson's essay "The Mechanics for a Literary 'Secession,'" a manifesto on contemporary aesthetics. "Mr. Costyve Duditch," "White Arrow," and "Reflections" appear in *The Dial* in 1929; second printing of *Cane* in 1927. *Balo* appears in Locke and Gregory's *Plays of Negro Life* (1927), and "York Beach" is published in *New American Caravan* (1929). His "Lettre d'Amérique" appears in *Bifur* in France. "Race Problems and Modern Society" is published in *Problems of Civilization*, edited by Baker Brownwell, in New York in 1929, and *Essentials* appears in Chicago in 1931. But Toomer fails to publish a book of stories written between 1924 and 1929 and some of the plays and novels he wrote during those years and in the 1930s. Among his major unpublished fictions of these years is "Transatlantic," written in 1929, which evokes his transatlantic journey in 1924 when he went to France; revised as " Eight Day World" in 1933, it is one of his longest pieces, whereas "Caromb" (1932) recalls the time spent in Carmel, California, and the racial incident and scandal his first marriage had created then. Only the long poem started in 1921 as "The First American" is published with a new title, "Brown River, Smile," in *Pagany* in 1932, and as "The Blue Meridian" in *The New Caravan* in 1936.

1936–1940 Toomer starts a new experiment in Doylestown, the Mill House experiment, but fails to carry it through.

1939 Takes his family on a pilgrimage to India. Interest in Edgar Cayce and in scientology.

1940s and 1950s Applies to join the Society of Friends in 1940. Writes for the *Friend's Intelligencer* and lectures. Publication of *An Interpretation of Friends Worship* and of *The Flavor of Man* in Philadelphia in 1947 and 1949, respectively. 1949: Interest in Jungian analysis; 1953: Renewed interest in Gurdjieff's work.

1950s and 1960s Long illness, frequent stays in a nursing home, and death on 30 March 1967 in Doylestown. Third printing of *Cane*.

Jean Toomer and the Harlem Renaissance

Tight-Lipped "Oracle"

Around and beyond Cane

GENEVIÈVE FABRE
MICHEL FEITH

THE MANY DEBATES that revolved around *Cane* and its author, Jean Toomer, are related to issues that were raised and much discussed in the 1920s. This was a time of "vicious modernism," intense experimentation, and artistic and literary activity when many small or bigger magazines and presses were intent upon publishing new writing, when writers and artists were attentive to one another, when several renaissances were blooming with their distinct circles, celebrities, sites, and manifestoes that were sometimes overlapping, clashing, or engaged in active interaction. In a decade framed by World War I and the Depression, everything had to be new and fast moving. New ideas and ideologies were tested: ideas about psychology, color and race, nationalism and identity, or more progressive political theories. Organizations like the National Association for the Advancement of Colored People (NAACP) took a new turn, new ones like Garvey's Universal Negro Improvement Association (UNIA) suddenly swept the stage, and scholarly research was conducted in many domains, thus nurturing social thinking at a time of postwar changes, even while racial violence raged in many cities. Intellectuals questioned new trends in modern civilization, worried about increased mechanization, and expressed their concerns about the spiritual damage caused by these mutations. Most importantly, artistic innovations or revolutions stormed the world on both sides of the Atlantic and raised the central questions of modernity and of the role and function of art in this swiftly moving age.

This volume attempts to show how Toomer was very much a man of his time: he was involved or immersed himself in many of these movements; emulating his uncle Bismarck's passion for knowledge, he read widely, from his early years—books, but also new journals and magazines; became acutely aware of current social, intellectual, and artistic issues; was intensely curious and eager to carry experiments into many domains; joined circles and groups; and was in contact with many leading minds and artists. Alternately admired and misunderstood, this man, who seems to have stood apart from his contemporaries, who followed a solitary path and took stands that went against the grain, belongs in many respects to both the Lost Generation and the Roaring Twenties, to the Harlem Renaissance and to the American modernist movement. He was both harbinger and follower, anticipating and heralding trends, yet was often perceived as a renegade or dissenter.

To this day Toomer remains a rather enigmatic figure. When in tune with the spirit of the era, keeping up with its tempo and moods, aware of its problems and promises, he seems to be one of its representative men. Interested in socialism, in cubism and modernist movements, as well as in the development of mind and body, he ventured into many trades and associations, was attracted to the folk spirit as well as to more elitist enterprises, suddenly encountered his Negro heritage and concurrently claimed his Americanness, or proudly delcared himself the first conscious member of a new, emerging race. He was eager to participate in his epoch and, in a word, to belong. He befriended many prominent artists and joined an avant-garde that attempted to negotiate a new equilibrium between organic life and a mechanical future, between the machine and the garden. He was painfully aware of the rise of xenophobia and racial violence and dreamed of a society where color would no longer be a stigma. Yet, in many ways, he was at odds with the times, torn between contradictory impulses and commitments, driven to take a rather singular and solitary course, and forced to clarify positions that were often puzzling or disconcerting.

It is especially rewarding to examine this rather elusive figure at a decisive moment, that of the publication of *Cane,* when he was forced to deal with situations that entrapped him in labels and also confronted him with the image in the mirror. We thought it was important to focus first on *Cane* itself and offer close readings of the text. These could help understand Toomer's place as a writer in these early twenties and that of *Cane* in the literary history of the era, a place that is being constantly debated. This assessment had also to take into consideration what Toomer wrote, in his correspondence and in his autobiographies, about the experience of writing *Cane,* about ways of reading it and about its reception and misreadings.

Toomer's writings "around" *Cane* receive here critical examination: at times suggestive and illuminating, they can also be misleading and contradictory and often do not do justice to the creativeness of the artist. His feelings about his work ranged from enthusiasm or confidence to distrust and perplexity, ending at times in denial and neglect. Born of many encounters—with the Negro folk spirit and soul and with the modern desert—*Cane* was also his swan song and the song of an end; artistically as well as spiritually, in 1923 he was ready to move in different directions. Although eager to be published in little avant-garde magazines, he was reluctant to be included in *The New Negro* (just as he was later opposed to figuring in Nancy Cunard's *Negro*); he was unwilling to be called a Negro writer, but blamed Waldo Frank for not taking into account the African American presence in his book *America*.

When the Harlem Renaissance was gathering momentum and its leaders were calling for a common effort to promote racial equality through the development ot art and letters, Toomer, who is now seen as one of its precursors, followed his own individual path. Although he had close relations with some New Negro writers, he seems to have had greater affinities with white authors (although he did exchange letters with McKay and Hughes). Many contributors here insist on Toomer's associations with white circles; the most often quoted names are those of Waldo Frank, Margaret Naumburg, Gorham Munson, and Sherwood Anderson, but we know he also met, among many other personalities, Van Wyck Brooks, Edwin Arlington Robinson, Hart Crane, and Kenneth Burke.

Toomer's place in the Harlem Renaissance has to be reconsidered even if he denied having strong connections with the movement. He may have been more implicated in it than has been usually assumed by those who saw him as a renegade, too marginal or eccentric to really belong there. Toomer's declarations—confidential or public—have often been misinterpreted or taken too literally; attention to his ideas and positions was, for a while, given precedence over examination of his work as a writer. Many essays in this volume attempt to give a more complete portrait of the artist: as one who knew the power and limits of "pure words," was experimenting with their kinetic, musical, or visual dimensions, and was very much aware of the trends of his time and of what other artists were doing; as a man also who was haunted by many unanswered questions and had conflicting loyalties. Toomer's ideas did find their way into *Cane;* there, they were expressed more indirectly, but with greater poetic density and complexity than in the pronouncements we find in his later writings.

Toomer's definition of his identity—as of mixed ancestry, blue blood, and as American—at a time when the term mulatto had disappeared from census forms and when curiosity for, or loathing of, anything Negro were intense, was somehow disconcerting. Yet his declarations were more properly affirmations than denials and forced attention on the composite ethnic makeup of most

Americans, as well as on the arbitrariness of boundaries and categories that defined individuals as either/or. He experienced at his own expense the difficulty of proclaiming oneself neither white nor black; this is most evident in his dealings with editors and the publishing world.

The pressure to be "tagged" was so great that he spent much time justifying his positions in often ambivalent pronouncements, but it never deterred him from his conviction that his approach and treatment must be first and foremost artistic, regardless of other considerations. The answer to the dilemma he faced (and with which the framers and actors of the Harlem Renaissance were also confronted) is to be found as much in a careful study of the *Zeitgeist* of the twenties as in an attentive reading of *Cane* and of Toomer's other writings. There is a need to place Toomer in the context of another renaissance—the emergence of a new racial discourse in the 1920s and 1930s reclassifying America into two colors only. The new biracialism strangely became the shared premise of both white supremacists and some New Negro activists and replaced the older, romantic equation of race and nation, to which Toomer was still attached. His famous retort to editors and publishers, "I am chiefly concerned with . . . a position above the hypnotic divisions of America into white and black," expresses his reaction to a period when a form of pluralistic nationalism was predicated on the belief that racial differences were a functional necessity. Several trends—the rise of racist theory, the Great Migration, the intensification of modern life—combined to entail irrevocable changes in American polity and in the handling of "darker peoples." It is against this background that one can best appreciate the boldness of Toomer's depiction of the black world—"jazzed, strident, modern."[1]

Yet, the debates on race did not go in one direction only: the rich interaction and exchanges that took place in the artistic and intellectual world led to challenging the definitions of identity through racial categories, even if in some cases the vogue for anything Negro and for African art was not immune from certain stereotypes. For Toomer the temporary solutions were found in his adhesion to schools of thoughts on the future of America or to political ideas or philosophical doctrines or groups. That made him shift constantly from one experiment in writing to another and try to combine these with experiments in living . What is fascinating about Toomer is movement—we are reminded here of the expression he used to describe Karintha in *Cane:* "Karintha running is a whir."[2] His explorations or pilgrimages may betray his dissatisfaction and instability or, by contrast, testify to his incessant quest "for harmonious development" or to his hunger for knowledge. If his involvement with the Village Renaissance, with the Progressive group that Waldo Frank introduced him to, with socialism, and with the Gurdjieff school have been studied, if his interest in scientology, in Jungian thought, or in Buddhism are sometimes mentioned, his association with the Society of Friends later in his life and his writings for the *Intelligencer* need to be further investigated. But one is struck by the fact that all his activities as reader and student, writer and lecturer, revolved round a few "essentials," as he would say: his preoccupation with body, mind, land, and soul. And they all converge in his primary engagement with art, his determination to find the most compelling and modern expressions to the ideas, thoughts, feelings, and emotions that his personal or collective experiences or experiments inspired in him. His enrollment in courses on physical training, dance, or agriculture nourished his fascination for body and soil and were inseparable from the other, more philosophical or intellectual teachings; and his conviction of the interrelatedness of all aspects of life, of the necessary struggle to keep it whole and save it from dislocation, from physical or spiritual destruction, founded his poetics. What seems most amazing and perplexing to us today, is that all this found its premature, prophetic, and most forceful expression in *Cane*, a work that appeared so early in his career and whose excellence he would never be able to surpass. Toomer's failure after *Cane* to meet the challenge he had then set for himself, in spite of the fact that he continued to write with the same dedication and obstinacy, has led biographers and critics to many speculations. It has encouraged us in this volume to look carefully at *Cane* as a landmark, a significant moment in Toomer's life and career as a writer, but also as a stepping stone for his activities beyond his early success. *Cane* and later writings mutually illuminate one another, just as *Cane* highlights, through its striking innovations, an epoch that teemed with artistic and intellectual creativity.

Cane is thus a work of unresolved tensions. Generally speaking, one of the main traits writing shares with myth is an attempt to "provide a logical model to solve a contradiction (an impossible task when the contradiction is real)."[3] This statement holds even truer for *Cane* and gives it a special place both in American modernism and in the Harlem Renaissance. *Cane* partakes of the "double-voicedness"[4] of African American literature, which finds its origin and inspiration in Western formal writing as well as in vernacular forms of expression. This ties in with the depiction of the African American "double-consciousness" that W.E.B. Du Bois made in his landmark work *The Souls of Black Folks* (1903).[5] Thus, the split in the work parallels that of the writer himself as an heir to more than one culture, several literary traditions, and many "races." The specificity of *Cane* in the context of the Harlem Renaissance lies in the widening of the split, which evolves into a state of formal fragmentation. The body of the work is "torn asunder" under the pressure of "unreconciled strivings." Toomer's book stages a radical breakup of the unifying principle of form. A mixture of poetry, prose vignettes, and short stories connected by a web of thematic echoes, it embodies a rare yoking together of two opposite strains, "high" and "low" modernism.[6]

Cane offers many clues to Toomer's questioning of the issue of race and identity, dramatizing it through many situations, and figuring it through an idiosyncratic grammar of motives, a multiplicity of personae and voices, and an intricate web of images. This haunting problem is clearly connected with the nature of the narrator(s) of *Cane*. Nellie McKay turns the poetic voice of the poems into an overall narrator, who becomes a reflection of the involvement of "Jean Toomer, artist" in the work. The underlying theme is therefore the creator's quest for reconciliation with, and expression of, African American culture. This progression follows a dialectical pattern: from the return of the (alienated) prodigal son in part 1 ("Song of the Son") to the depiction of the contradictions of urban life in part 2, to a rounding up of Black experience, brought about by the "poet emergent" at the end of "Kabnis."[7]

In contrast with N. McKay's interpretation, one might argue that the aesthetics of collage and the kaleidoscopic effect of a composition by fragments also apply to narrative instances, engendering a general polyphony, in which each piece creates its own voice. There is often a shift in enunciation within the stories: "Becky," for example, evolves from a third-person to a first-person narrative. Most of the sketches include the recurrent appearance of short passages in verse, fragments of songs whose origin remains ever mysterious: are they moments when the narrator breaks into song, collages of folk expressions obliquely commenting on the plot, or an illustration of the call-and-response pattern of traditional African American singing and storytelling? If the narrators of *Cane* do concur in composing a "portrait of the artist" of sorts, it must then be a cubist, syncopated type of portrait.

The cyclical, organic design of the book is an attempt to transcend the many contradictions that are staged in it. The divergences between North and South, the city and the country, men and women, body and soul are all symbolically related to that between black and white, and the latter does not hold, as evidenced by the generalized *métissage* that pervades the book as it pervades America. Induced by his interest in both Oriental philosophy and Gurdjieffian idealism to "renounce the idol of duality" (Ouspensky) in the perceptual, conceptual and political senses of these terms, Toomer made *Cane* redolent with transitional images and states so as to shape it into a rite and a site of passage, of passing into a more integrated vision of life.

Could one picture Toomer's world as one of gradations, variations along a continuum that deny the validity of polar opposites? Yet, even though they are constantly subverted, contradictions still exist; they constitute the structuring pattern of the work and, probably, of the mind behind it. There is neither fusion nor dialectical resolution. The clearest illustration of this unalleviated tension is the failure of all the encounters between men and women in the book. Love, as symbol of the harmonious conjunction of opposites, is strikingly absent from *Cane*. Operating in the twilight zone between the political, the existential, and the poetic, the unresolved tensions in the work might not be the mark of a refusal, on the part of Toomer, to acknowledge his "real" black self—since his very existence disproved the idea of clear-cut categories, racial and otherwise—but rather the product of a writer's excruciating sincerity.

If one looks beyond *Cane*, one sees how persistently Toomer came back to the same question to express his views of the modern social order. Although he got more involved with theoretical issues and tried to develop his own positive ideas of a new race, he never lost sight of the day-to-day, actual experience of those who faced the drawing of the color line. Noting "the deadlock existing in the American situation" in essays like "The Crock of the Problem" (1928) or "Race Problems and Modern Society"[8] (1929), he enumerates "all manners of aggressions, resistances, oppositions, oppressions, fears, prejudices, hatreds," not to speak of "stoning, burning of houses, riots and lynchings" (66).These experiences are overwhelmingly present in *Cane*, but treated more elusively and artistically and with greater and more incisive poetic irony.

Perhaps the greatest irony of Toomer's career is precisely the publication and the reception of *Cane* that set him on a long crusade "as a member of the new race." In 1929 he wrote, "Since the publication of *Cane*, my name has been included among those who are also called Negroes. So what I am now going to say will not only be contrary to the general tendency to locate people in racial groups but it will also disturb the notion about me which people have as a result of *Cane* and my connection with the Negro Art Movement. . . . I am at once of no one of the races and I am all of them. I belong to no one of them and I belong to all. I am, in a strict racial sense, a member of the new race."[9] The process of discovery, "transforming rejections to acceptances, denials to affirmation," at work in "The Negro Emergent" (1924) thus finds its more assertive expression in 1929 and continued till the end of his public career, when in 1949 he gave a William Penn keynote address in Philadelphia, "The Flavor of Man," which echoes his earlier indictment of American society, his famous "Letter from America."[10] Under the influence of Gurdjieff, which intrigued many scholars, but also that of Waldo Frank's circle and later of the Society of Friends, Toomer viewed himself more and more as a spiritual reformer and forsook some of his artistic endeavors, but never gave up writing.

"Harvest Song" already expresses Toomer's doubts about his work and literature in general. The oats are reaped, but not bound: *Cane*, in spite of the organic project and imagery, remains fragmented. The announcement of success is at the same time an acknowledgement of failure or, at least, of incompleteness. Art, which was supposed to bring wholeness, only reveals the finitude of the man and the creator: "I fear knowledge of my hunger" (Toomer, *Cane*, 71).

Immediately after *Cane* Toomer bartered his irresolution and internal chaos for philosophical certainties and discipline, and his subsequent writings bear this dogmatic imprint. *Cane* may well have been an immensely taxing exercise in "negative capability"—the ability, in Keats's words, to be "in uncertainties, mysteries, doubts, without any irritable reaching after fact and reason."[11] Such painful soul-searching is the key to the enduring life of the book, but at the same time the price was so high that Toomer could not persevere in this course: "In truth, [*Cane*] was born in an agony of internal tightness, conflict, and chaos. . . . Harvest Song, better than any other of the book's content, gives an idea of my state at that time. After finishing *Cane*, I swore that I would never again write a book at that price."[12]

"Harvest Song" dramatizes a failure to reconcile the opposites presented in "Kabnis" through Lewis's words: "Cant hold them, can you? Master; slave. Soil; and the overarching heavens. Dusk; dawn. They fight and bastardize you" (Toomer, *Cane*, 108–109). The deep-rooted ambivalence towards racial and cultural heritage, modern-day America, and artistic creation itself, which are so prominently featured in *Cane*, are never resolved. If *Cane* purports, as the epigraph has it, to be "oracular", it is a tight-lipped oracle, in which the hope for a revelation of ultimate truth and wholeness of being remains ever elusive.

Toomer's landmark book may have been oracular in at least one more way, pointing straight at the contemporary evolution of the "reception side" of his creation. Each work of art creates its own implied audience, which it might or might not actually find. According to Ross Posnock in his *Color and Culture*, the waning fame of writers like Toomer or Zora Neale Hurston toward the end of their lives and their inability to get their late production published was only partly due to the failing of their creative powers.[13] The real reason might have been the discrepancy between their attempts to transcend or erase racial categories and the publishing world's exclusive demand for stories that "featured Negro" (213). In this respect, the Toomer revival, which occurred at the height of the Black Arts movement and was part of a nationalistic drive for unearthing forgotten African American writers was as much of an ironic misunderstanding as the Boni and Liveright advertising campaign of the 1920s. Both privileged identity matters over more inclusive literary or social concerns.

Posnock detects a turn of the tide in the criticism of the 1990s, a move away from the essentialist remains of the identity politics of postmodern multiculturalism, toward a "post-identity" epistemology, a new cosmopolitanism taking its origins in the pragmatism of men like William James, W.E.B. Du Bois, and Alain Locke: "Refusing the paradigm of identity/difference, pragmatist pluralism escapes the circular logic of cultural pluralism: becoming a mirror image of what it sets out to repudiate—racialist, nativist thinking. These alleged enemies both fetishize difference" (24). Considering Toomer as an "antirace race man"(5), an intellectual and artist confronting the color line but refusing to accept the validity of its exclusivist logic, Posnock contends, might help clarify our appreciation of *Cane* and reevaluate his later writings. The author may at last have found the public he had attempted to create for himself. Yet again, more than the critics' attempt to uncover the last word of an artist's life and works, it is Toomer's complex and contradictory involvement in the intricacies of the identity question that makes him resonate with contemporary preoccupations and provides for infinite readings of his creations.

The present volume, originating from a conference held in Paris in January 1998, reflects the enduring interest in Toomer both in Europe—especially among young scholars from major universities—and in the United States, in a common effort to reassess his artistic and literary accomplishments and reexamine his ideological positions. The impression one received of the participants was that of innovative, challenging, stimulating give-and-take; it is this feeling of novelty and interest, born of the oral moment, that we would like to "put in writing."

The tensions and contradictions in *Cane* allow for an inexhaustible wealth of interpretations. The readings in this volume hope to expand the range of the Toomer critical canon, without claiming to define its limits.

Werner Sollors insists on Toomer's powerful contribution to the stream of modernism; he sets *Cane* and its author's intellectual and artistic itinerary in the aftermath of World War I and interprets it as an attempt to find literary expression for the dislocation that modernity had wrought in a bleak new urban world still not far from slavery. Sollors sees Toomer's mission as a search for spiritual unity and views the interrelatedness of fragmentation and quest for wholeness as the core structure of the book. The essay examines its movement and designs, its swift change of scenes, its orchestration of images, of narration and song, and its musical and rhythmic effects and shows how Toomer's stylistic choices are an expression of his refusal to endorse certain ideas on the racial divide. A lucid observer of the gradual "whitewashing" of African America—*Cane* was actually conceived as a swan song for the dying culture of the rural South—the writer was also confronted with the increasing racial polarization of life in the United States. Drawing attention to echoes of Brecht, T. E. Hulme, Stein, and Joyce and pointing out analogies with Eisenstein's film montage technique, the article confronts aesthetics with theoretical pronouncements and includes discussions of Toomer's little-known correspondence with J. McLure, Dubose Heyward, Nancy Cunard, Claude McKay, and Max Eastman, as well as his "post imagist collection of aphorisms," *Essentials* (1931), and his essay "Race Problems in America" (1929).

Complementing Werner Sollors's essay, George Hutchinson sees Toomer's work from a different perspective and emphasizes the way in which Toomer was able to abstract himself from the labels and guises imposed on him. Hutchinson examines Toomer's singular personal history, his early upbringing, his curiosity, his intellectual and literary development, and sporadic activities and, pointing to their incessant fluidity, he shows how there was direction and growth in all these movements. Toomer was a careful reader, an accomplished writer, a critical and enthusiastic observer and, Hutchinson insists, was confronted with the same issues as many of his contemporaries and shared their sentiments on these realities. The essay also looks at Toomer's correspondence and highlights the tension between his intuitions of what writing should be about and the situation he found himself in. Many other writers—one might think of Langston Hughes or Zora Neale Hurston—found themselves in the same predicament and vehemently claimed their right to pursue their activities regardless of pressures from editors or critics or theoreticians of race.

The unity of *Cane* largely depends on recurrent themes and imagery. Two contributors have focused on the transformative and performative power of symbols and, more specifically, of elemental symbols. Fluidity is the key word of Charles Yves Grandjeat's article. A close analysis of transitional topography and of a constant, alchemical transmutation of elements serves to support a vision of *Cane* as a rite and site of passage, of passing—not in the narrow racial sense, but on the more general level of a refusal of exclusive dichotomies. The intermediate hues of the dusk, of the color purple, tie in with a fluctuating symbolic landscape in which crossings and connections—railways, roads—are as prominent as separations. A rhetoric of circularity, displacement, and balancing, emphasized by doubly connecting images, transgresses the dividing line between poetics and politics, hinting at the fictional nature of ethnic categories. "Renouncing the idol of duality" might therefore also mean healing the past split in Toomer criticism between an ideological and a strictly literary perspective through an awareness of the interdependence of both dimensions in the book, as part of a "logic of symbolic integration as opposed to one of segregation."

Françoise Clary finds in water one of the keys to the author's inspiration. On the subjective level, the fluidity of water gives birth to echoing metaphors of a sensuous, variegated quality, allowing for the intuitive fusion of a complex experience with words. Images become events, and the emotional quality of these visions evokes a certain wistfulness verging on metaphysical insight and longing. On the mythic level, the waters in *Cane* are related to death and resurrection patterns, which are part of black cultural tradition. Weaving intertextual connections in which "the construction of a network of interactions supersedes the literal meaning of the narrative," they also help define a sphere of communal identity and belonging based on memory even more than on history, a nonlinear sense of heritage to which "water, the metaphor of life, provides both dynamism and unity".

Cécile Coquet identifies the central problem of the work as that of communication with the other, as that of the soul's maladjustment to external reality. She shows the complex relationships between two cardinal figures in the text, the dreamer and the preacher: each embodies a different attitude to both world and word. The language of the former seems to be self-enclosed and ineffectual: vision replaces dialogue without overcoming the "opacity" of the soul; the individual stands aloof from the spontaneous expression of the folk spirit. The preacher, by contrast, utters "truths to live by," uses speech as a means to produce changes in his audience and the order of things. The call-and-response he institutes is a celebration of the beauty of blackness and black folk religion. But the treatment of these types in the work reveals that they are also two facets of the figure of the poet and that the sharp opposition between them has to be replaced by a more balanced vision expressed in terms of mutual distanciation and reinforcement.

The problematic articulation between modernism, racial politics, and artistic achievement constitutes the core of Monica Michlin's contribution. Her close reading of "Karintha" shows that this first sketch introduces the main themes and stylistic effects of the work. The sexual conflict announces the racial one and is depicted with Toomer's characteristic avoidance of moral and racial categorization. Nevertheless, she states, "the many ambiguities of the text can be interpreted as either an experimental desire to transcend worn-out clichés or as political irony." By simultaneously endorsing and deflating a pastoral setting that naturalizes the woman's victimization at the hands of society, the narrator might be diluting the issues presented in the story. Pervading images of death and stillbirth also point to uncertainties about poetic voice and identity. The fragmented, polyphonic structure of the piece is therefore associated with a double-edged staging of primitivism, in an attempt to redefine blackness, at a cost. The cost is the woman's voice: the latter is never heard and constitutes the "hole" around which the story revolves. Ultimately, the story aborts.

Dramatic and musical structures are all carefully elaborated in each piece of *Cane*. From "Karintha," where lyrical prose serves as counterpoint to the drama and where the beauty of visual and musical images offsets the real tragedy, to "Rhobert," where music and drama seem to merge to express the irrevocability of fate, Toomer had been playing metaphorically, figuratively, and literally with the idea of the stage ("theater," "box seat") and experimenting with musical forms that could enhance, subdue, or control the tensions. Drama was also a permanent concern for some writers of the time. In the years that saw the emergence of a Negro theater, when major authors like Ridgely Torrence and O'Neill were portraying black characters, Toomer was fascinated by the potentialities offered by the medium and conducted his own experiments in *Natalie Mann*, "Kabnis," *Balo* and other unpublished plays. *The New Negro* featured a play by Willis Richardson, who was to edit the first anthology of Negro plays, and an essay by Montgomery Gregory, "The Drama of Negro Life," praising the talents of African American comedians such as Sissle, Blake, Miller, Liles, and Florence Mills, as well as the work of new groups of actors like the Ethiopian Art Theatre, founded in 1923 in Chicago. It also urged the further development of a more serious and legitimate Negro theater. Langston Hughes saw *Shuffle Along* as the landmark of the era and joined Zora Neale Hurston to create a Negro folk drama. It is in this context that Toomer's own early interest in the theatre and his decision to include "Kabnis" in *Cane* must be seen. Michael Soto analyzes the vaudeville element present in the volume, a little-heeded aspect that was much derided by critics in 1923; Werner Sollors reminds us that Toomer submitted a play to O'Neill's Provincetown Playhouse and corresponded with DuBose Heyward.

The question of voice is therefore crucial in Toomer's literary project. A multiplicity of speaking, singing, moaning, and crying voices, whether "dicty" or vernacular, shapes a Bakhtinian textual heteroglossia perhaps best illustrated by Fern's speaking in tongues in the canefield. *Cane* is a book haunted, possessed by conflicting attempts at vocalization.

In her essay Geneviève Fabre focuses on "Harvest Song" and "Kabnis" to study dramatic and musical structures. She argues that their interaction is very much part of Toomer's aesthetics and enabled him to deal with the complexities he strove to express. His own experience while writing *Cane* was fraught with ambivalent feelings about the communion with land and soil (as well as with fading or newly emerging cultures) and about the future of the race and the future of art itself. This sense of unfulfilled hopes, ambitions, and promises—the dramatic core of *Cane*—found its expression in the song and solitary call of the harvester, which is so antinomic to the "Song of the Son." In "Kabnis" it was conveyed through a variety of more or less burlesque or serious situations and dramatis personae, a diversity of ironic, mock-heroic, or parodic modes. These theatrics, acted or imagined mostly by the central character, indicate the moods in which Kabnis's encounters are staged. Monologues, dialogues, and narrative and dramatic sequences weave a web of images and alternate with songs that enhance or create counterpoints to the drama by introducing other verbal or musical explosions and climaxes.

Claude McKay and Toomer appeared on the American literary scene in the early 1920s. *Harlem Shadows* (1922) was not McKay's first book, he had previously published both in the Caribbean (*Constab' Ballads*) and in London (*Spring in New Hampshire*); in New York he was first known as a poet. The publication of *Cane* (often referred to as Toomer's prose poem) the following year led critics to see them both as precursors of the Harlem Renaissance, breaking new grounds and creating a new tradition of black poetry after a long silence from African American writers. Both were attracted to socialism, both also remained marginal to the New Negro movement. Their paths met briefly, until they parted geographically, artistically, and ideologically.

Wolfgang Karrer examines the various grounds on which their encounter took place and their respective positions and ambiguous responses to the debate on racial formation, to the pressures of a modernist field, and to readers, patrons, and editors who had specific demands and expectations. The two writers shared a distrust of urban settings and did not believe in a black Mecca that would bring hope to the rural masses. Although they contributed to the flowering of poetry at a time dominated by the novel, their work and ideas seem to question Harlem's claim to become the center of the renaissance. The essay assesses Toomer's modernism through an analysis of his subversion of tradition and the genesis of *Cane;* each piece is seen as a stage in the artist's development, each finds its place in a design that suggests the principles behind the work. A close reading of two poems, "Conversion" by Toomer and "The Little Peoples" by McKay, throws further light on the two writers and their common concerns and distinctive techniques.

Cane, for all its richness, never was the be-all and end-all of Toomer's life and writings. His essays and relations with the intellectual world of his time, especially other Harlem Renaissance authors, can shed light on the whole period, on the issue of black modernism, and on the racial question that still divides America. In the "Negro Emergent" Toomer discusses the step the white world has taken toward the Negro and "the discovery of the Negro by creative America": "The influence of this discovery is mutual . . . each brings to the other an essential complement: a living contact made from different levels of experience."[14] While he was writing *Cane*, during his stay in Georgia, he confessed his fascination for his own Negro past and legacy ("my seeds were planted there") and the debt he owed to the rural South and its folk spirit for his artistic development. Although, as Michael Soto points out in this volume, he was irritated when labeled as a primitivist writer, he nevertheless participated, like most intellectuals of his time, in an artistic movement that associated primitivism with modernism; yet he did so in his own, singular way.

For many years Toomer exchanged letters with Alfred Stieglitz and Georgia O'Keeffe; their correspondence and enduring friendship gave him the occasion to discuss the role of the visual arts and to reflect upon the way they could affect and transform "the craft of writing." Martha Jane Nadell examines, through a close reading of that correspondence, Toomer's relation to the photographer often called "the American seer" and to the painter, their affinities, and the affiliations he established through them. She draws a stimulating parallel between the achievements of these three avant-garde friends in different fields. Georgia O'Keeffe and Alfred Stieglitz pioneered a "new objectivity" that was situated between abstraction and figuration and whose aim was to bypass the observer's cultural assumptions in order to induce an immediate, affective response. Toomer especially admired Stieglitz's ability to seize life without mediation, to reach essential design, "pure form, pure color, pure black." He tried to find an equivalent to this project in his depiction of race as a surface aesthetic dimension of characterization, thereby escaping the traps of exclusive social categories. Dissatisfied with pure words, he was anxious to experiment with visual forms. He felt that as an artist he shared the experience of O'Keeffe, that of being mistreated and misread as a Negro writer as she had been as a woman painter. Nadell's reading of *Cane* draws attention to color scheme and vocabulary, to Toomer's experiments with competing modes of description, and to his composite portrait technique. The comparison between the three artists shows both the common modernist project of new vision and a more ethical and political approach of form in Toomer, reflecting the African American dimension of *Cane*.

The relation between primitivism and modernism—a much-discussed issue in the 1920s in the United States as well as in Europe—is picked up in the following essays that connect it more directly to the race question. Choosing a middle ground between cultural studies, whose flaws are noted, and at the other extreme a more textualist literary approach, Michael Soto considers the role of the publishing market and its influence on the critical reception of *Cane*. This raises the larger problem of the situation of the black artist: the encouragement received from white patrons and the ensuing dependence and the acceptance or rejection of the racial label by writers like Toomer. The Boni and Liveright advertisement campaign, its confused policies and strategies, and the various steps in the preparation of the book, are closely examined: contacts and contracts, exchanges between writer and publisher, and the use of biographical sketch, foreword, jacket design, color, blurb, and advertisements that shaped the responses to *Cane*. Featuring Negro and primitivism were key elements in the marketability of the book, even though avant-gardist experimentation was also put forward. Taste and "race" crossed paths, which might explain why Toomer came to think that the message he was trying to convey had been betrayed. Solid documentation enables Soto to further highlight the history of the reception of *Cane* by contemporary critics and by later reviewers. He studies the assumptions underlying critical assessments by white critics as well as by Toomer's "peers": Du Bois who saw him as heir to a weakening African American tradition or Cullen who thought he had more to gain from English American poets "than from atavistic yearnings."

In 1923 Toomer's connections with white authors and his publications in little magazines put him among the avant-garde, so Liveright wavered in his campaign, advertising Toomer as modernist and later, in order to increase sales, mostly as a Negro writer. This essay, as others here, shows the need to examine a wider diversity of sources in order to reach a deeper understanding of *Cane* and of an era—be it called Jazz Age or Harlem Renaissance—that drew from many traditions. A close scrutiny of the Liveright-Toomer relationship throws light on the meaning of *Cane* in the 1920s, on the ambiguous connection between modernization and a modernity rooted in a critique of modernization. Writers like Toomer could only have ambivalent feelings toward a publishing industry that craved both modernity and primitivism, or what is now called racial exceptionalism, and that, under the impulse of men like Liveright, was undergoing a big change.

It was important to look at the racial discourse of the time and at Toomer's response to the ideology of racial purity or to white-black oppositions. Toomer tried to combine his own experience of a racially mixed status or ethnic indetermination with his inclination for racial transcendence or his yearning for what Toni Morrison called "racelessness."

In her provocative essay on Toomer's eugenic aesthetics, Diana Williams takes issue with critics like Hutchinson who read *Cane* as a biracial text and emphasize Toomer's attempt to go beyond the dualistic consciousness of a black-and-white America through his artistic representation of the taboo "interracial subject." Williams claims that Toomer's ideas were less transgressive, were influenced by Spencer, for whom he professed his admiration, and had eugenic implications, but with a difference—a difference graphically demonstrated in *Cane*. Basing her demonstration on a close examination of Toomer's writings on race ("Race Problems and Modern Society"), on eugenic theory, and on the racist practices and legislation of the time ("Race Integrity"), she shows that his idea of a new American identity was based on eugenistic premises and implied a careful selection of the best racial and cultural characteristics of individuals. She sees in the structure of *Cane* and in its racially ambiguous characters an attempt at acknowledging America's racial entanglements. She thus proposes new readings of "Kabnis," especially of Kabnis's and Lewis's brotherhood and of the ending. The essay suggests interesting analogies between buildings and women's bodies as central metaphors of the transition between old and new races. Toomer's description of his most famous work as the "song of an end" is set against his conception of a new race, and his (in)famous pronouncement, "As for being a Negro, this of course I am not," is seen against his poetic awareness of the greater complexity of the race situation.

Toomer repeatedly visited France and contributed to the avant-garde review *Bifur* in the 1920s, but he was mostly interested in Gurdjieff's sect at Avon, as Michel Fabre argues in his essay. In Europe, too, the Negro seems to have been "in vogue," since the aspects most early reviewers, scholars, and translators of his work chose to emphasize were the soulful rendition of the South and the primitivistic overtones of the work, at the expense of its experimental qualities. Though never widely known in France, he was hailed as a modernist black poet by a few critics and mentioned in such magazines as *La Revue du monde noir* and *Cahiers du sud*, while "Blood-Burning Moon" was published in a review. The pioneers of the *négritude* movement paid a different tribute to Toomer's achievement: Aimé Césaire stressed the elemental power and pride of race in response to oppression, while Léopold Sédar Senghor insisted on the pervasive rhythm and musicality. The latter greatly appreciated and translated "Song of the Son" and "Georgia Dusk" in the 1940s. Still, from the 1920s to the 1960s, only the poetry in *Cane* received widespread attention. French scholars started dealing with Toomer extensively only from 1960, with Jean Wagner's pioneering work on African American poets and his translation of *Cane*, entitled *Canne*, in 1977. Inasmuch as its diffusion is limited to Francophone African countries, no complete translation of the work is to be found on the French market to date. Michel Fabre's essay on the reception of *Cane* in France highlights the difficulties of cultural translation and aptly pleads in favor of a continued international exchange of multiple points of view on masterpieces of African American literature.

Notes

1. This paragraph is inspired by Matthew Guterl's communication at the Paris conference on Toomer and the Harlem Renaissance of January 1998. A revised version of this communication is to be featured in a forthcoming book by Guterl.
2. Jean Toomer, *Cane*, ed. Darwin T. Turner (New York: Norton, 1988), 3. All page references are to this edition of *Cane*.
3. "L'objet du mythe est de fournir un modèle logique pour résoudre une contradiction (tâche irréalisable quand la contradiction est réelle)." Claude Lévi-Strauss, *Anthropologie structurale* (1958; reprint, Paris: Plon, 1974), 264. (Translation M. Feith.)
4. Henry Louis Gates, "Criticism in the Jungle," in *Black Literature and Literary Theory, ed. Henry Louis Gates* (New York: Methuen, 1984), 12.
5. W.E.B. Du Bois, *The Souls of Black Folk* (1903; reprint, New York: Penguin, 1989).
6. This distinction is developed by George Hutchinson in *The Harlem Renaissance in Black and White* (Cambridge, Mass.: Belknap, 1995), 118.

   High modernism is usually associated with such expatriates as Gertrude Stein, T. S. Eliot, or Ezra Pound. Under the influence of the French symbolists, it advocates a separation of the social and personal spheres (the alienation of the artist) and a vision of the work of art as an autonomous object, an organic whole independent of the world of praxis. Its representatives engaged in widespread formal experimentation breaking with tradition. The "low" modernists in the United States were closer to the cultural nationalists in their attempts to find an accurate artistic expression for American identity in a changing world. This was expressed in a rehabilitation of the vernacular language, a focus on small-town and city life, and a voicing of social preoccupations. The Harlem Renaissance had many more affinities with the latter attitude to art than with "high" modernism.
7. Nellie McKay, *Jean Toomer, Artist: A Study of his Literary Life and Works, 1894–1936* (Chapel Hill: University of North Carolina Press, 1984), 171.
8. Robert B. Jones, *Jean Toomer: Selected Essays and Literary Criticism* (Knoxville: University Press of Texas, 1996), 55–59, 60–76.
9. Jean Toomer, "The Crock of the Problem," in Jones, *Selected Essays*, 56, 58.
10. *Bifur* (May 1, 1929): 105–114
11. John Keats to G. and T. Keats, December 21, 1817, quoted in Martin Gray, *A Dictionary of Literary Terms* (Longman, 1992), 192.
12. Jean Toomer, "Correspondence," in Toomer, *Cane*, 156.
13. Ross Posnock, *Color and Culture: Black Writers and the Making of the Modern Intellectual* (Cambridge: Harvard University Press, 1998), 12.
14. Jones, *Selected Essays*, 52.

Jean Toomer's *Cane*

Modernism and Race in Interwar America

WERNER SOLLORS

Time and space have no meaning in a canefield.
Jean Toomer, *Cane*

CANE IS A REMARKABLE expression of the modernist movement in literature that swept the United States and Europe in the first half of the twentieth century. Published in 1923 (before Ernest Hemingway's and William Faulkner's first important books were to appear), *Cane* was a powerful contribution to the stream of modernism that had begun with Gertrude Stein's *Three Lives* and James Joyce's *Dubliners* and continued with Sherwood Anderson's *Winesburg, Ohio,* Waldo Frank's manifesto, *Our America,* Hart Crane's poem *The Bridge,* and Eugene O'Neill's plays, a movement that was amplified by Alfred Stieglitz's photographs, Georgia O'Keeffe's paintings, the montage technique of the silent film, and the modern sounds of the blues and of jazz. The cultural historian Henry F. May called the watershed between Theodore Roosevelt and O. Henry on the one side and Greenwich Village and T. S. Eliot on the other a "cultural revolution";[1] the "revolution" in literature was spread by a younger generation of writers who loved the adjective "new," who chose many modern themes and settings, and who often looked to the other arts for inspiration. *Cane* is on our side of this transformation toward aesthetic modernism, psychological scrutiny, bohemian self-searching, increasing ethnic expression, and engagement with new ideologies.[2]

The author with the enigmatically androgynous name Jean Toomer (1894–1967) took up, but never completed, studies in history, anthropology, agriculture, and physical training; he was early attracted to atheism and socialism, later to the mystical and introspective Gurdjieff movement, to the Quakers, and to an Indian guru, and he spent important years in such artists' colonies as Greenwich Village, Taos, New Mexico, and Carmel, California.

He participated in an early experiment in group psychology in Portage, Wisconsin, that neighbors suspected was a free-love movement. He published poems, plays, and prose pieces on the pages of all the right small, experimental, and often radical literary magazines such as *Broom*, *Liberator*, and *Modern Review*. Toomer submitted a play to O'Neill's Provincetown Playhouse, befriended Sherwood Anderson and Hart Crane, and was intimate with Georgia O'Keeffe; his second wife, Marjorie Content, had previously been married to the editor of *Broom*, who was caricatured as Robert Cohn in Hemingway's *The Sun Also Rises*.

Not very well known outside of the United States, Toomer was a searcher among the modernist intellectuals of his time. His writing, most excellently embodied by *Cane*, represents an attempt to answer his close friend Waldo Frank's demand that American writers "study the cultures of the German, the Latin, the Celt, the Slav, the Anglo-Saxon and the African on the American continent: plot their reactions one upon the other, and their disappearance as integral worlds."[3]

Frank and Toomer spent some time together in Spartanburg, South Carolina. Inspired by this trip, Frank published his novel of perverted interracial lust and violence, *Holiday*. Toomer had previously worked as an acting principal in a black school in Sparta, Georgia, for two months—his first extended stay in the rural South—during which time the idea for *Cane* germinated. (He called Sparta "Sempter" in *Cane*.) He read the town newspaper, the *Sparta Ishmaelite*, and lived in an old cabin. This is the way Toomer remembered his emotional reaction to Sparta later on: "There was a valley, the valley of 'Cane,' with smoke-wreaths during the day and mist at night. A family of back-country Negroes had only recently moved into a shack not too far away. They sang. And this was the first time I'd ever heard the folk-songs and spirituals. They were very rich and sad and joyous and beautiful. But I learned that the Negroes of the town objected to them. They called them 'shouting.' They had victrolas and player-pianos. So, I realized with deep regret, that the spirituals, meeting ridicule, would be certain to die out. With Negroes also the trend was toward the small town and then toward the city—and industry and commerce and machines. The folk-spirit was walking in to die on the modern desert. That spirit was so beautiful. Its death was so tragic. Just this seemed the sum of life to me. And this was the feeling I put into *Cane*. *Cane* was a swan-song. It was a song of an end."[4]

Published the year before Horace Kallen coined the term "cultural pluralism," *Cane* was a meditation on what Toomer felt was the disappearing African culture on the American continent. It was also an aesthetic experiment of the first order.

Oracular.
Redolent of fermenting syrup,
Purple of the dusk,
Deep-rooted cane.

From the beginning to the ending of *Cane* the reader is drawn into a magical and mysterious world of pine needles and clay, of autumn leaves and dusk, of spiritual striving and human failing, of love and violence, but it also tells of the movement from country roads to city streets and from natural to industrial sounds.

Toomer achieves his effects by a carefully orchestrated system of verbal repetition and musical progression in a book whose very form resists classification. Is *Cane* a novel? A melange of experimental pieces of differing length? A synthesis of various forms of experimentation? A mosaic? Most of all, it is a book sui generis, a fusion of poetry, prose, and drama (in "Bona and Paul" and "Kabnis"), a text that appeals to all senses by presenting strong visual images and musical and rhythmic effects that evoke smells and powerful feelings of pain and suffering. Its very form is an attempt at finding a literary equivalent for the dislocations that modernity had wrought by moving people from soil to pavements, making them ashamed of their traditional folk culture or changing it into commercial entertainment, and radically altering the epic pace of sun and seasons, of sowing and reaping, into the accelerated and syncopated rhythm of trains and cars, the staccato of quickly shifting images and thoughts. Despite all the apparent variations in genres, the book has the effect of a long poem that is held together by recurring images. The book reflects on the country without idyllic nostalgia and on the city without teleological hope. Both are historically changing worlds of failed human understanding and of at times horrifyingly brutal encounters, since Toomer locates his work in the aftermath of World War I and in the white-black racial violence of the South and North. The modernist book *Cane* thus vies for the space of the spirit, of the human soul, that seems threatened under the rule of modernity—both in the country and the city. "We have two emblems, namely, the machine gun and the contraceptive," Toomer writes regretfully.[5] Can the lost soul of a fertile peasant past be found again in the elusively modernist form of a book that artistically, even artificially, reconstitutes life-asserting wholeness by resisting easy generalizations and a priori assumptions? *Cane* makes an attempt to do just that—even though Toomer articulated his keen awareness that there is no possibility of going back to a shared past.

> The modern world was uprooted, the modern world was breaking down, *but we couldn't go back*. There was nothing to go back to.

> Besides, in our hasty leaps into the future we had burned our bridges. The soil, the earth was still there, even under city pavements and congested sky scrapers.
>
> But such peasantry as America had had—and I sang one of its swan songs in *Cain* [*sic*]—was swiftly disappearing, swiftly being industrialized and urbanized by machines, motor cars, phonographs, movies. . . . "Back to nature," even if desirable, was no longer possible, because industry had taken nature unto itself. Even if he wanted to, a city person could not become a soil person by changing his locale and living on a farm in the woods.
>
> So then, whether we wished to or not, we *had to go on*.[6]

Toomer's answer to this problem could not lie in a return to traditional values, be they monarchy, religion, or mere conservatism, for "those who sought to cure themselves by a return to more primitive conditions were either romantics or escapists." No, going on, going on to create, searching for aesthetic wholeness and a new vision in a fragmented modern world, that was the only viable answer. The critique of modernity impelled Toomer to move forward the project of modernism.

Cane makes its readers self-conscious in order to let them yearn for a fresher and fuller look at the world. This effort is captured in the book's repeated allusions to St. Paul's Epistle to the Corinthians: "For now we see through a glass darkly; but then face to face; now I know in part; but then shall I know even as I am known"—a passage that Ralph Waldo Emerson and Nathaniel Hawthorne had also cherished and that Henry Roth and Ralph Ellison were to draw on later. Is it possible to have full knowledge and self-knowledge in the modern world? In pursuing this question in the United States, Toomer also searched for a more cosmic understanding of the wholeness of a polyvocal America as it was once sung by Walt Whitman and now proclaimed by Waldo Frank. And as many visionaries before him, Toomer espoused the fragmentary as the necessary part of larger totalities.

The interrelatedness of fragmentation and quest for wholeness structures *Cane*. The book is divided into three parts that are marked by parentheses: (,) and (). "Between each of the three sections, a curve. These, to vaguely indicate the design," Toomer wrote to Waldo Frank on December 12, 1922.[7] The two segments realign and aim for a circle without fully achieving its closure in the third part.

Part one is set in Georgia, the rural South. It is mostly focused on women, starting with Karintha, whose very name may represent a nod in the direction of Gertrude Stein's "Melanctha," or may allude to St. Paul's "Corinthians," ending with Louisa in "Blood-Burning Moon."

"Karintha" originally appeared in the context of the drama *Natalie Mann* (1922), in which Toomer's mouthpiece, Nathan Merilh, reads "Karintha" as evidence that historically grown, black sacred art remained a valid and important source of inspiration to the intellectual who found himself surrounded by modern Marxist and nationalist interrogators.[8] Yet Karintha is more of a modern Mary Magdalene than a conventional sacred figure. Men bring her money, and her imagistic constitution is that of a woman whose running is a "whir" and whose "skin is like dusk when the sun goes down"—a leitmotif of the story in the repetition of which Toomer visibly blurs the line between poetry and prose: it is typeset as a prose sentence and as a poem. In the play, Therman Law, a young man (who is also the friend of Nathan Merilh, who in turn is presented as the author of "Karintha") reflects:

> What should be the most colorful and robust of our racial segments is approaching a sterile and denuded hypocrisy as its goal. What has become of the almost obligatory heritage of folk-songs? Jazz on the one hand, and on the other, a respectability which is never so vigorous as when it denounces and rejects the true art of the race's past. They are ashamed of the past made permanent by the spirituals. My God, imagine the look on the face of Dvořák.[9]

The poems and the portraits of rural women that follow intensify the reader's sense of hearing Toomer's "swan song," of experiencing fragments of a passing rural world in which natural images, especially those of sunsets and autumn, and religious sentiments increasingly give way to such intrusions of modernity as railroad tracks and factories and to scenes of violence. Becky, introduced with a paradoxical subtitle reminiscent of Bertolt Brecht's dramatic strategies as "the white woman who had two Negro sons," lives on a "ground islandized between the road and railroad track" (18). Fern is presented as if narrator and reader were seeing her from a train thundering by:

> Besides, picture if you can, this cream-colored solitary girl sitting at a tenement window looking down on the indifferent throngs of Harlem. Better that she listen to folk-songs at dusk in Georgia, you would say, and so would I. Or, suppose she came up North and married. Even a doctor or a lawyer, say, one who would be sure to get along—that is, make money. You and I know, who have had experience in such things, that love is not a thing like prejudice which can be bettered by changes of town. Could men in Washington, Chicago, or New York, more than the men of Georgia, bring her something left vacant by the bestowal of their bodies?
>
> I ask you, friend, (it makes no difference if you sit in the Pullman

> or the Jim Crow as the train crosses her road), what thoughts would come to you . . . had you seen her in a quick flash, keen and intuitively, as she sat there on her porch when your train thundered by? Would you have got off at the next station and come back for her to take her where? Would you have completely forgotten her as soon as you reached Macon, Atlanta, Augusta, Pasadena, Madison, Chicago, Boston, or New Orleans? (18)

Esther, who has come to sexual maturity, walks into a jeering crowd like a somnambulist, and the story ends like a Franz Kafka tale: "She steps out. There is no air, no street, and the town has completely disappeared" (27). The undercurrent of violence emerges with the blood-stained blade of the scythe that has cut a rat in the poem "Reapers" and erupts at the end of the first section as the factory town mob lynches Louisa's black lover, Tom Burwell, whose steel blade had slashed his white rival Bob Stone's throat.

In part two *Cane* takes us to cities, especially Washington and Chicago in the age of mass migration and urbanization. (In 1910 about a quarter of all African Americans lived in cities, in 1940, half of them.) The rhythm changes abruptly in this world that is characterized by postwar disillusionment, by a proliferating entertainment industry, and by the syncopations of jazz that Toomer incorporates into his prose in order to render a life that is "jagged, strident, modern. Seventh Street, located in black Washington, is the song of crude new life. Of a new people" (41). The surrealistic Rhobert, who wears his house like a diver's helmet, is an urban counterpart to Becky, as the narration again repeats prose sentences as poems. The image of the man who sinks is connected with the World War I experience that reduced God to "a Red Cross man with a dredge and a respiration-pump" and makes the singing of the traditional spiritual "Deep River" seem out of place:

> Lets build a monument and set it in the ooze where he goes down. A monument of hewn oak, carved in nigger-heads. Lets open our throats, brother, and sing "Deep River" when he goes down.
>
> Brother, Rhobert is sinking.
> Lets open our throats, brother,
> Lets sing Deep River when he goes down.
> (43)

The self-conscious narrator of "Avey"[10] resembles that of "Fern." Again, the wish for a performance of the spiritual "Deep River," this time by the Howard University Glee Club, marks the contrast to rural religion, a contrast that shapes also the vignette of the young woman on the street in "Calling Jesus." "Theater" continues the jazz theme, and Toomer adopts some blues lines here:

"Arms of the girls, and their limbs, which . . . jazz, jazz . . . by lifting up their tight street skirts they set free, jab the air and clog the floor in rhythm to the music. (Lift your skirts, Baby, and talk t papa!)" (52). In "Box Seat," Dan Moore reflects on a man who saw the first Oldsmobile but was born a slave: "He saw Grant and Lincoln. He saw Walt—old man, did, you see Walt Whitman?" The new urban world is not even one lifetime removed from the Civil War and slavery; and this recent history also casts its shadow over the failed interracial romance between Bona and Paul in the story that ends the second part and corresponds most directly to "Blood-Burning Moon": just as Bob Stone wanted Louisa because she was black and he "went in as a master should and took her. Direct, honest, bold," so Bona in the new world of a Chicago gymnasium and the nightclub Crimson Gardens is attracted to Paul because she suspects he is black: "That's why I love" (72). Bona's (and Toomer's) lyrical labels "harvest moon" and "autumn leaf" cannot displace the racial slur "nigger" that is, for Bona, a source of attraction. The weight of such historical racial categories ("a priori" recurs here) impinges upon the consciousness of the youths: "Bona is one window. One window, Paul" (73).

In part three, "Kabnis," the artist himself is *seen* rather than having merely a stronger or weaker presence as observer. Like Toomer, Kabnis is a secular urban intellectual who goes to rural Georgia to teach. Partly inspired by Joyce's *Portrait of the Artist as a Young Man*, "Kabnis"—written as a play and submitted to O'Neill's associate Kenneth Macgowan—shows the development of a tortured mind through encounters with nursery rhymes, religion, and various role models such as a teacher, preacher, cartwright, radical, and visionary. There are many things Kabnis has to face about society, history, and himself, but the core of what he must come to terms with is a legacy of violence. When drunk and self-critical, Kabnis attempts to articulate his aesthetic against the avalanche of words that makes the country go down: "I want t feed th soul—I know what that is; th preachers dont—but I've got t feed it" (111). When he adds, "I wish t God some lynchin white man ud stick his knife through it an pin it to a tree," he likens his concept of the soul to the brutal story of the pregnant Mame Lamkins that the preacher Layman had told him earlier: when she tried to hide her husband, who was wanted, she was killed, and the living baby was torn out of her stomach and stuck to a tree with a knife, as if it were a perverse new crucifixion (92).[11] The ending of "Kabnis" is like a rebirth, and the book ends as a birth song with a sunrise.

The three parts of *Cane* confront the divisions of South and North, women and men, as well as black and white, whereas the structure of the book tends to bridge such divisions and strive toward unity. In a letter to Waldo Frank of December 12, 1922, Toomer suggested another sequence in which one might read the book: "*Cane*'s design is a circle. Aesthetically, from simple forms to complex ones, and back to simple forms. Regionally, from the South up into the North, and back into the South again. Or, from the North down into the South, and then a return North. From the point of view of the spiritual entity behind the work, the curve really starts with Bona and Paul (awakening), plunges into Kabnis, emerges in Karintha etc. swings upward into Theatre and Box Seat, and ends (pauses) in Harvest Song. Whew!"[12]

The book may then be said to follow at least a double curve: one that goes from beginning to end and one that starts in the middle and ends with "Harvest Song." Yet *Cane* could also be read in many other sequences, since many parts resonate with many other parts because of the book's poetic structure. Toomer's method also resembles the film montage technique of Eisenstein as it juxtaposes sequences that the reader/viewer must put together, must "suture." Unity is achieved by various repetitions and leitmotifs that create a sense of thematic cohesion and rhythm and shape the design of the text.[13]

Toomer aims for a particular kind of lyrical specificity expressed in strong and often enigmatic images that recur in repeated words, phrases, and shorter or longer sentences throughout the book. Although the precise meaning of an instance on a given page may be hard to define, the very fact that words are repeated throughout the book gives the reader a sense of acoustic and visual familiarity, a phenomenon reminiscent of *Three Lives*. For example, *Cane* is a book of repeated "thuds," harsh knocking sounds that syncopate the reading from "Becky" (8) to the end of "Kabnis" (117). In "Blood-Burning Moon" the thud is the sound of Bob's body falling and of the mob's action, giving a menacingly violent undercurrent of meaning to such later thuds as those in the gymnasium in "Bona and Paul." Similarly, there are trees throughout the book, but it is the tale of Mame Lamkins in "Kabnis" that gives them their precise sense of eeriness. *Cane* is a book full of sunset and dusk imagery that is virtually omnipresent in the poems and the prose, thus calling particular attention to the emphatic sunrise at the end. Karintha is described as a "November cotton flower"—the title of a poem appearing a few pages later.[14] The repetition of "pines whisper to Jesus" in "Becky" anticipates "Calling Jesus" and the whispering nightwind in "Kabnis." Read this way, the book is woven of recurring sounds and images in such words as sawmill, pine, cotton, dixie pike, street, smoke, wedge, window, moon, cloud, purple, cradle, sin, and, of course, cane. Robert Jones has stressed how Gertrude Stein's love for "-ing" forms also affected Toomer; he focused on "Seventh Street" with its reiterated "zooming cadillacs, / Whizzing, whizzing down the street-car tracks," its "thrusting unconscious rhythm"—all coming to a climactic moment in "Black reddish blood. Pouring for crude-boned soft skinned life, who set you flowing?" And: "Flowing down the smooth asphalt of Seventh Street, in shanties, brick office buildings, theaters, drug stores, restaurants, and cabarets? Eddying on the corners? Swirling like a blood-red smoke up where the buzzards fly in heaven?"[15] (39).

Additionally, many sections contain further patterns of repeated phrases and sentences within a single story or vignette. At times (as in "Becky" or "Calling Jesus") the phrasing with the central set of images appears at the beginning and the end, as prose or poetry. In stories like "Blood-Burning Moon" the internal repetition is remarkable; one can see how this works in Toomer's prose by looking at a few representative sentences:

> The full moon sank upward into the deep purple of the cloud-bank. An old woman brought a lighted lamp and hung it on the common well whose bulky shadow squatted in the middle of the road, opposite Tom and Louisa. The old woman lifted the well-lid, took hold the chain, and began drawing up the heavy bucket. As she did so, she sang. Figures shifted, restlesslike, between lamp and window in the front room of the shanties. Shadows of the figures fought each other on the gray dust of the road. Figures raised the windows and joined the old woman in song. Louisa and Tom, the whole street, singing:
>
> Red nigger moon. Sinner!
> Blood-burning moon. Sinner!
> Come out that fact'ry door.
> (33)

Many sentences contain words that echo earlier sentences. By the time we read the sentence, "Its yell echoed against the skeleton stone walls and sounded like a hundred yells" (36), most of the nouns are themselves echoes. This makes for a musical and visual progression. By using such words as "yell" as subjects of short sentences, Toomer also gives an energetic, imagistic quality to his descriptions, as he seems focused on a telling detail. "Fern" opens with a sentence in which "face" is the subject and that makes grammatical sense, contains only familiar words, and evokes a strong image, yet is also quite mysterious: "Face flowed into her eyes" (16).

Such a phrasing is reminiscent of Ezra Pound's "In a Station of the Metro." Toomer may, in fact, be consciously following F. S. Flint's and Ezra Pound's 1913 imagist maxims that exhorted poets to treat the "thing" directly, use absolutely no word that does not contribute to the presentation, compose in the sequence of a musical phrase, not the sequence of a metronome, and arrive at an image that presents an intellectual and emotional complex in an instant of time.[16] Toomer's images certainly are not ornaments; they *are* the speech.

The dialectic of the accustomed familiarity of given words that make physical things visible and vivid and the "oracular" strangeness of their precise meanings that surrounds the verbally constituted world with questions and ambiguity is given fullest play in Toomer's descriptions such as that of Louisa: "Her skin was the color of oak leaves on young trees in fall"[17] (30). This is a strongly visual image that makes the reader see things fresh, yet it would be hard to associate one specific color with such a description. It is no coincidence that for Toomer such lyricism also has the function of avoiding a label. Toomer shared with imagists such as T. E. Hulme a disdain for abstractions and a desire to let fresh metaphors make you continuously see a physical thing; thus Toomer does not call Karintha a "prostitute" (though reviewers like W.E.B. Du Bois did); the narrator only says that men bring her their money.[18] Yet Toomer brings to this program, again reminiscent of Stein's, a particular wish that goes beyond the aesthetic.

Louisa's skin color is an alternative to a racial label, a needling engagement with a reader's desire to know whether a character is black or white. Toomer's response is, "Her skin was the color of oak leaves on young trees in fall." We remember that Bona, too, saw Paul in the following way: "He is a harvest moon. He is an autumn leaf. He is a nigger." These are three grammatically parallel sentences, two of which offer lyrical perception and one of which is not just an abstraction and cliché, but the worst ethnic slur as a label (though for Bona this very abstraction is also a source of attraction). For Jean Toomer the worst aesthetic strategy was to employ a cliché—and he saw language as complicitous in racial domination.

> Damn labels if they enslave human beings—
> above race and nationality there is mankind.

Cane is a modernist work that has its specific milieu in the world of American race relations, polarized along the color line that divides black and white, whether in Sparta, Washington, or Chicago. Toomer's stylistic choices are an expression of his refusal to endorse this racial divide. To be sure, *Cane* was a book in which black life, rural and urban, was strongly thematized. But this was not all. His aesthetic was connected to a quest for unity, and one may say that Toomer was a spiritual searcher for all of his life. On May 16, 1923, Toomer wrote to DuBose Heyward: "Both black and white folk come into *Cane*'s pages. For me, this is artistically inevitable. But in no instance am I concerned primarily with race; always, I drive straight for my own spiritual reality, and for the spiritual truth of the South."[19]

This quest for wholeness and Toomer's own "spiritual reality" is related to the book's racial and historical thematic. If America is fragmented, black and white, male and female, Southern and Northern, rural and urban, Toomer sees his own mission, by contrast, as providing a ground for spiritual unity. His quest for union, for wholeness, for the circle is achieved precisely by thematizing the divisions that the book's author felt were so destructive and virulent in the modern world: race, sex, class, region. Toomer saw himself as a visionary who would try to redirect readers toward a wholeness—however elusive it might be—that they had lost in their differentiations by category. In other words, Toomer's aesthetic modernism was connected to an attack on false perceptions, prejudices, a priori assumptions, and labels. He was attracted to Waldo Frank, James Joyce, Eugene O'Neill (he submitted "Kabnis" to the Provincetown Players and wrote a rave notice on "The Emperor Jones") and Gertrude Stein (through Alfred Stieglitz, who had published some early Stein; both Toomer and Stein contributed an homage to Stieglitz in a volume published in 1934). Toomer found that modernist forms helped to complicate facile notions about social life. Georgia O'Keeffe had painted *Birch and Pine Trees—Pink* (1925) as a modern version of a "portrait" of her friend Jean Toomer, to whom she wrote, "There is a painting I made from something of you the first time you were here." The "dancing" trees were thus a "surrogate portrait of her close friend."[20] This was, of course, also a way of deflecting from portraits as realistic representations (including typical ones) to portraits as purely formal expression. Toomer wrote to Georgia O'Keeffe on January 13, 1924:

> Have you come to the story "Bona and Paul" in *Cane?* Impure and imperfect as it is, I feel that you and Stieglitz will catch its essential design as no others can. Most people cannot see this story because of the inhibitory baggage they bring with them. When I say "white," they see a certain white man, when I say "black," they see a certain Negro. Just as they miss Stieglitz's intentions, achievements! Because they see "clouds." So that at the end, when Paul resolves these contrasts to a unity, my intelligent commentators wonder what its [*sic*] all about. Someday perhaps, with greater purity and a more perfect art, I'll do the thing. And meanwhile the gentlemen with intellect will haggle over the question as to whether or not I have expressed the "South."[21]

This is most dramatically apparent in Toomer's notions of racial identity, including his own. A philosophical spirit in a world of race antagonisms, Toomer was bent on any verbal strategy that would promote the transcendence rather than the hardening of racial categories, all the more so since Toomer had a modern, analytical understanding of the mechanisms of racial differentiation. Racial tension to him was not an ancient survival but a new creation. In his essay "Race Problems and Modern Society," published in 1929, he writes that

> the new Negro is much more Negro and much less American than was the old Negro of fifty years ago. From the point of view of sociological types, the types which are arising among Negroes, such as the business man, the politician, the college student, the writer, the propagandist, the movie enthusiast, the bootlegger, the taxi driver, etc.—these types among Negroes are more and more approaching the corresponding white types. But, just as certain as it is that this increasing correspondence of types makes the drawing of distinction supposedly based on skin color or blood composition appear more and more ridiculous, so it is true that the lines are being drawn with more force between the colored and white groups.[22]

In an unpublished essay entitled "The Americans" he views America as the place

> where mankind, long dismembered into separate usually repellant groupings, long scattered over the face of the earth, is being re-assembled into one whole and undivided human race. America will include the earth.
>
> There is a new race here. For the present we may call it the American race. That, to date, not many are aware of its existence, that they do not realize that they themselves belong to it—this does not mean it does not exist; it simply means it does not yet exist for them because they, under the suggestion of hypnotic labels and false beliefs, are blind to it. But these labels and beliefs will die. They too must and will die. And the sight of people will be freed from them, and the people will become less blind and they will use their sight and see.
>
> This new race is neither white nor black nor red nor brown. These are the old terms for old races, and they must be discarded. This is a new race; and though to some extent, to be sure, white and black and red and brown strains have entered into its formation, we should not view it as part white, part black, and so on. . . . Water, though composed of two parts of hydrogen and one part of oxygen, is not hydrogen and oxygen; it is *water*.[23]

The logic of segregationism was all the more absurd to Toomer since he perceived that the old African American culture was disappearing, whereas the new American culture was a shared crossover culture. He asked himself: "Was Seventh Street Negro?" and answers: "Only in the boldness of its expression. In its healthy freedom. American. For the shows that please Seventh Street make their fortunes on Broadway."[24] Black culture was, for Toomer, an intricate part and tastemaker of American culture, and yet the mental (and social) boundaries between black and white were being reinforced rather than blurred.

What could a writer do to fight such racial blindness and ridiculousness as was prominent, for example, in the Virginia legislature, which passed the *Act to Preserve Racial Purity* in 1924, defining any person "in whom there is ascertainable any Negro blood" a colored person? The U.S. census after 1920 also no longer provided a category for interracial or biracial Americans.[25] Toomer was convinced that a rethinking of the power of language in creating group divisions was in order, especially for writers. His aesthetics had to work against, and his theoretical pronouncements had to attack and transcend, facile labels. In the essay "The Americans" he stressed, after having made the analogy with water, in a very modern way the sociological (not biological) nature of racial distinctions:

> There is only one pure race—and this is the *human* race. We all belong to it—and this is the most and the least that can be said of any of us with accuracy. For the rest, it is mere talk, mere labelling, merely a manner of speaking, merely a sociological, not a biological, thing. I myself merely talk when I speak of the blending of the bloods of the white, black, red, and brown races giving rise to a new race, to a new unique blood, when I liken the combination of these strains to the combination of hydrogen and oxygen producing water. For the blood of all the races is *human* blood. There are no differences between the blood of a Caucasian and the blood of a Negro as there are between hydrogen and oxygen. In the mixing and blending of so-called races there are mixtures and blending of the same stuff.[26]

In his postimagist collection of aphorisms, *Essentials* (1931), he draws the consequences from such reflections and writes about himself:

> I am of no particular race. I am of the human
> race, a man at large in the human world,
> preparing a new race.
>
> I am of no specific region. I am of earth.
>
> I am of no particular class. I am of the human
> class, preparing a new class.
>
> I am neither male nor female nor in-between. I am
> of sex, with male differentiations.
>
> I am of no special field, I am of the field of being.[27]

The fourth of these "definitions" might explain the reason why in 1920 he chose the name "Jean" over his baptismal name Nathan Eugene for publication; this choice made Toomer part of a 1920s penchant among modernists for gender ambiguity.[28]

Yet it was particularly the first maxim that remained his greatest concern. Toomer would express similar sentiments in his Whitman-inspired poem "Blue Meridian" (1936) and in his autobiographical writings. Toomer, who was in this respect, too, an heir to Walt Whitman's utopian hopes for the New World, tended to see both "America" and the first person singular "I" as potentially all-inclusive. He writes in "On Being an American":

> I had lived among white people. I had lived among colored people. I had lived among Jews. I had met and known people of the various nationalistic groups. I had come into contact with my fellow countrymen from the bottom to the top of the American scene.
>
> I had seen the divisions, the separatisms and antagonisms. I had observed that, if the issue came up, very few of these United States citizens were aware of being *Americans*. On the contrary, they were aware of, and put value upon, their hearsay descents, their groupistic affiliations.[29]

He therefore suggested to the editor of *Prairie* magazine: "It is stupid to call me anything other than an American."[30]

Toomer's identity choice was at odds, however, with the way in which race is defined in the United States. When Nathan Eugene Pinchback Toomer was born on December 26, 1894, he was born into a family with a longstanding tradition of racial ambiguity.[31] His father, Nathan Toomer, had been born in 1841 and may have been a slave or freeborn. He was the light-skinned son of a prosperous Georgia plantation owner of English, Dutch, and Spanish descent and a "woman of mixed blood, including Negro and Indian." Nathan Toomer lived on both sides of the color line: as a white man in the South, and as a Negro in Washington, D.C. He was a restless man and left Jean's mother, Nina Pinchback (1868–1909), a year after Jean's birth. Nina was the daughter of Pinckney Benton Stewart Pinchback (the son of a white father, Major William Pinchback, who also had a legal white wife and family on his Virginia plantation) and a Mulatto slave mother, Eliza Benton Stewart, who was, according to Toomer, "of English, Scotch, Welsh, German, African, and Indian stock." She bore William ten children, the first in 1829 at age fifteen or sixteen; after the sixth childbirth, William manumitted her and the surviving children. Pinckney was born in 1837 in Macon, Georgia, when the family was journeying west after the Jacksonian Indian removals. In 1846 P.B.S. Pinchback and his brother Napoleon were sent to Hiram S. Gilmore High School in Cincinnati, "a private academy catering to the offspring of just such unions as the Major and his mulatto helpmate" (Arna Bontemps). After Major William Pinchback's death, no money was forthcoming; Napoleon functioned as head of the family but went insane, and the family broke up. The twelve-year-old Pinckney was on his own and worked as steward on riverboats, became a gambler, and moved to New Orleans where, in 1860, he married Toomer's maternal grandmother, Emily Hethorne, an Anglo-French Creole woman who was light in appearance and about whose racial background there is conflicting information. Pinchback, too, was so lightskinned that his sister Adeline advised him in 1863 to pass for white. Pinchback became the first African American to serve as governor of a state when he was appointed in 1872 as acting governor of Louisiana. (At one point Toomer declared that Pinchback had only said he was black for the political motive of being appointed governor during Reconstruction.) In addition to their daughter, Nina, the Pinchbacks also had three sons, Pinckney, who was educated at Andover and the Philadelphia College of Pharmacy, Bismarck, a freethinker and lawyer, and Walter, who served in the Spanish-American War in Cuba and later became a doctor. Nina was sent to the private Riverside School in Massachusetts. After his parents' divorce in 1899 Jean Toomer lived with her and his grandparents in a black middle-class neighborhood in Washington, DC; his mother remarried in 1906. Her new husband, Archibald Combes (sometimes spelled Coombs), descended from the famous New Jersey Mulatto colony Gouldtown in Cumberland County, near Bridgeton (probably from Jacob Coombs, the son of William Coombs and Elizabeth Pierce Coombs, and Clara Gould Coombs, a direct descendant of the Gouldtown founders), yet both Nina and Combes were described as "white" on their marriage certificate. Toomer lived with his mother and stepfather in Brooklyn and in a white neighborhood in New Rochelle for three years when he was twelve to fourteen years old. After Nina Pinchback's death, Jean Toomer lived with his maternal grandparents in Washington, DC, and graduated from the famous black Dunbar (then called M Street) High School.

Obviously, his mysterious father's Georgia background and the Georgia birth of his overpowering maternal grandfather made Toomer's teaching experience in Sparta a much deeper quest: "When one is on the soil of one's ancestors, anything can come to one," he writes in *Cane;* and in "Song of the Son" it is hard not to think of an autobiographic significance to the lines of the son who comes to the soil "to catch thy plaintive soul."

> Thy son, in time, I have returned to thee,
> Thy son, I have in time returned to thee.[32]

Toomer's project in *Cane* was thus an aesthetic experiment, a study of a vanishing rural folk culture, a quest for the meaning of modern "America" and his own Americanness, and the expression of a profoundly personal and deeply felt genealogical engagement. He described his own background in a famous letter to Max Eastman and Claude McKay, the editors of the radical *Liberator,* in 1922, in order to explain *Cane:*

> Racially, I seem to have (who knows for sure) seven blood mixtures: French, Dutch, Welsh, Negro, German, Jewish, and Indian. Because of these, my position in America has been a curious one. I have lived equally amid the two race groups. Now white, now colored. From my own point of view I am naturally and inevitably an American. . . . Within the last two or three years, however, my growing need for artistic expression has pulled me deeper and deeper into the Negro group. And as my powers of receptivity increased, I found myself loving it in a way that I could never love the other. It has stimulated and fertilized whatever creative talent I may contain within me. A visit to Georgia last fall was the starting point of almost everything of worth that I have done. I heard the folk-songs come from the lips of Negro peasants. I saw the rich dusk beauty that I had heard many false accents about, and of which till then, I was somewhat skeptical. And a deep part of my nature, a part I had repressed, sprang suddenly to life and responded to them. Now, I cannot conceive of myself as aloof and separated.[33]

"American" as an ideal self-description meant for Toomer an identification for people of all backgrounds who could acknowledge their shared and mixed characteristics—in opposition to the silent usurpation of the term "American" to stand for "white American." The United States as a reality, however, was characterized by an emphasis on "groupistic" descent, which drew Toomer both closer to a deeper experience of black life and to a more profound claim on his Americanness. Like many nineteenth-century New Orleans Creoles, Toomer lived—and responded intellectually and aesthetically to—the paradox of American racial construction that simply defined him as "black," all his other "ascertainable" ancestry notwithstanding. When he and the novelist Margery Latimer, a descendant of Anne Bradstreet, got married in March of 1931 (after the group psychology experiment at Portage, Wisconsin), he issued the following, familiar-sounding statement, entitled "A New Race in America":

> There is a new race in America. I am a member of this new race. It is neither white nor black nor in-between. It is the American race, differing as much from white and black as white and black differ from each other. It is possible that there are Negro and Indian bloods in my descent along with English, Spanish, Welsh, Scotch, French, Dutch, and German. This is common in America, and it is from all these strains that the American race is being born. But the old divisions

> into white, black, brown, red are outworn in this country. They have had their day. Now is the time of the birth of a new order, a new vision, a new ideal of man. I proclaim this order. My marriage to Margery Latimer is the marriage of two Americans.[34]

The *World Telegram* headline read "Negro Who Wed White Novelist Sees New Race." Whatever Toomer saw, the newspaper failed to see—and the headline seems like a translation of one of Toomer's *Essentials* into a journalistic cliché.[35]

Toomer would not only deplore such sensationalist and hostile labeling at a time that interracial marriage was prohibited in the majority of the United States; upon the completion of *Cane* he also came to reject the label "Negro writer." He received largely favorable reviews and comments from black intellectuals: for example, the authoritative Du Bois praised Toomer for daring to "hurl his pen across the very face of our sex conventionality," noted that he painted things "with an impressionist's sweep of color," and admired the book's "strange flashes of power" even when it was difficult to understand it; and the aesthete Alain Locke thought that *Cane* was, with Wright's *Native Son* and Ellison's *Invisible Man*, one of the three best works of the modern period and found that in Toomer's text "the emotional essences of the Southland were hauntingly evoked in an impressionistic poetic sort of realism."[36] Yet Toomer questioned—as we saw in his letter to O'Keeffe—his role as a representative of "the South," and, more controversially, he did not wish to be included in anthologies such as Nancy Cunard's *Negro*.[37] He was also apprehensive of friendly writers who, like Sherwood Anderson, saw him too exclusively as "Negro." He wrote to Waldo Frank around March 1923: "Sherwood limits me to Negro. As an approach, as a constant element (part of a larger whole) of interest, Negro is good. But try to tie me to one of my parts is surely to [lose] me. My own letters have taken Negro as a point, and from there have circled out. Sherwood, for the most part, ignores the circles."[38] Conversely, Toomer would also question Frank's failure to include the Negro more fully in *Our America:* "No picture of a southern person is complete without its bit of Negro-determined psychology."[39]

For Toomer, black and white were linked together like twins, like yin and yang; but racist labels, lazy thinking, and faith in clichés prevented this reality from finding universal creative expression. And it is here that Toomer perceived his own avant-garde position. In the ideal American world of racial reciprocity, Toomer conceived of his art as a spiritual sort of racial amalgamation, which he explained in his letter to McKay and Eastman: "I have strived for a spiritual fusion analogous to the fact of racial intermingling. Without denying a single element in me, with no desire to subdue one to the other, I have sought to let them function as complements. I have tried to let them live in harmony."[40] A few days earlier, he had similarly written to John McClure: "I alone, as far as I know, have striven for a spiritual fusion, analogous to the fact of racial intermingling. It has been rough riding. Nor am I through. Have just begun, in fact. This, however, has neither social nor political implications. My concern is solely with art. What am I? From my own point of view, naturally and inevitably an American."[41]

Toomer thought that *Cane* was only the beginning of a long road. Though, indeed, many projects and fragments, long manuscripts, a few literary publications, and published essays and aphorisms followed, no second Toomer book to equal the brilliance of *Cane* ever appeared. *Cane* united aesthetic experimentation, the contemplation of African American folk culture in modern America, the themes of genealogical origins, migration, and interracialism, while it challenged easy labels and insisted on the need for a new spiritual wholeness. It remains Toomer's outstanding contribution to modern literature.

Notes

1. May, *American Innocence*.
2. For a full discussion of Toomer in the context of the American avantgarde, Lost Generation, and Harlem Renaissance, see Soto, "Literary History."
3. Frank, *Our America*, cited in the context of the Frank-Toomer correspondence by Terris, "Waldo Frank," 306.
4. From an autobiographical sketch cited by Darwin T. Turner in the Norton critical edition of *Cane* (New York, 1988), 141–142, from which I cite parenthetically in the text. Further references to other sources in this edition will be made as Turner, *Cane*. A larger excerpt appears in Darwin T. Turner, ed., *The Wayward and the Seeking*, 121; this collection will be referred to as Turner, *Wayward*.
5. Toomer, *Essentials* (1931; reprint with an introduction by Rudolph P. Byrd, Athens, GA: University of Georgia Press, 1991), xxxii.
6. Turner, *Wayward*, 129. Kerman and Eldridge, *Lives*, 116, also call attention to this passage.
7. Excerpted in Turner, *Cane*, 152.
8. The play was published in Turner, *Wayward*, 243–325. See also the discussions by McKay, *Toomer*, and Byrd, *Years*, as well as Terris, "Waldo Frank."
9. Turner, *Wayward*, 290.
10. Jones, *Prison-House*, 42, suggests that "Avey" is reminiscent of Joyce's "Araby." He also links the story's theme of the modern woman's indifference to men's sexual advances to Eliot's *Waste Land*.
11. The tale may go back to an incident Walter White reported in his book *Rope and Faggot*. White writes: "In the ten years from January 1, 1918, through 1927, American mobs lynched 454 persons. Of these, 38 were white, and 416 were coloured. Eleven of the Negro victims were women, three of them at the time of lynching with child" (20–21). White gives a detailed account of the lynching of Mary Turner (the pregnant wife of Hayes Turner, who had been killed by a mob): "Securely they bound her ankles together and, by them, hanged her to a tree. Gasoline and motor oil were thrown upon her dangling clothes; a match wrapped her in sudden flames. . . . The clothes burned from her crisply toasted body, in which,

unfortunately, life still lingered, a man stepped towards the woman and, with his knife, ripped open the abdomen in a crude Cæsarean operation. Out tumbled the prematurely born child. Two feeble cries it gave—and received for answer the heel of a stalwart man, as life was ground out of the tiny form" (28–29).

12. Excerpted in Turner, *Cane*, 152. This letter is also cited and perceptively discussed by McKay, *Toomer*, and Byrd, *Years*, among others.
13. Bone, *Negro Novel*, McKay, *Toomer*, John M. Reilly, and Patricia Watkins (both in Turner, *Cane*) are among the critics who have developed aspects of the unity of *Cane*. As Turner suggests, names also recur from one section to another: John Stone in "Becky" is the father of Bob Stone in "Blood-Burning Moon," and David Georgia also appears in both of these tales; Barlo appears in "Becky" and "Esther," and the Dixie Pike in "Carma" and "Fern." For a concise statement of elements that contradict a unifying reading of *Cane* see Byrd, *Years*, 15ff.
14. John M. Reilly, in Turner, *Cane*, 198.
15. See Jones, *Prison-House*, 47. The question is repeated three more times and served as inspiration to Farah Griffin's study "*Who Set You Flowin'?*"
16. Darwin T. Turner and Rudolph P. Byrd, among others, have briefly discussed imagist aspects of Toomer's work. Flint's and Pound's maxims are cited in William Pratt, ed., *The Imagist Poem* (New York: Dutton, 1963), 18.
17. The description continues in drawing out tree imagery—which has a sinister undertone in view of the lynching that is coming and the Mame Lamkins story in "Kabnis."
18. T. E. Hulme cited in Pratt, *Imagist Poem*, 28. Du Bois review reprinted in Durham, *Merrill Studies*, 40–42; also excerpted in Turner, *Cane*, 170–171.
19. Cited in Kerman and Eldridge, *Lives*, 95.
20. Eldredge, *O'Keeffe*, 44. For a full analysis of Toomer's literary work in relationship to O'Keeffe's and Stieglitz's visual arts, see Nadell, "Experience."
21. Rusch, *Reader*, 280–281.
22. Toomer, "Race Problems," 98–99. This essay, reprinted in *Theories of Ethnicity: A Classical Reader* (New York: New York University Press, 1996), 168–190, has not received much attention by Toomer scholars. See, however, Williams, "Eugenics," 1–12; and Lindberg, "Raising *Cane*."
23. Rusch, *Reader*, 107–108.
24. Letter to Waldo Frank, late 1922 or early 1923, excerpted in Turner, *Cane*, 151. Toomer's view of black culture as prototypically American culture prefigures the thought of Albert Murray in *The Omni-Americans* and Ralph Ellison in *Shadow and Act*.
25. For an excellent discussion of Toomer in this context see Hutchinson, "Racial Discourse," 226–250.
26. Rusch, *Reader*, 109.
27. Toomer, *Essentials*, xxiv.
28. One thinks, for example, of Man Ray's portrait of Marcel Duchamp as Rrose (1921) or of Anton Räderscheidt's doubling self-portrait (1928).
29. Turner, *Wayward*, 121.
30. Toomer to Samuel Pessin, cited in Kerman and Eldridge, *Lives*, 99.
31. The biographical information is derived from Turner, *Cane*, from Bone, *Down Home*, from Onita Marie Estes-Hicks, "Jean Toomer: A Biographical and Critical Study (*Cane*)" (Ph.D. diss., Columbia University, 1982), and from conversations with the late Marjorie Content Toomer. See also Hicks, "National Identity," 22–44.
32. W. Edward Farrison, in Turner, *Cane*, 179, argues, however, that "thy son" need not be identified as Toomer.

33. Cited in Arna Bontemps's introduction to Toomer, *Cane* (New York: Harper and Row, 1969), viii-ix. The latter part of this letter is included in Turner, *Cane*, 128–129, and cited in Kerman and Eldridge, *Lives*, 96.
34. Rusch, *Reader*, 105.
35. Lindberg, "Raising *Cane*," 73 n. 17, comments on this passage: "Toomer is not even a writer, but simply a Negro looking for a new race through (dread) miscegenation." North, *Dialect*, 163, describes the "almost hysterical" reaction of *Time* magazine to Toomer's marriage to Latimer: *Time* "quoted his idea about the new American race with scorn and affected alarm under the ironic title of 'Just Americans.' The article suggested that some states, like Wisconsin, where Toomer and Latimer were married, were insufficiently vigilant against marriages between the races." See Kerman and Eldridge, *Lives*, 202, for other responses.
36. Such other important black American writers as Countée Cullen, James Weldon Johnson, William Stanley Braithwaite, Jessie Fauset, and Claude McKay also responded enthusiastically to Toomer's *Cane*, as McKay, *Toomer*, 238, has shown. In addition, Rudolph P. Byrd cites a letter by Sterling A. Brown describing *Cane* as "one of the most beautiful and moving books of contemporary American literature" and discusses Toomer's influence on Langston Hughes, Michael Harper's "Cryptograms," Alice Walker's *Meridian*, Ernest J. Gaines's *The Autobiography of Miss Jane Pittman*, and Gloria Naylor's *The Women of Brewster Place* (Byrd, *Years*, 183–189).
37. See McKay, *Toomer*, 46–50; Byrd, *Years*, 97, cites the Toomer letter to Cunard of February 8, 1930: "Though I am interested in and deeply value the Negro, I am not a Negro. And though I have written about the Negro, and value the material and the art that is Negro, all my writings during the past seven years have been on other subjects. In America I am working for a vision of this country as composed of people who are Americans first, and only of certain descents as secondary matters." Toomer did, however, contribute to Sterling Brown's *Negro Caravan* (1941), perhaps because Brown had praised *Cane* as an *American* book.
38. Cited in Kerman and Eldridge, *Lives*, 97.
39. Toomer to Frank, April 26, 1922. Cited in Kerman and Eldridge, *Lives*, 87.
40. Cited in Arna Bontemps's introduction to Toomer, *Cane*, viii; Turner, *Cane*, 128; and Kerman and Eldridge, *Lives*, 96.
41. Toomer to McClure, July 22, 1922, cited in Kerman and Eldridge, *Lives*, 96.

Identity in Motion

GEORGE HUTCHINSON

Placing Cane

THE APPEARANCE OF *Cane* in 1923 was greeted by influential critics as the brilliant beginning of a literary career. Presenting an unprecedented perspective on the South generally and on black Southerners in particular, *Cane* was "wholly unlike anything of this sort done before," a reviewer in the *New York Tribune* wrote.[1] Many stressed the "authenticity" of Toomer's African American characters and the lyrical voice with which he conjured them into being. His treatment of blacks contrasted starkly with both the stereotypes of earlier work by (mostly) white authors and the then current limitations of African American "problem fiction." As Montgomery Gregory pointed out in an effusive review for the new black journal *Opportunity*, Toomer had avoided "the pitfalls of propaganda and moralizing on the one hand and the snares of a false and hollow race pride on the other hand."[2] Many agreed with Waldo Frank's statement in the foreword to the book: "It is a harbinger of the South's literary maturity: of its emergence from the obsession put upon its minds by the unending racial crisis—an obsession from which writers have made their indirect escape through sentimentalism, exoticism, polemic, 'problem' fiction, and moral melodrama. It marks the dawn of direct and unafraid creation."[3] As these comments reveal, part of what made the book seem so amazing was that the author had been able, allegedly, to abstract himself from the constant pressure of American race consciousness in order to explore the beauty of the South and of black people in a purely "artistic" fashion. That Toomer's own background allowed him special insight into the South may have been a precondition of his accomplishment, but this was not the point; what set him apart, said critics both black and white, was that he was able to drop the self-consciousness of writing as a "Negro"—or as a white man, or as an American, or under the guise of any other "limiting" identity. Precisely this sort of negative capability had made possible an evocation of beauty and of "Life" that catapulted *Cane*'s author into the front ranks of American art and made his book an inspiration to a new generation of African American authors.

Key to the unusual features and effectiveness of *Cane* was the fact that its author was in rapid transition, vocationally, geographically, socially, and intellectually, between identities. His unsettled position derived from both a complicated personal history and the unusual cultural moment and places in which he emerged as an artist. Indeed, *Cane* is a striking example of how the texts that do most to renovate literary traditions are often subversive of the very notion of tradition; their authors are not so much unitary figures inhabiting fixed cultural coordinates as liminal figures who straddle the thresholds of social difference and, like their multivalent texts, are difficult to pin down.

Born just two years after his famous grandfather had moved from a palatial home in New Orleans to a smaller, though fashionable, house in Washington, Toomer never really knew the father for whom he was originally named.[4] His mother, Nina, gave birth to him just nine months after a wedding of which her father disapproved and then found herself abandoned when Nathan Pinchback Toomer (as Jean was first named) was only a year old. Nina had little choice but to move back home and accommodate to at least some of her autocratic father's conditions, which included changing the boy's surname to Pinchback and his first name to anything other than Nathan. Eventually, the first name became Eugene, after a godfather; but friends called the boy "Pinchy." His mother called him Eugene Toomer and his grandparents, Eugene Pinchback. Ambiguity of identity and a strong intuition of the arbitrary nature of social labels came quite naturally to Toomer.

Toomer would later represent the social world of his youth as peculiarly unmarked by racial consciousness, yet he attended a segregated "colored" primary school on U Street while his white friends attended a different school. After his mother's 1906 remarriage, a move to a white neighborhood in New Rochelle on Long Island Sound, and then his mother's death in 1909, Jean returned at age fourteen with neither father nor mother to the Pinchback family in Washington, where his grandparents now lived in his uncle Bismarck's home on Florida Avenue, in a mostly black neighborhood. He would later remember this milieu as one of a genuine distinction in culture, manners, and learning. Yet his family belonged to a group that considered itself "above" most black people. After graduation in 1910 from the famous black M Street High School, he began to consciously think of himself as neither black nor white—or both black and white, belonging to both worlds and yet, precisely because of that, removed from each. There can be no doubt that he felt adrift and that his physical appearance, childhood experiences, and family situation had much to do with this. He decided, he would later insist, to simply let people take him for what they wished while he maintained a sense of being outside their clumsy categories.

Toomer entered an agricultural program at the University of Wisconsin—where he was apparently taken by many for a Native American—but dropped out after only a year. He then started to enroll at the Massachusetts College of Agriculture at Amherst but changed his mind. Nonetheless, Toomer's interest in scientific agriculture would have some bearing on his notion of the transformation of the rural South that informs *Cane*. His subtle observations about the changing agricultural economy are everywhere evident in the first and last sections of the book. (Toomer no doubt knew, too, that sorghum—the "cane" of his book—first came to the Americas with captives from Africa.)[5]

In January 1916 Toomer entered the American College of Physical Training in Chicago. Meridel Le Sueur, later a famous left-wing poet, attended the school at the time and would remember Toomer as "reserved, isolated, perceived as an Indian by the rest of the students."[6] A boxing instructor introduced him to socialism, and he began attending lectures by Clarence Darrow and others on naturalism, atheism, and social radicalism which overturned his prior notions of the world, initiating an intense intellectual pilgrimage. The attempt to find a comprehensive theory of contemporary reality had a special significance to this young man who did not know who he was or where he fit in. Toomer never completed his second year at the college; he enrolled at the University of Chicago but dropped out after only a few months. Returning East, and inspired by Lester Ward's *Dynamic Sociology*, he took a sociology course at New York University's summer school, then studied history at City College while he stayed with his uncle Walter. He explored Bernard Shaw. World War I broke out and he went back to Chicago, where he sold Ford automobiles and began writing, still reading Shaw. Then he took a short-term job as a substitute physical education director in Milwaukee. The story "Bona and Paul" was surely inspired by Toomer's experiences in these years, if an early version of it was not first drafted then.

After returning to Washington with neither a job nor a vocational plan and with his family understandably upset with him, Toomer once again moved to New York to take a clerk's post with a grocery firm. He attended lectures at the left-wing Rand School (as did a number of other soon-to-be "New Negro" authors) and there met radicals and writers associated with journals such as *The Liberator* and the New York *Call*—the first to which he would soon begin submitting his work. Influenced, apparently, by Romain Rolland's fictional hero Jean-Christophe (a composer-prophet fusing German and French "spiritual" inheritances into a pan-European music), he decided to become a composer and took a second job as a physical education director in a settlement house to pay for music lessons and piano rental. About this time he adopted the name "Jean," inspired by Rolland's hero and Victor Hugo's Jean Valjean. He heard the socialists and cultural radicals like Scott Nearing and Alfred Kreymborg speak; read Ibsen, Santayana, and Goethe; bummed around upstate New York during the summer of 1919; and placed two pieces with the *Call*—evidently his first appearance in print.[7]

In his later autobiographical manuscripts, Toomer played down the extent of his interest in socialism. His two pieces for the *Call*, a voice of the Socialist Party in New York, clearly reveal, however, that he had found in socialist theory a compelling framework for understanding racial as well as class exploitation.[8] The socialist strain remains evident in references within *Cane* to "powerful underground races" threatening the foundations of bourgeois Washington. In a letter to his publisher while *Cane* was in press, Toomer described a new book project about "this whole black and brown world heaving upward against, here and there mixing with the white. . . . This upward heaving is to be symbolic of the proletariat or world upheaval. And it is likewise to be symbolic of the subconscious penetration of the conscious mind."[9] Even in the late 1920s, when Toomer had little interest in political solutions to human problems, being thoroughly engaged with religious/psychological development based on the system of G. I. Gurdjieff, he would write of how existing economic, political, and social systems formed the ground of racial division and exploitation. Yet racialized modes of thinking and feeling had taken on a semiautonomous life of their own that prevented any intelligent grappling with the basic inequities of modern society and merely contributed to the "trap" in which all Americans were caught. To Toomer, the answer was to combat "mutually repellent" psychological tendencies among different groups. He thus turned increasingly to psychological and spiritual exploration, guided in part by a theory about the emergence of a new "American" race of which he considered himself the first conscious member. Spiritual and psychological transformation, Toomer believed, would be the first step toward social reconstruction.

This kind of thinking was not unusual between 1919 and 1929, a period in which political conservatism had turned back the forces of progressive reform and many left-wing thinkers turned to cultural radicalism as well as psychological and "spiritual" programs as routes toward the desired social transformation. In the same year that Toomer published his first two pieces in the *Call*, Waldo

Frank's *Our America* appeared; fitting the general drift of Toomer's intellectual trajectory, it would prove an important catalyst for many of the basic ideas behind *Cane*.

In Frank's vision, young writers and artists were to play a crucial role in bringing a new America into being. Borrowing from Van Wyck Brooks's notion that "Puritan" and "pioneer" traditions in the United States had prevented the emergence of a genuine American culture, Frank argued that the United States had no "rooted" peasant traditions out of which a national art might be expected to develop. The social elite looked to "imported" culture as a mere mark of status, and the immigrant working classes had discarded what spiritual heritage they had brought with them in the mad dash for "Americanization." Religion as a "mystical consciousness" had not survived the transatlantic voyage. Anglo-Americans had never put down roots in the continent, and the cultures of the Indian and Mexican had succumbed to white, industrial civilization. Thus the American people were reduced to automatons serving capitalist overlords and their machines. Industrialism and materialism took over as gods, leaving the nation a cultural and spiritual wasteland. Yet Frank believed the "American chaos" would finally give birth to the living culture prophesied by Whitman. The "spiritual pioneers" of the rising generation were answering the call of *Democratic Vistas*, he proclaimed, moving beyond naturalism and critical realism to a fusion of revolutionist and artist-prophet into the "bringer of a new religion."[10]

Like most white intellectuals of the time, Frank failed to take any notice of African American culture, as Toomer would point out to him in 1922, prompting Frank to plan a new edition of the book with a section on "the Negro." W.E.B. Du Bois had proclaimed as early as 1903 that black Americans offered the only "indigenous" spirituality, the only folk song and sense of simple reverence, the only genuine "culture" in "a dusty desert of dollars and smartness."[11] Just as he tended in later life to downplay the influence of socialism on his thinking, Toomer covered up much of his apparent indebtedness to African American thought in his early intellectual development. He clearly had read Du Bois, for example—indeed, the controversy between Du Bois and Booker T. Washington (who had occasionally stayed at the Pinchback home) would surely have been a topic of conversation within his family—and the way in which he imagined African American culture fitting into, yet transforming, Frank's cultural nationalist program seems to owe much to *The Souls of Black Folk*. Alain Locke, a philosophy professor at Howard University, knew Toomer at least by 1919 and acted as an early mentor of sorts; indeed, Locke may have been the first person with whom Toomer shared some of the sketches that went into *Cane*. Locke's ideas had been developing along lines parallel to Van Wyck Brooks's and Waldo Frank's since at least 1911, and probably earlier. In his foreword to the famous anthology *The New Negro* (1925), a key text of the Harlem Renaissance, Locke would connect the Negro's "spiritual coming of age" with what Brooks had termed "America's coming of age" in a famous book of that title: "The New Negro must be seen in the perspective of a New World, and especially of a New America. . . . America seeking a new spiritual expansion and artistic maturity, trying to found an American literature, a national art, and national music implies a Negro-American culture seeking the same satisfactions and objectives."[12] Toomer's relations with white New York intellectuals seem to lie behind Locke's hopeful statement in the foreword to *The New Negro* that white authors are turning with "unbiassed interest" to African American culture, prepared for a "common vision of the social tasks ahead." Conversely, the New Negro no longer, says Locke, allows "social segregation to segregate him mentally, and a counter-attitude to cramp and fetter his own living."[13] These were precisely Toomer's sentiments.

Georgia Douglas Johnson was also an important contact and source of moral support before Toomer had connected with white modernists. They read each other's work and he shared his developing ideas with her; indeed, she was quite impressed by how much he had "improved" through his contact with New York intellectuals. Toomer directed study sessions at Johnson's home on the history of slavery, the social and economic forces behind racial ideology, and the position of the "mixed race group" in the United States, hoping to develop an ideal that would be "both workable and inclusive"; about this time Johnson seems to have written her poems of the "new race" that would appear in the climactic section of her book entitled *Bronze*.[14] The sessions initiated by Toomer apparently formed the beginning of her regular "Saturday Nighters"—meetings of black writers and intellectuals interested in contemporary issues and literature. These would continue for several years and were among the incubators of what came to be called the "Negro Renaissance." Thus Toomer drew upon two different communities of thinking, roughly centered in black Washington and white Manhattan, in the years immediately preceding *Cane;* and Toomer epitomized the interconnections between these communities in his life and in his work.

By 1920, Toomer was living in New York and working for a grocery firm, when his grandfather sent him six hundred dollars from the sale of his house. Toomer quit his job to devote his time to reading, writing, and music. Gradually he realized he would have to choose between writing and music as his vocation. Goethe's *Wilhelm Meister,* he would later claim, decided the matter in favor of writing and committed him to a program of becoming an "aristocrat of culture, of spirit and character, of ideas, of true nobility."[15] He then returned to Whitman "because he was of America." Toomer spent days in the library, reading everything he could get his hands on concerning Whitman and spending the rest of his time writing. The impact was enduring—from the search for an "American" language and creative use of slang to the development of a sensual mysticism, to the notion of a new race of Americans. In the fall of 1920, at a party given by the editor of *Broom*, Toomer met Waldo Frank, who showed interest in him, read some of his work, and said that he had promise as a writer.[16] By winter, however, Toomer had run out of money and returned to Washington. His grandfather agreed to put him up in exchange for household duties; this allowed Toomer to concentrate on reading and writing. By now, at least, he felt he had a purpose in life.

During this period of intense self-development in Washington, when Toomer was feeling a growing sense of difference from, and superior perceptiveness to, those around him, he immersed himself in Buddhism, theosophy, occultism, and various other "Eastern" religious modes of thought, strains of which play throughout *Cane*. His religious character intensely aroused, he turned back to literature in the desire to learn the craft of writing. Here Frost's poetry appealed to him in its precision and localism; Sherwood Anderson's *Winesburg, Ohio* suggested a "spiritualization of the immediate" in a lyrical prose departing from prior models of fiction. The economy of the Imagists and their stress on "fresh vision" attracted him (Toomer, "Outline," 55). He worked on his writing, sharing it with his black friends in Washington. And at the same time he read works of racial theory or studies of the "race problem" in the United States, which he found informative in some cases but blind to what he regarded as the formation of a "new race" that would transcend current divisions. Having lived between the white and black worlds, Toomer clearly believed he had a superior perspective on the "realities" of race in American society, particularly with respect to its psychological dimensions.

Exhausted from caring for his grandparents and his intellectual labor, and short of money, through his grandfather's contacts Toomer was offered a short-term position as substitute principal of Sparta Agricultural and Industrial Institute, beginning in September 1921. Located a mile or so outside of Sparta (the "Sempter" of *Cane*) in east central Georgia, the school trained young black men and women chiefly for jobs in agriculture and light industry.[17] Toomer spent only two months there before the principal returned, but the experience was pivotal. Indeed, the brevity of the experience (together with Toomer's "outsider" status) may help account for its psychological intensity.

Toomer was a careful observer of the social structure and mores of the community around the institute. Much of the first and last sections of *Cane* refers to specific geographical and sociological features of Hancock County, as Barbara Foley has demonstrated ("Jean Toomer's Sparta," 747–76). His experiences there also confirmed Toomer's suspicion that the folk culture would soon die out: "The fact is, that if anything comes up now, pure Negro, it will be a swan-song. Dont let us fool ourselves, brother: the Negro of the folk-song has all but passed away: the Negro of the emotional church is fading. . . . America needs these elements. They are passing. Let us grab and hold them while there still is time."[18] The experience in Sparta unleashed a steady creative surge in Toomer, and he began sending things out. He returned to Washington excited about his work.

In Washington Toomer took on the care of his elders again while he continued working on the pieces that went into *Cane*. He finished the first draft of "Kabnis" in December 1921—the day before his grandfather died, according to a later autobiography (which, if not literally accurate, is psychologically revelatory). He and his uncle took the body to New Orleans and put it in the family vault beside Toomer's mother's remains—an experience, surely, that intensified and personalized his awareness of generational change, of an old order giving way to a new (Toomer, "Outline," 59). The personal transition through which Toomer was living seemed intimately connected with a fundamental transformation of U.S. society. In this transformation, his unique personal history, Toomer believed, endowed him with a prophetic role.

In August 1922 Toomer wrote to his love interest, Mae Wright: "I believe that we are at the beginning of one of the great cultural phases of world history. I have my part to play in it, and you have yours." He found Washington stagnant, but beneath he felt a "quickening of higher impulses, an awakening to values that concern the soul."[19] The life of Seventh Street, where Southern black migrants settled and recreated themselves as an urban working class, now captured Toomer's attention in a new way. It seemed to Toomer to express a stage in the ultimate "absorption" of the folk spirit into the modern "chaos," at the same time transforming the dominant culture itself.[20]

Toomer's letter to Wright also expressed the notion that Americans must overcome "the Tyranny of the Anglo-Saxon Ideal," an ideal that included both white superiority in all things and the notion that greatness consisted of success in conquering the material world. Thus whatever had inhibited that conquest had been considered sinful, particularly the expression of emotions and imaginative creation. A new generation of young white Americans, however, had abandoned the old ideal and stressed "the supreme position of the arts." Moreover, they had overcome belief in Anglo-Saxon superiority and grown receptive to all peoples: "They have successfully transcended the narrow implications of the entire Anglo-Saxon ideal."[21]

It was time for African Americans to do the same: "Paradoxical as it may seem, we who have Negro blood in our veins, who are culturally and emotionally the most removed from Puritan tradition, are its most tenacious supporters." Not only did (bourgeois) black Americans judge a man's worth by his possessions, but they were skeptical of art, suspicious and often ashamed of their own emotions, convinced of the greater beauty of Anglo-Saxon physical features. Without denying the beauty of white people, African Americans must learn to love "the charm of soft full lines. Of dusk faces. Of crisp curly hair. Their ears must learn to love the color and warmth of mellowed cadences, of rounded southern speech. They must be made aware of the subtile [*sic*], intuitive natures of their own minds. They must learn to prize these qualities. Their souls must feel (and glory in the feeling) the abundance and power of Negro-derived emotions." They must "create a living ideal" of their own.[22] Toomer's awakening to the black-folk South owed nearly as much to his artistic development from 1920 on—and specifically to his engagement with the concepts promoted by Frank, Anderson, and others—as his artistic inspiration owed to his two-month stay in Sparta; for his reading had taught him to find value where the older generation of his class and caste had not. Significant in this letter is Toomer's positioning himself as both connected to and different from other "Negroes"; he possesses "Negro blood" but is evidently not one of "them." What he refers to as his "unique racial and social status" has enabled him to crystallize a new Negro ideal.

In December of the same year, in a letter to Sherwood Anderson that makes mention of African American tendencies either to accept the "Anglo-Saxon [white] ideal" or to overemphasize "what is Negro," Toomer expressed the belief that his art would "aid in giving the negro to himself," and he proposed starting a new magazine, "American, but concentrating on the significant contributions, or possible contributions of the Negro to the western world. A magazine that would consciously hoist, and perhaps a trifle overemphasize a negroid ideal."[23] No doubt he felt that once the Negro ideal had achieved its full development, transforming all Americans, it would be transcended and absorbed into a new and greater ideal—an ideal for which he was a sort of Jean the Baptist. He was disappointed when Anderson misunderstood his racial self-conception and responded to him as a Negro.

As he told the *Liberator* editors, "From my own point of view I am naturally and inevitably an American. I have striven for a spiritual fusion analogous to the fact of racial intermingling. Without denying a single element in me, with no desire to subdue, one to the other, I have sought to let them function as complements." Nonetheless, his "growing need for artistic expression" over the previous two to three years had pulled him "deeper and deeper into the Negro group. And as my powers of receptivity increased, I found myself loving it in a way that I could never love the other. It has stimulated and fertilized whatever creative talent I may contain within me."[24]

From the time of his return to Washington, Toomer wrote constantly and sent manuscripts to such journals as *The Double Dealer, The Liberator,* and other "little magazines" with which authors such as Sherwood Anderson and Waldo Frank were connected. Frank responded enthusiastically to the pieces Toomer sent him and also asked Toomer for help with the "southern" novel he was working on, *Holiday*.[25] The bond between the men quickly grew extremely intense—they greeted each other as "brother" and "brother mine." Toomer seemed to find himself working his way into his proper milieu. He clearly found, as well, an emotional outlet and bond that he deeply needed. Frank seemed not only to understand him but to admire and learn from him at a time when many people to whom he expressed his thoughts and feelings apparently thought them strange.

By the summer of 1922, Toomer felt ready to publish a book, to be entitled *Cane* and composed of three parts. The sketches of the South (now in section 1 of *Cane*) and "Kabnis" would become "Cane Stalks and Choruses." The poems would be collected under the heading "Leaves and Syrup Songs." The Washington vignettes would make up "Leaf Traceries in Washington."[26] Whitman's method of clustering poems in *Leaves of Grass*, with an overall symbolic structure interconnecting them, seems to have been a partial model.

Meanwhile, Frank was planning a trip south for the fall of 1922 to gather more material for *Holiday*, and he invited Toomer to join him. They ended up going to Spartanburg, South Carolina, where the bond between them intensified under the pressure of the ubiquitous color line and where Frank, significantly, "passed" as a Negro.[27] About this time the two men began thinking of their books as closely interrelated efforts to bring the South to artistic fruition.

When Toomer returned to Washington from this second trip south, he took a job for two weeks as assistant manager at the Howard Theater, a popular black-managed theater in the heart of what later came to be known as Washington's "Little Harlem," where African American revues destined for fame in New York at the outset of the Harlem Renaissance had trial runs during the very period that Toomer worked there.[28] From this experience he got the inspiration for "Theater" and "Box Seat" (Kerman and Eldridge, *Lives*, 90). He remained in contact with Alain Locke, who helped him place "Song of the Son" in the magazine brought out by the National Association for the Advancement of Colored People, *The Crisis*. Thereafter, other pieces from what is now *Cane* began appearing in *The Liberator, Broom, Double Dealer,*

Little Review, *Modern Review*, *Nomad*, *Prairie*, and *S4N*. The series of magazines in itself indicates a shift in Toomer's primary vocational and intellectual affiliations from overtly socialist politics to aesthetic and psychological experimentalism. His political and social interests were being reconfigured in relation to, and absorbed by, other interests.

Toomer had read Anderson's *Winesburg, Ohio* and *The Triumph of the Egg and Other Stories* just before going to Sparta and asserted that these books had nourished his artistic response to the folk life there. Not surprisingly, then, much of Toomer's work owed a great deal to Anderson's method of deemphasizing plot in his fictional prose and developing instead a "lyric fiction," using symbolic and metaphorical matrices, as well as repetition and refrain, to provide the structure of the work. Each sketch thus came to have an essentially musical or poetic structure. This characteristic is even more pronounced in Toomer's than in Anderson's work. Interspersed poems and songs often function as refrains to establish a basal rhythm and mood throughout a story or sketch.

Like *Winesburg*, the first and last sections of *Cane* (which Toomer initially planned to form the whole of his book) presented a series of semi-independent stories or sketches, focusing on different characters, all set in the same locality. Behind most of the pieces in both books, moreover, one finds a sense of spiritual and emotional frustration, failure of basic communication between individuals, repression of "natural" energies—all of which reveal the futility and "chaos" of contemporary American life and the need for a spiritual awakening, a bursting of unconscious forces through the desicated crust of residual Puritan and pioneer traditions. The "voice" of each work, moreover, strives for specific regional inflections and habits of speech—the Midwest in Anderson's work, the South in Toomer's.

Toomer aspired to go beyond both Anderson and Waldo Frank, however, in response to the forces of industrialization and modern technology. The introduction of the machine, he believed, had destroyed humanity's balance with Nature, creating spiritual conflicts to which artists had responded either by rejecting "the Machine" and suggesting back-to-nature programs or by accepting the machine as a necessary evil and creating aesthetic "counter-forms" or "anti-bodies" against its destructive features. Toomer proposed instead that artists must create new forms that would spiritualize machinery and absorb its sublime power.[29] Whitman himself had, after all, sung the "body electric" and installed the soul amid the kitchenware; Toomer would do him one better and install dynamos in his prose, electrical wiring in his poetry. Hence such pieces as "Her Lips Are Copper Wire" in the second section of *Cane*, which use the new "machine" forces as potentially positive metaphors of human connection:

"with your tongue remove the tape / and press your lips to mine / till they are incandescent" (57).

Also important for Toomer's prose style was an attempt to advance toward a "classic American prose," a dynamic and adaptable fusion of heterogeneous rhythms, words, and forms of pronunciation currently differentiated into conflicting racial and class dialects. Like jazz, slang and colloquialisms kept pace with the introduction of new forces into society; literary artists should do no less. Hence Kabnis's tortured attempt to find words to "feed his soul"—the soul of the South, fed by words of "white folks," "black niggers," "yaller niggers": "This whole damn bloated purple country feeds it cause its goin down t hell in a holy avalanche of words. I want t feed the soul—I know what that is; the preachers dont—but I've got t feed it" (*Cane*, 111). Kabnis's need to create "golden words" to transmute the nightmare of southern history into aesthetic value and spiritual awakening is Jean Toomer's as he worked toward his own voice under the pressure of southern life. But "Kabnis" ends before its central character achieves what Toomer and Waldo Frank would call "fusion." Toomer intended "Kabnis" as the dramatization of a phase from which both he and the United States were about to emerge. Thus he ends the book on a note of uncertainty, transition—rather than resolution and achieved "identity" in either comic or tragic mode.

Some notion of Waldo Frank's fictional method is worth attending to in coming to terms with Toomer's book, particularly its second section and its overall design. Toomer wrote Gorham Munson in October 1922 that, except for Anderson earlier, "(and to a less extent Frost and Sandburg) Waldo is the only modern writer who has immediately influenced me. He is so powerful and close, he has so many elements that I need, that I would be afraid of downright imitation if I were not so sure of myself."[30] Particularly in such narratives as "Theatre," "Box Seat," and "Kabnis" (which is dedicated to Frank), Toomer structured the plot around "slopes," "curves," and "crescendos" of cognition, physical action, and emotion, to use the contemporary lingo of Frank, Gorham Munson, and himself. Swift, dramatic shifts, soliloquies in rapid transit between different thoughts, moods, and physical impressions were to suggest a dynamic structure and explosive forces, with chaotic "fluxes" terminating in decisive statements. The effect was to be kaleidoscopic. "Lyrical crystallizations" would bring several moving elements of a piece to a sudden, brilliant integration, as when, in "Box Seat," for example, a jagged series of interpenetrating actions, thoughts, and statements by different characters ends with the character Dan Moore suddenly crying out, "JESUS WAS ONCE A LEPER!" Even Toomer's moments of integration tend to bring into focus a liminal figure.

Moreover, Toomer believed the larger structure of a work should be itself a "lyric crystallization of which the interior poems and images are the facets" (Toomer, "Critic," 26). The overall structure of a work should have an underlying "spherical form," with a "curve" cementing the various parts together and "giving the Whole a dynamic propulsion forward," to borrow from Toomer's own phrasing with regard to Frank's novels *Rahab* and *City Block* (Toomer, "Critic," 27). Thus in a letter to Frank about *Cane*, written just after Toomer had completed it and sent the manuscript off to his correspondent, Toomer noted that "from three angles, *Cane*'s design is a circle. Aesthetically, from simple forms to complex ones, and back to simple forms. Regionally, from the South up into the North, and back into the South again. Or, From the North down into the South, and then a return North. From the point of view of the spiritual entity behind the work [that is, Toomer's own spiritual development], the curve really starts with Bona and Paul (awakening), plunges into Kabnis, emerges in Karintha etc. swings upward into Theatre [*sic*] and Box Seat, and ends (pauses) in Harvest Song."[31] To reinforce the design, Toomer included a series of arcs before the three divisions of the book.

Also important to the structure of Toomer's more complex tales and dramatic sketches is the differentiation between characters in relation to the multiple dimensions of human consciousness that control their actions. Because of the disintegrating forces of modern society, these different dimensions—intellection, physical passion, emotion, dream—rarely were in balance either within or between individuals. In "Theatre," for example, Dorris and John fail to coincide spiritually and complement each other, to a great extent because of urban class differences that block communication and because they do not have a proper balance of physical, intellectual, verbal, and emotional capacities.

The frustration of many characters in *Cane* owes much to the chaotic and unsatisfying state of male-female relationships, a constant theme in *Cane*. Toomer's personal ideal of the relationship between a man and a woman stressed inherent differences between them, with the woman often in the role of muse and pupil, inspirer of the male prophet-creator. Men, Toomer believed, are dynamic and aggressive by nature, women primarily lyrical and receptive.[32] Both are incomplete in themselves. Yet Toomer is capable of endowing some of his female characters, such as Carma, with remarkable strength, and in much of *Cane* female sexuality either overpowers or nearly overpowers the male characters. The man must be strong enough to control his response, to be attentive to woman's needs, and to lead the relationship toward a "fusion" of complementary elements. Nonetheless, *Cane* also reveals the damage done to women by the restriction of their lives, particularly by men's use of them as mere vessels of meaning, routes to "higher consciousness," or means of sexual satisfaction—roles that women often played in Toomer's own life. *Cane* critiques its narrators' own ambivalence about female sexuality, as Megan Abbott has argued,[33] an ambivalence revealing a basic insecurity about masculine identity at the very heart of the desire for "fusion" of male and female energies. A desire for domination and control competes with, and is thoroughly intertwined with, a desire of the male to lose himself in the sublime embrace of the female. It is difficult not to notice a correspondence in the book between this complex of masculine desire and the ambiguity of racial and class identities with their frustrated or repressed longings for self-transcendence. Such transcendence Toomer associated with spiritual "fruition," an ecstatic transformation of human being.

Although Toomer admired the imagists and other "high modernists" for their precision and economy and for the mystery they could evoke with sharp sensory details (evident especially in such poems as "Face," "Nullo," "Portrait in Georgia," and "Storm Ending"), he found their work lacking in "substance" and spiritual significance. Their intellectual acuity came with a sterility of soul, offering sharp irony but no "affirmative creation."[34] Yet he agreed with them that art should not be a mere transcription or reflection of life; it should be "the most vital and thrilling experience that life has to give."[35] Human life must be used but transformed toward a new "dimension" by the sort of experience that only words can precipitate.[36] And the result of the precipitation, Toomer hoped in the case of his own work at least, was "spiritual" germination. It was precisely the liminal potential of literary expression, in other words, its ability to mediate between realms of possible experience, that appealed to Toomer as he completed his book. The most powerful poems in *Cane*—such as the lovely sonnet "November Cotton Flower," "Song of the Son," and "Georgia Dusk"—extend Frost's subtle transformation of traditional poetics, as well as his evocation of a landscape's human history, to achieve a remarkable fusion of the mood of the spirituals and other folk song with almost traditional English metrical and stanzaic forms. This creates an effect that is entirely original; the mood is reverent, suggesting a spiritual dimension that makes itself known in sudden revelations.

To say this is not at all to deny the material reality of the life that went into *Cane* and the social relations Toomer criticizes. But Toomer's goal was "mystical realism"; naturalism and "surface realism" were not enough (Toomer, "Critic," 27). *Cane* does function as a critique of contemporary society, and the "spiritual" force he wanted his work to have was no disembodied "transcendence" of history but, to Toomer's way of thinking, a total engagement with it.

Cane sold well below a thousand copies, and Horace Liveright never made back the $150 advance he had paid Toomer for signing with him; Toomer, moreover, never composed the books he had planned and described to Liveright as *Cane* was in press. He made a decisive turn, perhaps provoked by the reception of *Cane*. In "The Significance of Jean Toomer," a 1925 essay for the black magazine *Opportunity*, Toomer's close friend and intellectual ally Gorham Munson pointed out that "shortly after writing *Cane*, [Toomer] formed two convictions. One was that the modern world is a veritable chaos and the other was that in a disrupted age the first duty of the artist is to unify himself."[37] The literary vocation in its current state seemed to Toomer part of the problem of modernity rather than a solution. An old "slope" of consciousness needed to be dissolved through spiritual self-development and then the seeds planted for a new one. Soon after *Cane*'s appearance Toomer temporarily abandoned "literature" and turned to the program "The Harmonious Development of Man" developed by the Russian mystic G. I. Gurdjieff, which had much in common with beliefs Toomer already held about the need for a balance of intellectual, emotional, and instinctual aspects of the self.[38] Part of the reason for Toomer's shift, however, seems to have been a reaction against the insistent identification of himself as a Negro that *Cane* provoked and upon which its publication may well have depended. His disaffection with the "literary" vocation seems intimately intertwined with a sense of his failure to free words from limiting forms of consciousness and social institutions—including the institution of race.

The drama surrounding the publication of *Cane* is a unique and revealing instance of the problem that no person considered "Negro," according to the one-drop-rule of the U.S. regime of race, could get a hearing *except* under the sign of blackness, even if they did not consider themselves black. Horace Liveright probably was interested in the book partly because it was by someone he considered black. Waldo Frank, who delivered the manuscript to the firm in December 1922, undoubtedly identified Toomer as an author with "Negro blood." One suspects, in fact, that Toomer introduced himself to Frank—or introduced himself to someone who introduced him to Frank—as a person with "Negro blood." Horace Liveright considered the "race" of the author crucial to marketing *Cane*. Toomer objected, and Liveright (who was Jewish) then expressed wonder at why he would wish to "dodge" the fact of his racial identity, infuriating the author. Nonetheless, washing his hands of the advertising aspect of *Cane*'s publication, Toomer explicitly allowed Liveright to market the book as one written by a Negro.[39] At the same time, Toomer insisted that all representations of the book to reviewers and the like and anything purporting to reflect Toomer's own views must not refer to him as a Negro but reflect his own "fundamental position."

Being identified as a "Negro" author not only violated Toomer's philosophy and personal self-conception but also would lead people to interpret his work entirely in relation to issues of racial identity. He would later accuse Waldo Frank of helping fix the "Negro" label on him in the foreword to the book, but the correspondence between the men shows that Frank virtually wrote the foreword to Toomer's order and that Toomer, after reading it, raved about it, telling Frank, "I knew you could do the thing. You *have*."[40] Frank was careful not to call Toomer a Negro, although most readers would have been led to think of him as such. Certainly many of Toomer's black readers already thought of him as a Negro, knew his family as a Negro family, and would not have welcomed his self-description any more than Horace Liveright did.

The truth is, however, that he only gradually firmed up his position against allowing himself to be seen as a Negro. He even wrote an essay entitled "The South in Literature" in which he paired his own book with Frank's *Holiday*, pointing out that "Since the juxtaposition of the white and black races is so typical of Southern life, it is of real interest to know that the authors of these books are personally expressive of this racial contrast. For Waldo Frank is of white, while Jean Toomer is of Negro descent."[41] Toomer sent a copy of this essay to Horace Liveright, just as *Cane* hit the bookstores, in hopes that the publisher could place it in a magazine.[42]

The "Negro" label became more firmly attached when Alain Locke, allegedly without Toomer's permission, included pieces from *Cane* in his landmark anthology of the Harlem Renaissance, *The New Negro*. He also got Toomer to sit for a portrait by Winold Reiss that was included in the anthology, along with similar portraits of a range of black authors and intellectuals of the day whose work appeared in the book. It is hard to believe that Toomer did not have at least some inkling of how this portrait would be used.

Nonetheless, none of Toomer's seeming compromises about letting people come to their own conclusions about his racial identity permits us to neglect his commitment to the idea of a "new race"; *Cane* is full of inarticulate members of this new group of "Americans" who have yet to become "conscious" of themselves, in Toomer's phrasing. It presents others in whom violation of the color line provokes ostracism or death as Americans resist the "merging," haunted by wraiths of the past. This feature of his book remained virtually invisible to critics for over half a century.

Americans were not going in Jean Toomer's direction. Indeed, the great irony of Toomer's career is that modern American racial discourse—with an absolute polarity between "white" and "black" at its center—took its most definite shape precisely during the course of his life. The United States would be more segregated at the time of Toomer's death than it had been at the time of his birth, despite the dismantling of some of the legal bulwarks of white supremacy.[43] It is a sign of the fundamentally segregated nature of American society that *Cane* could only be understood as a "black" text and in relation to African American identity. Toomer's connection with the Harlem Renaissance largely accounts for the availability of his work today. When Georgia O'Keeffe and other friends (including Toomer's former roommate from the University of Wisconsin) were inspired to bring out a new edition of *Cane* in 1953, Toomer apparently would not cooperate (Kerman and Eldridge, *Lives*, 324). Only after he died was the book reissued, in the midst of rising interest in the "black aesthetic." It was in this context that the book entered the academic "canon." In an often quoted statement of 1966, Arna Bontemps remembered the excitement with which, four decades earlier, "practically a whole generation of young Negro writers then just beginning to appear" reacted to *Cane;* the book "marked an awakening that soon thereafter began to be called a Negro renaissance."[44] Not surprisingly, then, it was interest in African American literature, and the Harlem Renaissance in particular, that brought *Cane* back to public attention—and into print—some forty years after its second small printing.

It must be allowed that Toomer might be upset; it must also be allowed that this connection is not inappropriate. Not only was *Cane* a tremendous influence upon the Harlem Renaissance and later African American writing, it was produced by the same confluence of institutions and even individuals that helped produce the Harlem Renaissance. But although it is entirely fitting to read *Cane* in the context of African American literary tradition—and as one of the most important texts of the Harlem Renaissance—it is important to recognize that Toomer's relation to that tradition is ambivalent at best and that *Cane* also needs to be read in relation to other traditions and movements. Indeed, it is precisely the ambiguity—and mobility—of Toomer's "identity" in a society obsessed with clarity on this score that motivated the restless searching through which *Cane* came about, through which Toomer left it behind, and without which there could be no book like it.

Notes

This essay is a revised version of an introduction to a 1999 edition of *Cane* for Penguin Twentieth Century Classics, which was withdrawn from publication after the U.S. Congress passed a copyright law extending copyright protection from seventy-five to ninety-five years.

1. John Armstrong, "The Real Negro," *New York Tribune*, 14 October 1923, 26; reprinted in Durham, *Merrill Studies*, 28.
2. Gregory, "Our Book Shelf," *Opportunity* 1 (1923): 374.
3. Waldo Frank, foreword to *Cane*, by Jean Toomer, ed. Darwin T. Turner (New York: Norton, 1988), 139.

4. Except where noted otherwise, for biographical information I have relied on Cynthia Earl Kerman and Richard Eldridge, *The Lives of Jean Toomer: A Hunger for Wholeness* (Westport, Conn.: Avi, 1970), 416–433.
5. Wall and Ross, *Sorghum*, 416–433.
6. Kerman and Eldridge, *Lives*, 66.
7. See Scruggs, "Chosen World," 103–126.
8. For a fuller discussion of Toomer's engagement with socialism, see Scruggs, "Chosen World"; and Foley, "Toomer's Washington," 289–321.
9. Jean Toomer to Horace Liveright, 9 March 1923, Jean Toomer Papers, series 1, box 1, folder 16, James Weldon Johnson Collection, Beinecke Rare Book and Manuscript Library, Yale University.
10. Frank, *Our America*.
11. Du Bois, *Souls*, 11–12.
12. Locke, foreword, xxv–xxvi.
13. Locke, "New Negro," 9–10.
14. Hutchinson, "New Negroes," 683–692.
15. Jean Toomer, "Outline of the Story of an Autobiography," 44, Jean Toomer Papers, series 1, box 20, folder 515.
16. Waldo Frank to Jean Toomer, 21 October 1920, Jean Toomer Papers, series 1, box 20, folder 515.
17. For helpful discussions of the school and its environs, see Kerman and Eldridge, *Lives*, 81–82; and especially Foley, "Sparta," 747–775.
18. Jean Toomer to Waldo Frank, n.d., 2, Jean Toomer Papers, series 1, box 3, folder 84.
19. Jean Toomer to Mae Wright, 22 July 1922, Jean Toomer Papers, series 1, box 9, folder 283.
20. Jean Toomer to Waldo Frank, n.d., 3, Jean Toomer Papers, series 1, box 3, folder 84.
21. Jean Toomer to Mae Wright, 4 August 1922, Jean Toomer Papers, series 1, box 9, folder 283.
22. Toomer to Wright, 4 August 1922, 2.
23. Jean Toomer to Sherwood Anderson, 29 December 1922, Jean Toomer Papers, series 1, box 1, folder 1.
24. Jean Toomer to *The Liberator*, 19 August 1922, quoted in Rusch, *Toomer Reader*, 15–16.
25. Waldo Frank to Jean Toomer, 16 January 1922, Jean Toomer Papers, series 1, box 3, folder 83.
26. Jean Toomer to Waldo Frank, 19 July 1922, Jean Toomer Papers, series 1, box 3, folder 83.
27. See Waldo Frank to Jean Toomer, 17 July 1922; and Jean Toomer to Waldo Frank, 25 July 1922, Jean Toomer Papers, series 1, box 3, folder 83. See also Onita Estes-Hicks, review of *Lives*, by Kerman and Eldridge, *CLA Journal* 31 (1988): 493.
28. See Green, *Secret City*, 178.
29. Jean Toomer, "The Critic of Waldo Frank: Criticism, an Art Form," in *Jean Toomer: Selected Essays and Literary Criticism*, ed. Robert B. Jones (Knoxville: University of Tennessee Press, 1996), 28, 29. The essay originally appeared in *S4N* 30 (January 1924).
30. Jean Toomer to Gorham B. Munson, 31 October 1922, in Rusch, *Toomer Reader*, 19–20.
31. Jean Toomer to Waldo Frank, 12 December 1922, in Rusch, *Toomer Reader*, 26.
32. See Kerman and Eldridge, *Lives*, 358–361.
33. Abbott, "Dorris Dances," 455–474.

34. Toomer, "Notes for a Novel," Jean Toomer Papers, series 1, box 48, folder 1002. The content of these notes suggests that Toomer wrote them soon after completing *Cane*.
35. Jean Toomer to Kenneth Macgowan, 21 March 1923, in Rusch, *Toomer Reader*, 23.
36. Jean Toomer to John McClure, 22 July 1922, in Rusch, *Toomer Reader*, 12–13.
37. Gorham Munson, "The Significance of Jean Toomer," *Opportunity* 3 (1925): 262–263, quoted in Durham, *Merrill Studies*, 99.
38. Kerman and Eldridge, *Lives*, 126–127. Toomer's involvement with the Gurdjieff work is dealt with at length in Byrd's *Years*.
39. Jean Toomer to Horace Liveright, 5 September 1923, Jean Toomer Papers, series 1, box 1, folder 16.
40. Jean Toomer to Waldo Frank, n.d., Jean Toomer Papers, series 1, box 3, folder 83.
41. Jean Toomer, "The South in Literature," in Jones, *Selected Essays*, 12.
42. Horace Liveright to Jean Toomer, 27 September 1923, Jean Toomer Papers, series 1, box 1, folder 16.
43. Massey and Denton, *Apartheid*.
44. Arna Bontemps, "The Negro Renaissance: Jean Toomer and the Harlem Writers of the 1920's," in Durham, *Merrill Studies*, 76.

The Poetics of Passing in Jean Toomer's *Cane*

CHARLES-YVES GRANDJEAT

READING CRITICAL essays on Toomer and, more specifically, on *Cane*, can prove a rather puzzling experience. At least it was for this candid European reader. I was at the time a relatively fresh crossover from another field of academic inquiry, and I had got to Toomer's poetic prose without being fully aware of the fierceness of the debate raging around his positions on racial identity. Of course this is no longer the case. But I remember how absurd the controversy seemed to me in the light of a work that had so immediately and powerfully struck me as, more than anything else, a rite and a site of *passage*. I could not understand how so many critics could chose to position themselves along the very either/or divide that Toomer's prose so persuasively rejected as dangerous and inadequate. Against Toomer's advice that walls should be left porous, that they should let music "soak in" or "seep out" (Toomer, *Cane*, 52), scholars seemed intent on erecting soundproof partitions. This seemed a rather preposterous stance in the light of Toomer's portrayal of himself, in his autobiographical writings, as an essentially hybrid crossover: "I am a chicken; I am a hawk. A sheep, a wolf. A reliable person and a pirate. I am a home-man and a wanderer, a patriarch and a lone nomad. A devil and a saint . . ." (Turner, *Wayward*, 21). The divisive approach seemed even more absurd in light of Toomer's unflagging resolve to offer, in *Cane*, a defense and illustration of the virtues of dynamic communication.

Now, in addition to taking sides for or against Toomer's racial positioning, readers also gathered into two schools. There were those who opted for an ideological approach centering on Toomer's racial pronouncements and his public persona. Then there were those who chose to focus on form, structure, theme, imagery, as well as the poetic, lyrical qualities of his prose. And there were a few, but not many, in between, trying to link up the two. Of course, the common argument, since the New Critics, is that formalist or close textual analysis is a form of political denial that serves the interests of white, male, bourgeois hegemony. I would like to show that this is not necessarily the case and that Toomer's textual poetics and his racial politics are intimately linked, though not necessarily in the way that they have been made out to be.

It is my contention here that close attention to form and imagery, i.e., the poetics of *Cane*, does not just shed light on Toomer's racial politics. Rather, it helps clarify how his poetics involve a choice of textual politics. Of course, the major question stands: how are we to assess his racial politics? Should they be viewed as a rejection of race or as a rejection of racism? In this regard, it would be easy to argue that his positions are no different from, say, those of John Wideman—who can hardly be labeled a traitor to his "race"—in the opening section of his essay *Fatheralong*: "It's impossible to pin down the definition of race because race is a wild card" (xvi); 'Race' and 'racism' are equally predatory, destructive" (xvii); "Our power lies in our capacity to imagine ourselves as other than we are" (xxii); or "I do hate the paradigm of race—a vision of humankind and society based on the premise that not all people are created equal and some are born with the right to exploit others" (xxiv). Assessing the value of his rejection of racial classifications—in general, and as applied to himself—may still be of interest at a time when postcolonial intellectuals have breathed new life into the debate on "racial identity." In this light, his position, as stated in his autobiographical writings, because it denies the concept of "race" any epistemological validity, chimes in with those who struggle against racial "essentialism" in its various guises. On the other hand, it will irk other postcolonial intellectuals (e.g., bell hooks, recently relayed by Kadiatu Kanneh) who, while dismissing "race" as an epistemological tool, may wish to retain it as an empowering political weapon in the struggle against oppressive colonial power structures. The debate is too broad to be correctly addressed in the scope of this essay. Suffice it to say that, rather than calling upon the terms of the debate to either validate or invalidate, praise or condemn these statements, one could be tempted to call upon these statements to throw light on seemingly insolvable contradictions in the terms of the debate.

At one end of the critical spectrum we find David Bradley who, in an essay entitled "Looking Behind *Cane*," argues that "what was glossed over whenever possible was Toomer's apparent repudiation of blackness" (101). Bradley then goes on to bolster his claim by engaging in just this type of glossing over. The same question had been addressed at great length earlier by Arna

Bontemps, as well as by Henry Louis Gates Jr. (Gates, *Figures*, 196–224), who made the most of a keen sense of irony and contended that, insofar as "the trope of blackness in Western discourse has signified an absence," then *Cane* and Toomer are perhaps "the blackest text and author of all" (200). Despite Gates's claim, however, blackness is far from absent either from Toomer's non-fictional writing or from *Cane*. Rather, one is tempted to agree with Toni Morrison that "race is unequivocally the overriding preoccupation of Jean Toomer's life: not blackness or even being a Negro, but having (or having to have) a race at all" (Gates, *Figures*, 222). At the other end of the spectrum, critics such as Melvin Dixon, Bernard W. Well, Robert Bone, and Michel Fabre turned their attention to the literary qualities of the text of *Cane*. The most rewarding readings were those that tied up the formal, the imaginative, and the ideological. Robert Bone's contention that "the style [of *Cane*], which is modernist and highly metaphorical, supports the author's philosophical intentions. For metaphor destroys perceptual categories, demanding of the reader a fresh and imaginative response" (Bone, *Negro Novel*, 221) was an insightful one, although Bone did not go on to elaborate on this. One could add that metaphor does not just disrupt "perceptual categories" but displaces categories in general, be they perceptual, intellectual, or just semantic. In this regard, Bone's point is illustrated by Michel Fabre's point that Toomer uses "symbolism as a way towards synthesis," showing how opposites are "inextricably related" (Fabre, "Notes," 14), as for instance in the overriding motif of "dusk": "Dusk(y) is a kind of chiaroscuro, neither white nor black yet both, blurred and mulatto-like" (17).

Indeed, it all begins and ends in dusk. Dusk is the prevailing in-between, transitional hue in *Cane*, in keeping with Toomer's preference for secondary colors; purple is his most-favored one. Readers of *Cane* are consistently plunged into the realm of the intermediate. Purple is the melancholy, transitional color that mediates between day and night, black and white—in "Bona and Paul"—but also between blue (sky) and red (earth, flesh, and blood)—in "Fern"—as orange bridges yellow (sunlight) and red (passion) in "Theater." In this regard, a phenomenological reading suggests that Fabre's point about dusk could be extended to most of the constitutive elements of Toomer's imaginative landscape and elemental cosmogony, which are ruled by such intermediate elements as smoke, dust, haze, scent, and cane itself. These transitional elements constantly reactivate a poetic momentum that transgresses dividing lines. Meaning does not arise from a hermetic partitioning of semantic or symbolic units that, like Becky's shack, would be "islandized" (Toomer, *Cane*, 7), but from a process of cross-pollination from one unit to the other. This is the case with similes, as in the opening line of the text: "Her skin is like dusk on the eastern horizon," where the semantic focus is definitely on intermediate surface (skin), time of day (dusk), and space (horizon), and where meaning is lifted from the semantic and musical displacement of "skin" into "dusk," then on to "eastern horizon," toward which it is sent on an endless errand. From the very outset, then, the construction of meaning inclines the reader to look at *Cane* as, primarily, an open site of passage.

Such phenomenological reading, I would argue, does have political implications. Because the poetics of *Cane* privileges processes of elemental transfer or transformation, it implements an aesthetics and a textual and imaginative ethics of interaction, rather than division. Metaphorically projected onto the stage of racial relations, the text of *Cane* thus enacts a logic of integration as opposed to one of segregation. This of course does not just occur on the metaphorical plane. The relation between, on the one hand, an emphasis on a poetic logic that designates translation as its fundamental mode of signification and, on the other hand, the question of racial identity is bolstered by Toomer's forceful contention, in his autobiography, that race is not a natural, biological fact but a cultural, social construction based on rhetorical force. When seeking to "trace" the genealogical basis for his racial identity, Toomer can only come up with references to various discursive acts: Pinchback's father was "what is *called* a white man"; Pinchback himself "*claimed* he had Negro blood"; "All of this concerning my family *was told* to me"; "Most of it is *hearsay*"; and so forth. Toomer then feels authorized to conclude that "thus most of what we speak or write is *fictional*" (Turner, *Wayward*, 22; my emphasis) including the so-called facts of our racial genealogy. If "race" is grounded not in nature but in discourse, then, it makes sense to look at poetic discourse as an appropriate means of shaping an alternative—perhaps idealistic and utopian—racial consciousness, based not on confrontational antagonism but, rather, on an evolutive conversation.

This is not, of course, to belittle the very real and ghastly consequences entailed by the rhetorical and imaginative acts leading to racial classifying. And Toomer certainly did not, in *Cane*, screen out the white-on-black violence that prevailed in the South: the lynching of Tom Burwell in "Blood-Burning Moon," the killing of Mame Lamkins in "Kabnis," the poem "Portrait in Georgia" are cases in point. Still, Toomer also sought to offer his readers a glimpse of a world that would not abide by the disastrous logics of racial antagonism—a glimpse of the color-free utopia that he envisioned in his autobiography, a world where one would be "subject to few of the rigid conventions and fixed ideas which contract the human psyche and commit people to narrow lives ruled by narrow preferences and prejudices" (Turner, *Wayward*, 61). Rather than fighting the enemy on the latter's terms, thus validating those terms, Toomer often chose to fight the terms—fight them either by deconstructing them, as he did in his autobiographical writings or, as he did in his lyrical prose, by substituting them with what I would call imaginative action: guiding his readers through processes of transmutation, setting them adrift among the various elements of a decidedly unstable, fluctuating symbolic landscape where images and metaphors take on philosophical, even political, value, as their power rests on a coupling of difference and inclusiveness, not exclusiveness.

Having to decide between politics and poetics would rather put the reader in a position reminiscent of Paul's predicament in "Bona and Paul": "Paul is in his room of two windows. Outside, the South-Side L track cuts them in two. Bona is one window. One window Paul" (73). Here is one among a number of images that, throughout the collection, figure a splitting of personality that affects most male protagonists and that refers to racial, social, sexual, and psychological considerations. Another arresting image is that of John, the protagonist of "Theater": "One half his face is orange in it. One half his face is in shadow" (52). Toomer's approach of such divisiveness is all but obscure. His stories do warn against the damage wreaked by various forms of splitting. One thinks of "Seventh Street": "Split it! Into two! Again! Shred it!" (41) or in "Box Seat": "Break in. Get an axe and smash in. Smash in their faces" (59). As for "Blood-Burning Moon," it makes clear that murderous urges feed racial divisiveness: "His black balanced, and pulled against the white of Stone" (30). But the text does not just denounce oppositional thinking. It also consistently deflates it, replacing it with processes of *conversion*—to quote the highly significant title of one of the poems included in the volume. Conversion may be of a violent, murderous sort as in the poem "Portrait in Georgia": "And her slim body, white as the ash / of black flesh after flame" (29), or it may result from a more gentle imaginative alchemy, as in most of the lyrical, descriptive fragments in the volume.

Thus, the double severing of the perspective in "Bona and Paul" is offset by the passing of the L train by the windows thrown "in swift shadows." In addition, this passing rumble echoes with many other strains and trains—the ghost train that brought Becky's shack down, the one whose chugging engine, in "Carma," brought the repair gang home (12), the evening train whose searchlight, in "Fern," could be seen miles up the track (17), then was heard as it "thundered by," the engine that was heard whistling and sobbing in "Avey" as it ran up the valley (46). That engine pulls a train of thoughts and images that runs from one story to the next. The train acts not just as a link with the tradition of the blues, but also as a connecting element from one story to the next—a symbolic vestibule or a key "conductor," to borrow one of Gaston

Bachelard's illuminating metaphors—in a chain of images rippling through the text. The "Fern" piece well illustrates how such doubly connecting images as the train or the road (means of communication also connect various sections of the text as they migrate from one segment to another) are conjured up in response to the logics of racial division: "I ask you, friend (it makes no difference if you sit in the Pullman or the Jim Crow as the train crosses her road), what thoughts would come to you . . . had you seen her in a quick flash, keen and intuitively, as she sat there on her porch when your train thundered by?" (18).

The "crossing," of course, is also laden with disquieting religious connotations arising from an ever-present biblical subtext. But the porch, the door, the fringe of pines, the edge of the forest, the side of the road are mostly part of a liminal topography placing emphasis on thresholds or passages from one space to another, while roads, trains, tracks, streets are supports for the crossing or passing momentum. This symbolism has obvious psychological implications that other critics have analyzed, involving a tension between repression, burial, confinement, and, on the other hand, expression or liberation. But psychology here is part of a broader worldview, in keeping with Toomer's adhesion to the thinking of P. D. Ouspenski and G. I. Gurdjieff, the two esoteric masters whose teachings aimed at integrating the various parts of the human being into a dynamic whole. In "Bona and Paul," the image of the "hurtling Loop-jammed trains" that throw the window-protagonists "in swift shadows" triggers an imaging process that weaves through the text. The reader's eyes are invited to follow Paul's gaze from "gray slanting roofs of houses tinted lavender in the setting sun" in Chicago to imagined "slanting roofs of gray unpainted cabins tinted lavender" on a "pine-matted hillock in Georgia" where "lush melodies of cane and corn"(73) are heard. The stream of images follows semiconscious associations conjured up by a euphemistic lexicon: "slanting," not falling; "tinted," not painted; "lavender," not blue; a "hillock," not a hill. This, again, is the realm of the intermediate. Then Paul's mind returns to Chicago to realize that he has shifted from one window to the other: "He is at Bona's window." The slanting roofs and the lavender tint have acted as transitional elements bridging the space between the two windows and temporarily healing the rift in Paul's divided self.

The short subliminal interlude in this tale of love and war provides a poetic alternative to the racial and emotional rift staged in the rest of the story. The dominant motion is one of ascending "over the stockyards where a fresh stench is just arising, across wheat lands that are still wavering above their stubble," before looping the loop and spiraling back not exactly to the starting point, but not very far from it either. It illustrates the extent to which

circularity, displacement, and balancing rule the book, from dusk and dust and up to dust and dawn and down. Integrating opposites by means of mediating elements: this, I think, is what *Cane* is all about. One may view the book as based on a series of oppositions as Gérard Cordesse does in his paper "The Two Models in *Cane*," which takes up the argument that the text dramatizes a tension between the archaic and the modern, the agricultural and the industrial, the organic and the mechanic. However, it is equally clear that Toomer works to sidestep opposition. Opposition generally rules on the dramatic, narrative levels, particularly as regards characterization as well as sexual and/or racial relations. On those levels protagonists are, as another critic, Alain Solard, argues, often "unable to achieve a fusion of opposite poles" (Solard, "Myth," 137). However, on the poetic, descriptive level, integration is effectively and systematically performed, so that the two levels are made to balance each other out. Toomer's text unfolds on a dual stage. On the psychological stage, *Cane* dramatizes a logic of division. But on a romantic, natural stage, it promotes a model where transition, penetration, and fluctuation prevail.

In "Seventh Street," for instance, the rift opened with the "Split it!" exclamation is immediately bridged with an image of circulation, evaporation, and dissipation: "ribbons of wet wood dry and blow away" (Toomer, *Cane*, 41). Toomer's dramatic oppositions are thus rhythmically cushioned and deflated by images of release. Hardening and crystallization—"Wedges are brilliant in the sun" (41)—are typically offset by softening and liquefaction—"who set you flowing?" (41). The constant alternating between the realms of the solid and of the volatile is a form of imaginary gymnastics that brings to mind the blocking, then releasing, of energy generated by the breathing and dancing exercises of Gurdjieff followers.

One could argue that *Cane* is, throughout, the site for the release of a dynamic imagination that cuts across material or mental categories. The best case can be made from a close analysis of the elemental images. They would substantiate Gaston Bachelard's principle that imagination is "essentially open, evasive. It is, in the human psyche, the direct experience of openness" and that its essential quality is "mobility" (Bachelard, *Songes*, 5–6). On the other hand, these images would invite us to qualify Bachelard's other principle that there is a virtual law that "of needs assigns to each creative imagination one of the four elements: fire, earth, air and water" (13). Indeed, while constantly stressing processes of expansion and diffusion—recurrent verbs include "spread," "drench," "soak," "flow," "pour," "flood," "splash," "throw," and "rise"—that bring one element—water—to impregnate another—earth or air—Toomer keeps his elements in motion to facilitate the conversion of one element into another. Karintha sets the key with an image blending three elements: "At *sun*set, when there was no *wind*, and the pine-smoke from over the saw-mill hugged the *earth* . . . " (3) (my emphasis), with smoke acting not only as a nostalgic, romantic trace of fire but also as a link between air and earth. Coming close to this, a second image: "Karintha's running was a whir. It had the sound of the red dust that sometimes makes a spiral in the road" (3) plays on synesthesia to enhance the implicit coupling of earth and wind lifting the spiral of dust off the road. Perceptions are brought together and set in motion, as is the case with the "cloudy rumble" in which Carma vanishes "at some indefinite point along the road" (13).

In "Blood-Burning Moon," the dynamic landscape provides an antidote to the murderous racial and sexual confrontation: "Up from the deep dusk of a cleared spot on the edge of the forest a mellow glow arose and spread fan-wise into the low-hanging heavens" (31). The borderline in between space, the half light, the lifting and spreading momentum, the balancing between high and low are typical of Toomer's intermediate realm. Just as typically, the transitional setting is the stage for a transmutation process that, predictably enough, involves the central motif of cane: cane stalks fed into the grinder give out juice that is boiled and thickens into a syrup from which steam arises and turns into a scent that drenches the whole scene so that one can taste it as if it were solid. Solid turns into liquid, which in turn changes into vapor, then into gas, then back to solid. The eponymous cane thus acts as a support for an alchemy involving a chain of elemental conversions, not to mention textual circulation, as this scene from "Blood-Burning Moon" reiterates an image from "Becky"—that of "Old David Georgia, grinding cane and boiling syrup"(8).

One could make a fairly convincing case about the symbolic intricacy of a text where elements keep migrating from one piece to another in varying combinations. The poet, like smoke from the "spider sawdust pile" in "Carma," spins his own fine imaginary web. In "Kabnis," pines are bathed in dusk, "the solid dusk bank of pines" (93), then they reappear at sunrise: "Shadows of pines are dreams the sun shakes from its eyes" (117). Dusk and the color purple link up with the cane motif, as in "Fern": "dusk settled with a purple haze about the cane." In "Carma" (as in "Georgia Dusk"), cane is also associated with singing and with the wind—"wind is in the cane"—as well as with earth "tracks dissolving in the loose earth about the cane" (13). Canebrakes recurrently border on roads. Roads are often covered in dust. Dust is kin to smoke when in the shape of sawdust, as in "Karintha": "its pyramidal sawdust pile smoldered" (4). The "sawdust pile" reappears in "Carma," with a "marvelous web spun by the spider sawdust pile" (12), then in "Georgia Dusk": "Smoke from the pyramidal sawdust pile / curls up" (15). Smoke is seen to curl up as well in "Becky" and "Karintha."

Furthermore, Toomer keeps using or coining lexical compounds whose effect, apart from imparting a powerful energetic beat to a text that is then made to bridge reading and listening, sight and sound, is to implement the combinative logic on the lexical level as well, such as "near-beer," "mass-heart," "space-dark," to lift just three from the first paragraph of "Theater."

Of course, combination operates on every level, from the lexical to the imaginative to the generic. An image such as "the sun shoots primitive rockets into her face" ("Carma") explicitly blends the primitivistic with the modernist. "Carma" draws on the romantic, the surrealistic, the spiritual, and the black vernacular to achieve a polymorphous fabric. For all the references to jazz, Toomer's symbolic landscape is also in keeping with standard romantic or even gothic conventions. His "Blood-Burning Moon" is standard gothic; it brings to mind Coleridge's Kubla Khan: "A savage place! as holy and enchanted / As ever beneath a waning moon was haunted / By woman wailing for her demon lover!" or Poe's "Sleeper": "At midnight, in the month of June / I stand beneath the mystic moon," among others. Karintha's smoke, as it "curls up and hangs in odd wraiths about the trees" may recall Frankenstein's view of "vast mists . . . rising from the rivers and curling in thick wreaths around the opposite mountains" (Shelley, *Frankenstein*, 94). Primitivism blends with fin-de-siècle nostalgia into a melancholy setting that also bears traces of Robert Frost's death-ridden pastoral. There also, as everywhere else, circulation is at work.

In this regard, and no matter how preposterous serious-minded academics may judge anything that smacks of the esoteric, one should not underestimate the extent to which *Cane* puts to practice the ideas expounded by P. D. Ouspenski, a Russian philosopher, who joined forces with Gurdjieff in 1915, and whose *Tertium Organum*, first published in 1920, we know Toomer had read before writing *Cane*. In this book, Ouspenski declares:

> We, in order to comprehend the world of many dimensions, must renounce the idol of duality. But the application of monism to practical thought meets the insurmountable obstacle of our language. Our language is incapable of expressing the unity of opposites. . . . We must train our thoughts to the idea that separateness and inclusiveness are not opposed in the real world, but exist simultaneously without contradicting each other. (239–240)

Cane, with its constant resort to imaginary shifters, symbolic passers, lexical compounds, and generic hybrids is precisely geared toward finding a language capable of renouncing the "idol of duality." In this respect, the writing of *Cane* might be a preparatory exercise for Toomer's involvement with the teachings of Gurdjieff. The text of *Cane* precisely integrates, symbolically, what Gurdjieff identified as the three centers of human activity: thought, emotion, and "motor," thus preventing the reader from turning into what Gurdjieff called a "unilateral being" (Gurdjieff, *Récits*, 343). Toomer's images are integrating impulses that send forth a flow of psychic energy, "flowing," "eddying," "swirling," and "flowing" again (41). They are the trembling site for an alchemy of expansion, impregnation, evaporation, diffusion, dissolution.

They illustrate that, as Gilbert Durand wrote, "the symbolic function is the human site of 'passage,' of the merging of opposites" (Durand, *Imagination*). They also cast an eerie light on the debate on Toomer's racial "passing." Toomer never attempted to "pass" for white, although he did persistently object to being labeled a Negro. Or to be labeled anything, for that matter. Of course Toomer was a fervent advocate and practitioner of all forms of passing. But he did not pass just once, from one point to another. He kept passing over and over again, eluding the deadly grip of definition. As a writer, then as a man, he made a point of testing Ouspenski's principle that "truth itself is motion, and can never lead to arrestment, to the cessation of search" (Ouspenski, *Tertium Organum*, 306). Toomer's claim that he was "an American" was a rhetorical gesture dismissing reductive definitions. Was Toomer colorblind? Certainly not. *Cane* is alive with colors. But if anything, the book is neither black nor white—it is a tremulous purple. It does not shine, it glows. No sooner is it glimpsed than it is gone, like Karintha, whose "sudden darting past you was a bit of vivid color, like a black bird that flashes in light" (3), as if to validate, again and again, Bachelard's contention that "imagining means absconding, disappearing into a new life" (Bachelard, *Songes*, 8). Which Toomer did.

Works Cited

Bachelard, Gaston. *L'air et les songes: Essai sur l'imagination du mouvement*. Paris: Jose Corti, 1914.

Bone, Robert. *The Negro Novel in America*. New York: Knopf, 1958.

Bontemps, Arna. "The Negro Renaissance: Jean Toomer and the Harlem Writers of the 1920s." In *Anger and Beyond: The Negro Writer in the U.S.*, ed. Herbert Hill. New York: Harper and Row, 1966.

Bradley, David. "Looking behind *Cane*." In *Afro-American Writing Today*, ed. James Olney. Baton Rouge: Louisiana State University Press, 1985.

Clary, F., and C. Julien, eds. "*Cane*," *Jean Toomer and the Harlem Renaissance*. Paris: Ellipses, 1997.

Cordesse, Gérard. "The Two Models in *Cane*." In "*Cane*," *Jean Toomer and the Harlem Renaissance*, ed. F. Clary and C. Julien. Paris: Ellipses, 1997.

Durand, Gilbert. *L'imagination symbolique*. Paris: P.U.F., 1964.

Fabre, Michel. "Notes towards a Hypothetical Lesson on Jean Toomer's *Cane*." In "*Cane*," *Jean Toomer and the Harlem Renaissance*, ed. F. Clary and C. Julien. Paris: Ellipses, 1997.

Gates, Henry Louis, Jr. *Figures in Black: Words, Signs, and the "Racial" Self*. Oxford: Oxford University Press, 1987.
Gurdjieff, G. I.. *Récits de Belzébuth à son petit-fils*. Paris: Denoël, 1976.
Hooks, Bell. *Yearning: Race, Gender and Cultural Politics*. London: Turnaround, 1991.
Kanneh, Kadiatu. *African Identities*. London: Routledge, 1998.
Lindberg, Kathryne V. "Raising *Cane* on the Theoretical Plane: Jean Toomer's Racial Personae." In *Cultural Difference and the Literary Text*, ed. Winfried Simmerling. Iowa City: University of Iowa Press, 1996.
Ouspenski, P. D. *Tertium Organum: A Key to the Enigmas of the World*. New York: Vintage Books, 1970.
Shelley, Mary. *Frankenstein*. London: Penguin Books, 1992.
Solard, Alain. "Myth and Narrative Fiction in *Cane*: "Blood-Burning Moon." In "*Cane*," *Jean Toomer and the Harlem Renaissance*, ed. F. Clary and C. Julien. Paris: Ellipses, 1997.
Toomer, Jean. *Cane*. Ed. Darwin T. Turner. New York: Norton, 1988.
Turner, Darwin T., ed. *The Wayward and the Seeking: A Collection of Writings by Jean Toomer*. Washington, D.C.: Howard University Press, 1980.
Wideman, John Edgar. *Fatheralong*. New York: Random House, 1994.

"The Waters of My Heart"

Myth and Belonging in *Jean Toomer's* Cane

FRANÇOISE CLARY

"Full moon rising on the waters of my heart"
Jean Toomer, *"Evening Song"*

THE TRADITIONAL VIEW of the Harlem Renaissance, which Jean Toomer's *Cane* is said to have launched, is that of the "Black Twenties," the days when black literary and historical studies were in vogue. Foreshadowed by W.E.B. Du Bois's poem "Song of Smoke" (1899), the first stirrings of the Negro Literary Renaissance are also visible in James Weldon Johnson's *Autobiography of an Ex Colored Man* (1912), in "The Negro Speaks of Rivers," the poem Langston Hughes had already published in *Crisis* when he arrived in New York in 1921, and in Claude McKay's *Harlem Shadows* (1923). What makes Johnson's description of the attempts of a light-skinned black to live first as a black, then as a white, man, or McKay's exploration of the pathos of black ghetto life, or again the trend of tragic irony in Langston Hughes's early poems, and finally Toomer's insight into the dilemma of the black artist so fully significant is that they all illustrate the inward look that characterized the black literature of the 1920s.

In the nineteenth century, the "divine plan" idea and the myth of white paternalism were central to the thought of the black race's spokesmen, for whom Western culture represented the quintessence of advanced culture. As the mood changed with the growing influence of the literature of white racial apologists—a literature that ranged from the pseudoscientific arguments of John H. Van Evrie's *White Supremacy and Negro Subordination; or, Negroes a Subordinate Race* (1867) to the theological theorizing of the Reverend G.C.H. Hasskarl in *The Missing Link: Has the Negro a Soul?* (1898)—black writers produced works in defense of their race by combining scriptural and historical arguments like Edward A. Johnson or by turning to philosophy, ethnology, and Egyptology to prove the past greatness of the blacks, as did George Washington Williams. The key to understanding the thought of black spokesmen during the 1890s and the early years of the twentieth century is the shift from an outlook of hope to one of a sense of alienation from white society. While Hughes attempted to capture the black spirit in the blues, Toomer, along with McKay and Johnson, offered a description of black life, resorting to the use of local color. As they used their art to search for the roots of the black experience, these writers contributed to laying the literary foundations of the Harlem Renaissance. Toomer can be considered as the one who actually defined the literary quest of the Black Twenties. By asking fundamental questions—echoed by Countee Cullen, Zora Neale Hurston, Nella Larsen, Rudolph Fisher, and Wallace Thurman—about the meaning of the black man's slave heritage, about his being torn between the urban North and the rural South, and about his desire to achieve wholeness, Toomer undertook a deeper quest, a search for the truth about mankind to be reached by holding up a mirror to the black artists and, beyond them, to the readers.

In a poetic novel with a Hegelian construct reminiscent of the dialectical opposition between the master and the slave, Jean Toomer, expressing much of the same emotion as Claude McKay in "Harlem Dancers," achieves a powerful dramatization of the struggle of African Americans for a new self-image. The identity quest of the black man is conveyed through a process of rebirth leading from a collective to an individual standpoint, that is to say, from a historical sense involving a common perception of the past to an expression of longing striking the keynote of personal experience. The choice of the image of water as a vehicle of emotion and meaning unites, in the same essentialist vision of the black man, Toomer's *Cane* and Hughes's poem "The Negro Speaks of Rivers." Whether it is the darkness of water or the gleam and the shifting of water in sunlight, the value of the passages of description is not in the visual images they arouse but in the far-reaching suggestiveness that belongs to the words and clings about the fragments of water imagery. As he urges the water metaphor closer to the impalpable forces of life and soul, Toomer gets in touch with the spiritual as well as with the earth, a closeness that enables his characters to transcend the limitations of their physical existence and arrive at a higher consciousness of themselves.

In *Cane* the imagistic symbol serves as an organizing principle, a means of gathering the intellectual and the emotional into a pattern of sensuous perception, and a vehicle for expressing the narrator's understanding of the world, both aesthetically and emotionally. Although a number of contemporary critics have examined how Toomer called up emotions through the use of symbols, so far there have not been any studies about the significance of the water metaphor in the work of a novelist who used it not for its representational value but to create states of mind. Toomer, who values words more for their connotative than their denotative meaning, illustrates, with the use of water imagery, both the fleeting quality of the sense of perception of the symbolists and the exact perception of the imagists. For these reasons, I think the water metaphor can be meaningfully approached as a key to the understanding of a novel that achieves an artistic fusion of Christian myth and Afro-American experience while distilling the essence of life.

The use of the visual representation of water in Jean Toomer's *Cane* poses fundamental questions about the delineation of meaning. Are the images Toomer develops—rain, ripples, water and mud, sleepy waters—free and autonomous, coinciding with nature, describing physical reality, or do they form an association of ideas related to metaphysical meaning? In the following example, Toomer's identification of ideas with the iconic power of words evocative of watery flux suggests a shaping of water imagery determined by symbolic significance:

> Bleeding rain
> Dripping rain like golden honey—
> And the sweet earth flying from the thunder
> ("Storm Ending," 90)

To explore this suggestion and its relation to meaning in *Cane*, three complementary lines of study are necessary. First, these concern the metaphoric expression of a subjective vision regardless of mimesis. Second, as the images in *Cane* are primarily expressive rather than imitative, we will study how they become evocative forces, or centers from which radiates a plurality of meanings. This plurality gives Toomer's water metaphors the symbolic quality of myth and makes them adequate vehicles to express the complexities of experience. Third, we will examine how this myth making provides a sense of shared aesthetic interests and moral values, thus fostering a cultural capital that contributes to the definition of identity and belonging.

Water Imagery as the Projection of Inner Truth

Water metaphors in *Cane* contribute to emotive discourse by distilling the sublime that informs figurative language.

> Life is water that is being drawn off.
> Brother, life is water that is being drawn off.
> Brother, life is water that is being drawn off
> ("Rhobert," 73)

As these lines show, Toomer's water imagery is not a projection of reality; instead, Toomer manipulates language through the use of such images in order to tell an inner truth. Because his use of water as metaphor confirms the tension between the pictured world (represented by the permanence of black memory) and the real one (represented by human existence in a society ridden by racism), the watery flux of images does not merely provide a means for lyric escape in *Cane*, but traces the movement from external nature to the poetic mind. "Murky water" and "sleepy waters" are metonyms of the self (73, 35). A function of the metaphoric process in a narrative sequence, they convey the idea of a self sinking down into life and are related to issues of cause and effect, part and whole.

Jean Toomer opens his discourse to emotion through figures of speech that evoke a hazy fluidity and a flux of dark waters. Among the numerous examples of this technique, we find "the ripples blown by pain" (14), "the mist of tears" (14) echoing "the smoke . . . you tasted . . . in water" (4), and "the murk in the water" (73). The succession of these motifs related to the water metaphor where qualities are associated by similarity and made into sequences that develop through relations of contiguity, illustrates Jakobson's argument that metaphorical and metonymical processes are at the heart of verbal activity (Jakobson, "Statements," 453ff).

Focusing on the play of language in *Cane* reveals how a concrete situation—the oppression of black Americans or the narrator's ambivalence—fades behind a weight of metaphorical associations. Evoked by such phrases as "murky, wiggling, microscopic water" (73), "ripples blown by pain" (14), "bleeding rain" (90), "black reddish blood / Flowing down the smooth asphalt of Seventh Street / Eddying on the corners / Swirling like a blood-red smoke up where the buzzards fly in heaven" (70–71), these associations betray the state of the narrator's soul. An extreme subjectivity results, for Toomer's water metaphors form a vortex from and through which rush mingled ideas of hope and suffering that replace the actual situation in which the narrator and other characters find themselves. Thus, water imagery in *Cane* does not mirror external reality but, in the manner of a symbol, denotes the metaphysical.

All ten poems in part 1 harmonize their lyrical expression derived from the intricate pattern of water imagery with the religious core of stories where physical and spiritual energy coalesce. "November Cotton Flower" with its tragic images of vanishing water, spreading drought, and dried-up wells echoes the dramatic conflict of "Karintha" by the symbolic representation of death as tension:

> And cotton, scarce as any southern snow,
> Was vanishing; the branch, so pinched and slow,

Failed in its function as the autumn rake;
Drouth fighting soil had caused the soil to take
All water from the streams; dead birds were found
In wells a hundred feet below the ground—
("November Cotton Flower," 7)

Toomer's metaphorical and metonymical processes involve similarity, causality, and inclusion. When associated with drought, water becomes evocative of drained life, even of life tinged with death, or foreboding death. To give another example, the poem "Face" reinforces the religious symbolism of "Becky," The imagistic montage of sights and sounds centered on the water metaphor is not just functional. It does not merely serve to portray a woman's face but also to convey suffering while drawing on the typology of redemption through sacrifice:

Hair—
Silver-gray,
Like streams of stars,
Brows—
Recurved canoes quivered by the ripples blown by pain
("Face," 14)

In "Becky," whose structure is that of an impressionistic yoking of mystical forces, the white mother of two black sons who has become the victim of the Southern legacy of miscegenation is isolated on an "eye-shaped piece of sandy ground. Ground islandized between the road and the railroad track" (9). The precise use of metaphor is striking. The adjective "islandized" plays a dynamic role as it symbolizes estrangement and exclusion, fully expressing the isolation of Becky, rejected by both ethnic groups for refusing the Southern caste system.

The deployment of water metaphor throughout the sketches and poems of *Cane* conveys emotion by a process of juxtaposition of ideas that underscore the metaphysical nature of the narrator's quest:

Pour O pour that parting soul in song,
O pour it in the sawdust glow of night,
("Song of the Son," 21)

This example and others call on the palpable sensation of running water evoked by "stream," "ripples," "tears," "pour," "eddying," "swirling" to represent both beauty and pain. Water imagery is at the center of a montage of sounds and movements: "Life is a murky, wiggling, microscopic water that compresses him" (73); of sights: "Cloine, curled like the sleepy waters where the moon-waves start" (35); or of smells and sometimes tastes: "The smoke was so heavy you tasted it in water" (4) that translate the abstract notions related to the loss of youth, pain, and sadness.

In Toomer's predominantly metonymic narrative, water metaphors are often composites. The literal accompanies the metaphorical. Half thought, half experience, the sight of water, be it "rain" or "tears" or "ripples," expresses wistfulness and provides a way of remaining faithful to a shifting reality through the representation of fluidity. Thus we read in "Carma": "No rain has come to take the rustle from the falling sweet-gum leaves" (17). Toomer's frequent metonymic digressions from character to setting and from plot to atmosphere also exemplify the composite nature of his water metaphors. In "Karintha," for example, the sadness that weighs down heavily on Karintha's soul is projected onto the setting and visualized as smoke mingling with, and tainting, water: "The smoke was so heavy you tasted it in water" (4). The intricacy of the pattern of water images illustrates how one topic leads to another in *Cane* through relations of similarity and contiguity. Just as the taste of water is adulterated by smoke, so is Karintha wounded by men's desires. She, who has been married many times, indulges men when she is in the mood, but her soul is forever out of men's reach. "They will die not having found it out" (4).

The metonymic digression into which the water metaphor is here integrated involves an overlap from plot to atmosphere and a projection from character to setting in harmony with Karintha "carrying beauty perfect as dusk when the sun goes down" (1). The sun (mirroring Karintha) sinks beyond the horizon as it would into the sea, seeking oblivion:

> Her skin is like dusk on the eastern horizon,
> O cant you see it, O cant you see it,
> Her skin is like dusk on the eastern horizon
> . . . When the Sun goes down.
>
> Goes down . . .
> ("Karintha," 5)

This passage exemplifies how, far from referring to reality in the manner of ordinary language, iconic representation in *Cane* neutralizes reality. This function is operative at the level of individual detail as well, as when Toomer describes the eyes of his characters, inviting a comparison with the haunting fluidity of water. In "Fern" we read: "Face flowed into her eyes. Flowed in soft cream foam and plaintive ripples, in such a way that wherever your glance may momentarily have rested, it immediately thereafter wavered in the direction of her eyes" ("Fern," 24). Paralleling the use of water imagery to tell how captivated men were by Fern's eyes, Toomer describes the strangeness and vacuity of Dan's neighbour's look at Lincoln Theater in "Box Seat" by mentioning the blurred liquidity of his eyes: "The man's face is a blur about two sullen liquid things that are his eyes. The eyes dissolve in the surrounding vagueness" ("Box Seat," 121).

Representing sorrow, the withdrawal from life, or memory of the past, the metaphoric use of water—a nonverbal symbol and a colorless liquid—conveys intuitive relationships between imagery and meaning, while Toomer's sensuous use of the water metaphor offsets the distance between the verbal icon and reality. Marcus B. Hester's semantic theory and his ideas on metaphoric language offer us a means of understanding Toomer's metaphors as sensorial impressions evoked in memory. These can also be linked to Hester's notion of "seeing as," which he defines as "an intuitive experience act by which one selects from the quasi-sensory mass of imagery" (Hester, *Meaning,* 180). Such a definition involves intuition and, at the same time, experience and action. Therefore, as Hester emphasizes, "the same imagery which occurs also means" (188).

If we examine the grammar of water imagery in *Cane,* we see that water metaphors sometimes occur as individual words, but that they most often appear in the form of statements. These are not derived from mere associations, for the contextual action creates a new meaning that exists only in the immediate context of its utterance. As a result, water metaphor acquires the status of an event. Notably in "Karintha," "Fern," and "Rhobert," this use of water as icon involves meaning controlling imagery. As an innovation or emergent meaning, it is a linguistic creation that contributes to the history of language as code or system by expressing a new consciousness. This is conveyed through the magic of the word "water" (often darkened in color or adulterated in taste, always musical in sound) and through the repetitive use of metaphors, which infuse the subtle movement of symbolic actions and feelings with intensity.

Because they are recurring structures, water metaphors in sentence form contribute to the shifting rhythm, syntax, and diction of *Cane*. The power of these metaphors derives from the fact that they form a pattern that unifies concepts and impression while joining meaning to the musicality of words and the fullness of images. Toomer's striking ability to develop images in a metaphorical style throughout this intricately structured book makes meaning itself iconic. This is exemplified in "Seventh Street," where images of water constitute a frame within which the modifier "blood" occurs:

> Black reddish blood. Pouring for crude-boned soft-skinned life, who set you flowing? Blood suckers of the War would spin in a frenzy of dizziness if they drank your blood. Prohibition would put a stop to it.

> Who set you flowing? White and whitewash disappear in blood. Who set you flowing? ("Seventh Street," 71)

These fluid images coalesce in the representation of a frenzy of dizziness. From this point, Toomer's style evolves toward symbolism with the internal monologue of "Bona and Paul," to culminate in the allegory of "Kabnis":

> White-man's land.
> Niggers, sing.
> Burn, bear black children
> Till poor rivers bring
> Rest, and sweet glory
> In Camp Ground.
> ("Kabnis," 157)

"Kabnis" dramatizes the inability of the narrator-actor to face the tensions of his double consciousness. Unable to cope with the legacy of slavery and with racism, his tortured soul longs for the peace and rest that, symbolically, only soothing rivers can bring.

In Toomer's water imagery the nonverbal and the verbal are closely united at the core of metaphorical statements. The iconized meaning of these metaphors can best be understood through Ruth Herschberger's semantic theory of tension and fusion (Herschberger, "Metaphor," 434), as seen in Toomer's description of a storm:

> Bleeding rain
> Dripping rain like golden honey
> ("Storm Ending," 90)

Toomer's description stresses the tension grounded, at the literal level, in the contradiction between the terms of his statement: rain is neither "blood" nor "honey." But Toomer's incantatory style operates a shift from the literal to the figurative. This change in meaning is not restricted to certain words ("bleeding," "dripping," "rain," "honey") but, in a general sweep, extends to all signs. Their lexical value is lost in favor of a metaphorical meaning that the context creates. Because it bridges the verbal and the quasivisual, the pictorial quality of Toomer's language lends itself to a transposition of reality. The original tension between the terms of the water metaphors and the subsequent fusion of apparently incompatible words correspond to "picture thought," or thinking in pictures. To depict rain in terms of the characteristics of blood (evoking pain) and of honey (symbolizing delight) is to see rain (and therefore water) as a mixed symbol of darkness and light, suffering and pleasure, gloom and hope.

As Wittgenstein has pointed out, transposing reality through metaphors is altogether different from imagining: it is to govern iconic deployment and suggest something other than what is stated (Wittgenstein, *Investigations*, 73). Moreover, since Toomer's water metaphors create congruence between the subject "water" and the connotations of such modifiers as "blood," "honey," "mud," "smoke," and "drought," *Cane* also illustrates Beardsley's theory of the decisive role of "logical absurdity" in the innovative character of metaphorical statements (Beardsley, "Twist," 300). Yet water metaphors in *Cane* are far from weakened by the ambiguity of their contradictory terms. In fact, Toomer mixes the connotative values of his various modifiers in order to maximize the poetic realism of a wholly contextual emergent meaning that involves the use of regional matter and the black man's past.

In so doing, Toomer reflects his consciousness of both the beauty and the pain of his African American heritage and moves toward discovering myth as an appropriate sign system for expressing his dilemma about belonging.

The Symbolic Quality of Myth

Water metaphors in *Cane* do far more than suspend "natural" reality; they open up meaning to myth making, just as they open it up to the dimension of inner reality. For Toomer, water, rain, and tears symbolize regeneration as well as wistfulness. Water metaphors blend in a whole current of thought, whereas rhetorical figures typically refer to shared black experiences and produce shared cultural memories. These range from Africa, the middle passage, slavery, and Southern plantation life to emancipation, reconstruction, the migration north, urbanization, and racism.

Water metaphors are crucial to spatial and social referents in *Cane* and to the way Toomer combines communal and personal modes of storytelling into cultural patterns. These patterns constitute a code that acquires the symbolic quality of myth in an intricate work that is partly constituted by fragments of former pieces of African American literature and music: slave narratives, chants, spirituals, the blues, field songs, and fables. Using the political, literary, and musical history of African Americans as a guide, the reader of *Cane* can apprehend the meaning of the wistful fluidity of water imagery in the haunting refrains of songs: "A girl . . . sings. . . . Echoes, like rain, sweep the valley. . . . She does not sing; her body is a song" ("Carma," 17). Woven into the sketches, the songs perpetuate pastoral conventions that symbolize the spiritual resiliency of the black community. Significantly, the fragments of Negro spirituals in *Cane* contain water metaphors evoking Christian myths:

> Brother, Rhobert is sinking.
> Lets open our throats, brother,
> Lets sing Deep River when he goes down.
> ("Rhobert," 75)

Toomer sets his protagonists against archetypal patterns, emphasizing thereby the universal aspects of their quest. From a symbolical perspective, as salvation will come only by rising above the innate sinfulness of man, so the achievement of self-identity will come only by rising above the inherited conditions of locality or race. The linking of city life and of the greed of modern man with mud and death in "Rhobert" makes clear that man is struggling against universal forces:

> He is way down. He is sinking. His house is a dead thing that weights him down. He is sinking as a diver would sink in mud should the water be drawn off. Life is a murky, wiggling, microscopic water that compresses him. ("Rhobert," 73)

In "Seventh Street" the bustling and dizziness of city life is evoked through the image of an endless flux tainted red: "Black reddish blood. Pouring for crude-boned soft-skinned life, who set you flowing?" ("Seventh Street," 71).The symbolic identification of the flux tainted red with perversion and sin is extended in "Blood-Burning Moon":

> Red nigger moon. Sinner!
> Blood-burning moon. Sinner!
> Come out that fact'ry door.
> ("Blood-Burning Moon," 53)

The succession of metaphors and connotative words opposing fire to flux, red to white give these red and white colors their full biblical significance. Their symbolic meaning reminds the reader of the meaning red and white have for Isaiah: "Though your sins be as scarlet, they shall be white as snow." Toomer provides several images of red flux in "Blood-Burning Moon," such as Bob Stone's blood as he drives through the cane: "Cane leaves cut his face and lips. He tasted blood" (62) or Tom Burwell's blood: "He bit down on his lips. He tasted blood. Not his own blood. Tom Burwell's blood" (62), and further on when describing Tom Burwell's body bound to the stake: "His breast was bare. Nails scratches let little lines of blood trickle down and mat into the hair. . . . Now Tom could be seen within the flames" (66). Old Testament and Christian symbolism are combined to convey the full force of racial hatred and the step to salvation. Black and white men share the heritage of sin, and the blood of salvation is the color of sin. Extending the metaphoric association of flux and blood, the poem "Storm Ending" complements the image of suffering and Crucifixion ("Bleeding rain," 90) with an iconic reference to the water of Redemption and the gold of glory that evokes the vision John of Patmos had of the golden Jerusalem ("Dripping rain like golden honey," 90).

In the field songs and narrative passages controlled by a communal mode, Toomer also evokes the social myths rooted in black experience, thus reflecting rituals and the slaves' collective participation in community life. Drawing on the African American tradition of music as a structural device, this focus on the Southern past (mainly in part 1) heightens the nostalgia conveyed by the intricate pattern of water imagery in the work songs and fragments of spirituals.

It is crucial to point out that, although many water metaphors occur in Greco-Roman mythology, Toomer calls instead upon water imagery related to social myths rooted in slave narratives and thereby specific to the African American past. The pattem of water metaphors in *Cane* is particularly significant because it refers to the network of understandings that defines black American culture and informs black consciousness. A symbol of hope, life, and rebirth, water also ominously forebodes death. It perpetuates the Manichaean clash between good and evil, life and death, hope and despair in the projection of Toomer's mystical vision of life.

If the structure of *Cane* is to be considered, the metaphorical chain that binds the companion poems to the sketches and stories recalls the rhetorical and authenticating strategies of the slave narratives. On a structural level, then, a comparison with a typical slave narrative such as Douglass's *Narrative of the Life of Frederick Douglass, an American Slave* reveals some similarities in the use of water imagery. Just as Douglass chooses the image of water to symbolize his own search for life and truth (Douglass, *Narrative*, 67), Toomer's water metaphors are the writer's representation of a metaphysical quest and of spiritual anguish. The structure of Douglass's slave narrative generates dynamic energy between the tale and each of its supporting texts. Toomer recreates the same sort of dynamic in *Cane*, relying on the incantatory power of repetitive water images—found mainly in the echoes of the field songs and slave songs—to bind the various fragments of his book.

Toomer's novel differs from Douglass's slave narrative, however, in that his language is more acutely "performative," to borrow a term from Austin (Austin, *Words*, 30). And, if it is true that asserting always constitutes a kind of symbolical doing, Toomer's highly metaphorical style reports events and situations (as, for example, in "Seventh Street") in such a way that the construction of a network of interactions supersedes the literal meaning of the narrative. This network makes the water metaphors in *Cane* unique semantic innovations with a reality of their own.

Located at the intersection of several semantic fields, water combines with "blood", "death," "drought," "blood-burning moon," "mud," "smoke," and "dusk" to convey pain, estrangement, and sorrow. In the construction of such metaphors, all the associations work together to make a new kind of meaning created by a language whose aim is to arouse images and express nostalgia. The metaphorical "twist" in Toomer's writing does not coincide with what ordinary or everyday language attempts to convey, or translate, in its reference to reality.[1] Rather, it contributes to the strategy of reappropriating the African American past through the wistfulness of water imagery that itself reflects estrangement from the present and a yearning for bygone days. Water metaphors consequently closely concern the representation of the "I" shaping and controlling narration in Cane.

Identity and Belonging

Ruth Herschberger's semantic theory of tension and Marcus B. Hester's perspective of "seeing as" seem particularly appropriate when examining Toomer's water metaphors. Herschberger maintains that the text invites the reader to take account of the dissimilarities as well as the likenesses between the multiple referents of the metaphor, while Hester foregrounds the fusion of iconicity with sense: together, they offer a context for understanding how the density of images in *Cane* nourishes metaphorical meaning, expressing not only the black man's being but that of humanity. This phenomenon, in which the nonverbal predominates over the verbal, is also described in Bachelard's *The Poetics of Space*:

> The image becomes a new being in our language, expressing us by making us what it expresses; in other words it is at once a becoming of expression and a becoming of our being. Here expression creates being. (Bachelard, *Poetics*, xix)

This "new being in our language" corresponds well to Toomer's belief in the attainment of spiritual truth through intuition.

While the literal takes second place to the metaphorical in *Cane*, ontological affirmation follows a process of tension. Verbs conveying tension ("flow," "gush," "bleed," "sweep," "sputter," "gurgle," "sink") are at the core of metaphors that further elaborate into similes. These intricate, complex constructions lead to a concept of metaphorical truth that reflects the dilemma of the author's double consciousness and his slow progression toward self-discovery.

This process is at the fore of part 3, where Toomer explores the inability of Ralph Kabnis to face the legacy of slavery and racism, and thereby dramatizes the incapacity of a black man to cope with the paradoxes of his African American heritage. Toomer proceeds metaphorically, defining meaning in relation to words borrowed from the semantic field of water, flood, and fluidity. To show that by rejecting his slave past Kabnis loses his sense of belonging, Toomer confers a spiritual and intellectual meaning on the adjective "soil-soaked," making it symbolize the hero's ethnic and national identity. Toomer describes Kabnis, who represents the black writer, as symbolically suspended between two worlds, "a promise of a soil-soaked beauty; uprooted, thinning out. Suspended a few feet above the soil whose touch would resurrect him" (191). The meaning of this description largely depends on what the word "soil-soaked," evocative of the density of life-giving water, can make us understand, think, or feel. Its primary signification is that Kabnis avoids his African American culture, a culture whose beauty depends on its being fully permeated with the flux of past experiences, but he can acquire a sense of his identity only by relating to his roots.

Running from symbol to object, the orientation of reference in *Cane* is linked to several categories of symbols that vary from verbal to nonverbal, from description to representation. In "Rhobert," for example, Toomer depicts the agonizing struggle of a man trapped and smothering in the slimy darkness of mud. This struggle figures the ambivalence of his own double consciousness, his spiritual anguish, and his search for truth. Without going as far as the radical heterogeneity of language games that Wittgenstein proposes (Wittgenstein, *Investigations*, 11), it is important to recognize this plurality of forms in metaphorical discourse and its interaction with other modes of discourse, for the interplay of implicit and explicit allows us to explore and better understand the ontological aim of Toomer's metaphors.

If we take as our guide Heidegger's assertion that the metaphorical exists only inside the metaphysical (Heidegger, *Thinking*, 71), we observe that the metaphorical function of water imagery brings about Toomer's philosophical reflection on the multiple meanings of being. Toomer combines the communal and individual modes of narration in *Cane* by using collective songs to support thematically related writings. In this process, the impressionistic use of water images illuminates the graphic and the timeless. Against the backdrop of time, the haunting evocation of watery flux and fluidity ("flowed," "pour," "mobile rivers," "dripping," "falling," "sweeping rain") evokes a dynamic feeling that subordinates personal and ontological loneliness. As the development of water imagery contributes to the interplay between the supporting songs and the tale, the communal response to experience or social history is never excluded. This permits spiritual anguish to be not only controlled but also transcended through collective response. It also permits expressions of epiphany reflecting a sense of belonging, the unity of life, and spiritual rebirth.

> Pour O pour that parting soul in song
> . . . .
> An everlasting song, a singing tree,
> Caroling softly souls of slavery,
> What they were, and what they are to me,
> Caroling softly souls of slavery.
> ("Songs of the Son," 21)

Toomer's metaphysical quest and his metaphorical discourse constantly interact because his philosophical thought is linked to the semantic dynamism of metaphorical expression. However, the gain in meaning is not a full conceptual gain. It remains limited by the "twist" imposed on the words that make up the metaphor. To employ a Husserlian-style critique, we could say that metaphorical discourse encounters its limits in *Cane* because images and exemplification function through "similarity," whereas conceptual apprehension is synonymous with "identity." According to Husserl's *Logical Investigations*, signifying differs from representing, while interpretation, at the perceptual or imaginative level, plays nothing more than a "supportive" role (Husserl, 339).

Though the image admittedly introduces a moment of absence or neutralization in the conceptual process of identification, Toomer's metaphorical discourse includes not only mental images but also predicative assimilations and schematizations. Thus, interpretation concerns both the notion of concept and the constitutive intention of African American experience expressed in the metaphorical mode. Partaking of this doubleness and effecting it, Toomer's water imagery delimits the space of dream. Departing from narration, it contributes to an iconography of black and white, opposing waters blurred by mud or smoke to life-promising, life-giving waters. This iconography may either fully blend into or, at times, revise traditional cultural codes.

Using water metaphors to explore the transmission of the past and a sense of belonging, Toomer differentiates history from memory and connects the latter to the affirmation of cultural identity:

> Her eyes, if it were sunset, rested idly where the sun, molten and glorious, was pouring down between the fringe of pines. . . . Like her

> face, the whole countryside seemed to flow into her eyes. Flowed into them with the soft listless cadence of Georgia's South. ("Fern," 27)

This passage illustrates how water imagery in *Cane* reflects "sites" of memory that are pregnant with a figurative moment of cumulative, racial significance. Toomer discards history, with its linear, chronological movement, for just such "sites," projecting not only his protagonist but also the black writer back to the South and their cultural past and leading them to reassess their culture and racial identity. "Seem[ing] to flow into [Fern's] eyes," the "whole countryside," in the above description, is imbued with "the soft listless cadence of Georgia's South." Sites of memory in *Cane* evoke not only a sense of place but also collective black experiences anchored in African American memory, permitting a sense of identity and belonging to emerge. Within these sites, the metaphors attached to the notion of fluidity render Toomer's attempt to relate to his past and understand his heritage. They convey the idea that, if it is true that history is the memory of mankind, the emotional and direct apprehension of memory provides the deepest insight that human beings can have into themselves.

Moving in a nonlinear way, often laden with emotion, memory works in ways that closely resemble the workings of metaphorical discourse; in *Cane*, both combine in the fluidity of water imagery to create a dreamlike space. Toomer introduces water metaphors, so crucial to the depiction of this space, in order to show how places constitute sites of memory and how memory-generating experiences reflect the construction of an African American culture as well as the tensions of black Americans' double consciousness. In *Cane*, the metaphorical and the metaphysical, or philosophical, overlap. Through its arabesque pattern of imagery and the incantatory power of the repetitions present in the work songs, slave songs, and fragments of spirituals, water, the metaphor of life, provides both dynamism and unity. It is the "soul" of a language whose shifting rhythm and various meanings coalesce into a whole, posited as mediation between one human being and another and allowing the self to look within the self and the community.

Notes

This is a revised version of an essay published in *L3 Liege Language and Literature* (1998). Reprinted with permission of the publisher.

1. I borrow the idea of "metaphorical twist" from Beardsley, "Metaphorical Twist," 300.

Works Cited

Austin, John Langshaw, and J. O. Urmson, eds. *How to Do Things with Words*. Oxford: Clarendon Press, 1962.

Bachelard, Gaston. *The Poetics of Space*. Trans. Maria Jolas. Boston: Beacon Press, 1969.
Beardsley, Monroe C. "The Metaphorical Twist." *Philosophy and Phenomenological Research* 22 (March 1962).
Douglass, Frederick. *Narrative of the Life of Frederick Douglass, an American Slave*. 1845. Reprint, New York: Penguin, 1986.
Heidegger, Martin. *What is Called Thinking*. Trans. F. D. Wieck and J. C. Grey. New York: Harper and Row, 1968.
Herschberger, Ruth. "The Structure of Metaphor." *Kenyon Review* 5 (1943).
Husserl, Edmund. *Logical Investigations*. London: Routledge and Kegan Paul, 1970.
Jakobson, Roman. "Closing Statements: Linguistics Poetics." *In Style in Language*, ed. T. A. Sebeok. Cambridge, Mass.: MIT Press, 1960.
Toomer, Jean. *Cane*. 1923. Reprint, NewYork: Harper and Row, 1969.
Wittgenstein, Ludwig. *Philosophical Investigations*. Ed. G.H.M. Anscombe. 3d ed. Oxford: Basil Blackwell, 1968.

Feeding the Soul with Words

Preaching and Dreaming in Cane

CÉCILE COQUET

The form thats burned int m soul is some twisted awful thing that crept in from a dream, a godam nightmare, an wont stay still unless I feed it. An it lives on words. . . . I want t feed th soul—I know what that is; th preachers dont—but I've got t feed it.

Toomer, "Kabnis"

THIS FRAGMENT FROM Kabnis's confession dramatizes the dualism between two impulses running all through *Cane:* the need to exchange with others and the need, or reflex, of isolating oneself in dreams. The character of Ralph Kabnis is probably the one that best embodies the tension between the two when he proclaims himself to be a dream: "Ralph Kabnis is a dream" (83), even as he is trying to sing about the soul of the South and later confronts the only true preacher figure of the book, Father John, who appears as his exact counterpart.

Preaching and dreaming in *Cane* are antagonistic rather than radically opposed; their struggle within the souls of the characters often points to intimate contradictions between mind and desire, as is most clearly expressed in "Theater" when the author describes the feelings of John, who is to be halfspectator and halfdreamer all through the show: "John's mind coincides with the shaft of light. Thoughts rush to, and compact about it. Life of the house and of the slowly awakening stage swirls to the body of John, and thrills it. John's body is separate from the thoughts that pack his mind. . . . His mind, contained above desires of his body, singles the girls out, and tries to trace origins and plot destinies" ("Theater," 52).

Whenever "dreaming" overtakes the characters' minds in *Cane,* they are living out their visions in reality—which often implies that, although replete with beautiful words, speech and poetry will be muted and remain so in the face of the surrounding world. At the other end of the spectrum, in the African American religious experience, "preaching" essentially means trying to communicate visions through the effective sharing of words that build emotions. The people involved in this activity are engaged in a quest for peace and reconciliation with the world and their own sense of self, which they express in different ways of spiritual escape, such as shout, tears, and song.

In their literary transformations, both dreaming and preaching can provide the artist with characters and images telling of the soul and its maladjustment to the world. Perhaps one of the main problems shown by *Cane* in its mosaic of stories and songs is that of communication with the other, or the hunger and fear to call put into song in "Harvest Song": "I hunger. . . . I fear to call. What should they hear me, and offer me their grain, oats, or wheat, or corn? I have been in the fields all day. I fear I could not taste it. I fear knowledge of my hunger" (71). Toomer's complex use of the themes of dreaming and preaching illustrates this struggle between both the hope and fear to escape in different, yet parallel, patterns of calls and responses between the multiple characters.

In *Cane*, dreaming is everywhere to be seen as the sign of utter solitude. The characters most given to the practice of it may be (self-styled) seers like Dan in "Box Seat" or Paul in "Bona and Paul"; they strike us as being as tragically and ironically tongue-tied as the old preacher, Father John, is thought to be.

Their call to the other is a sudden urge to communicate that nothing but eyes can convey. In the scenes of confrontation between Dan and Muriel, Paul and Bona, the narrator and Fern, Kabnis and Lewis ("His eyes call, 'Brother'"; 98), Lewis and Carrie Kate,[1] the exchange of gazes is the only junction in space, time, and expression where love, contempt, or fear are not meant to be hidden by, or mistaken for, deceitful words. By the same token, when Dorris seeks her dance in John's face, she cannot perceive it because he, too engrossed in his vision of the two of them, remains in "the shadow which is his dream" (56) and does not meet her real eyes. The common point of *Cane*'s dreamers, when they do reach out to the person who might embody their secret hopes, is to believe they can read the soul in the eyes of the other and be seen as they are, in the sheer truth of the moment.[2] But if their call gives life to a form of true exchange, albeit ephemeral and frail, what response do the "dreamers" meet with when they themselves are called to action or speech?

As soon as they are back in the realm of words, they are intent on talking their vision out, without caring for the other's sensitivity. Their soliloquies are the reverse of call-and-response patterns; they hope to be understood, but instead their minds escape alone, leaving the listeners behind. As visions are forming with increased precision in their minds, gaining words and colors, they leave the loved one, or the "weakest" of the two protagonists, without any alternative but passivity.

This imposed muteness may be accepted by the other and take the form of sleep, as with Avey (48–49) or Cloine ("Evening Song," 21), whose dreams the lover-narrator cannot partake in; or it may turn into revolts of fear and misunderstanding at the very moment when the transmission of the (gift of) vision seemed possible—as between Muriel and Dan at Mrs. Pribby's, Bona and Paul at the end of their dance, Dorris and John at the end of the show, or Carrie Kate and Kabnis in their frightened refusals of Lewis.

It can also be dramatized as symbolical gestures appealing to God, thereby staging the listener's escape from an impossible dialogue—as when Carrie Kate prays over Kabnis (117)—or even as a form of death, involving the deepest, hopeless desires of the weak—as with Fern's trance (19) or Kabnis's catalepsy at the feet of Father John, who has gotten into him "by way o dreams" (114). In these examples, the radical meaning given to the escape from spoken exchange seems to point to an almost physical impossibility to bear another person's vision.

The paradoxical disregard of dreaming souls for the other they seek betrays a maladjustment to the world that handicaps them and makes them incapable of saving their loved ones—or even their own selves threatened with disunity. Often, characters mesmerized by their dreamscapes forget all about the actual setting and presence of others until, recovering consciousness, they are hurt by the palpable otherness, which is suddenly expressed by innocent words or appearances—as between Lewis and Carrie Kate ("Her soft rolled words are fresh pain to Lewis"; 104) or Kabnis and Carrie Kate ("Kabnis forgets that Carrie is with him. . . . Dont look shocked, little sweetheart, you hurt me"; 116).

The dreaming seekers and seers are, in fact, talking in their sleep like Kabnis (112) and meeting other sleepers, other dreamers with their own good or bad dreams. To paraphrase "Prayer" (70), the act of giving is painful and makes you weak, but does not save your body and mind from being opaque to your own soul.[3] And as Toni Morrison voiced it, "There is no gift for the beloved. The lover alone possesses his gift of love. The loved one is shorn, neutralized, frozen in the glare of the lover's inward eye."[4]

In such configurations, "words to fit m soul" have no power to fit the souls of others, just as dreaming eyes often look beyond the loved one. This distrust in words is poignantly rendered by the narrative voice in "Fern": "I tried to tell her with my eyes. I think she understood. The thing from her that made my throat catch, vanished. Its passing left her visible in a way I'd thought, but never seen" (19)[5] and in "Avey": "I began to visualize certain possibilities. An immediate and urgent passion swept me. Then I looked at Avey. Her heavy eyes were closed. Her breathing was as faint and regular as a child's in slumber. My passion died" (48).

Between the "immediacy" of love and the "listlessness" of dreaming minds[6] (contrasting ironically with the supposed "listlessness" or "laziness" of Fern or Avey, framed as so many reproaches), there seems to exist no space for direct verbal contact between the dreamers' and the real worlds that might make them visible to each other.[7]

To make the souls of certain protagonists more visible to the reader, Toomer has established a subtle poetical link between the words "soul" and "chill", which appears in scenes, poems, or songs where the theme of sleep is prevailing, as in "Calling Jesus" ("Her soul is like a little thrust-tailed dog . . . left in the vestibule, filled with chills till morning"; 58) or the opening scene of "Kabnis," where the protagonist, trying to "read himself to sleep," listens "against his will" to the Georgia winds that whisper about the soul of the South while he feels "the weird chill of their song" (83).

This chill is the mark of the opacity of the self,[8] of the dreamers' fear of being "too close" to beauty, as in the phrase "Muriel is too close" (68) and in Kabnis's prayer, which clearly associates this closeness (immediacy) of beauty to spiritual pain: "Dear Jesus, do not chain me to myself and set these hills and valleys, heaving with folk-songs, so close to me that I cannot reach them. There is a radiant beauty in the night that touches and . . . tortures me. . . . Whats beauty anyway but ugliness if it hurts you?" (85).[9] It is a key to identities and hopes, but the consciousness brought about by this physical reaction can be either quickening or deadening, perhaps in an odd parallel to the image of "chilly Jordan," which alluded both to the converts' spiritual awakening during baptisms and to the final crossing between life and the afterlife; this connection might be traced in the night winds' song in "Kabnis": "Till poor rivers bring / Rest, and sweet glory / In Camp Ground" (83, 87, 105).

But beyond the problem of being opaque to one's soul, beyond the difficulties to reach to others or relieve pain, the characters that are conscious of the weakness within themselves fear to be alienated by the words coming from the crowd. This is the other side of the coin; it shows that, even if dreaming cannot veer off threats to the unity of the self, it can be even worse to let oneself be put into words by the outer world alone: "Taking their words, they filled her, like a bubble rising—then she broke" ("Becky," 7). Muriel, too afraid to dream, chooses to plead silently with Dan, while trying feebly to avert alienation: "[Mrs. Pribby] *is* me, somehow. No she's not. Yes she is. She is the town, and the town won't let me love you, Dan" (58). Unlike other female characters such as Esther or Dorris (the former being a dreamer, whereas the latter is rooted in reality), she has no trust in her own willpower to obtain in the real world what she wishes in thought: "You could make it let me if you would. Why wont you? Youre selfish. I'm not strong enough to buck it. Youre too selfish to buck it, for me. I wish you'd go" (61).

The destruction or frustration of such souls in front of otherness is not so much a problem of giving as receiving, not so much a problem of reaching to the loved one as of defining themselves on their own terms. Kabnis, who is described by Lewis as one to whom life "has given . . . in excess of what he can receive" (101), proves it by stating that white and black folks feed his nightmare (and his soul, parasitized by it) with their looks, "because their looks are words" (111).

For these oppressed characters, the accomplishment of an envisioned liberation in love or communion—which would give their lives meaning at last[10]—is intimately associated with the fear of sin. It is this fear that makes young Esther wary of her first dream: "[The town fire department] rescues from the second-story window a dimpled infant which she claims for her own. How had she come by it? She thinks of it immaculately. It is a sin to think of it immaculately. She must dream no more. She must repent her sin" (24).[11] The same reflex, dissociating the will from the realm of the mind and the desires of the body,[12] puts a brutal end to her dream of becoming the mother of a Black Messiah: "The thought comes suddenly, that conception with a drunken man must be a mighty sin. She draws away, frozen" (27).

Such a freezing of the soul, more lethal than the chills experienced in dreams and awakenings, Carrie Kate undergoes too when the "sin-bogies of respectable southern colored folks" (103)—whose "clamor" she has integrated just as Muriel has integrated the prejudices and rumor of the town—drive her to reject Lewis's unspoken offer of love. The seers' hope of a messianic liberation capable of bringing about the advent of love by ignoring fear, hatred, and stifling social convention thus finds itself shattered by the mental incapacity of the other (within themselves or the loved one) to accept their dream—of beauty, shared passion, or a black baby—as the essence of their soul and the salvation of their unity and to give it the warmth of life.

Instead of meeting their ideals of beauty in the world and achieving their goals, the tortured dreamers forget the existence of the loved one like an unsolved problem[13] or displace their vision so as to make it an alien thing, a "twisted thing" both integrated into their bodies and belonging to someone else. Thus, the imagined sight of Mame Lamkins's baby living in her dead body, the narration of the atrocious lynching of this baby, the images of burnt bodies found in "Karintha," "Blood-Burning Moon," and "A Portrait in Georgia," and the phantasm of a malediction linked to procreation and the sin of slavery combine to make the figures of Esther and Kabnis strangely transparent to the reader as the most accomplished embodiments of the dreamer's soul, whose hunger is a very real need to be born.[14] But the kind of new birth, of "soul-rising," required by this soul ("its th soul of me that needs th risin," Kabnis confesses to Carrie Kate; 115) is not of the same nature as that which can be offered by preaching or by the preacher figures appearing in *Cane*.

Preaching is more concerned with the quest of truth in a vision, because the kind of message it means to convey points toward universal ideals that people try to live by in order to be saved. The words and gestures used by the preacher figures can reach the souls of the weak to the point of alleviating their fears, as with Esther after Barlo's sermon or with Carrie Kate when she "fearlessly . . . loves into" Lewis's "Christ-eyes" after he has stretched his hands forth to hers and has looked to her to offer her salvation (103). In both examples, the problem is not to determine whether or not the characters can legitimately lay claim to the title of "preacher figure," but to see in what way their gestures are consciously fraught with religious meaning, which differentiates the patterns of call-and-response from those existing in the configuration of dreams.

King Barlo's rising to his full height as he preaches about the African ancestor and calls on his listeners to convert (23) expresses an appeal to liberation in the same way as Lewis's stretching forth his hands to Carrie Kate: both are aesthetic allusions to the biblical prediction about Ethiopia stretching out her hands unto God (Psalms 68:31), and both offer a vision of glory to the weak or hopeless, challenging the life that awaits them in "the southern town." These gestures go further than the ideal communing in mental dreamshapes: the type of call that is directly or indirectly sent to the other in terms of salvation draws the other, ultimately, to an acceptance of the beauty of blackness.

Therefore, the immediate response to this call (before fear or loss of communication interrupt the call-and-response exchange) is in keeping with the expressions of black folk religion. Fern not only sings but shouts, although she is cream-colored and partly Jewish; other characters keep a sense of temporal continuity by nursing some hope in a promise, be it a new or an old one, that they can actively take part in: Esther dreams of begetting a Black Messiah with Barlo; Dan symbolically heals (or feeds the soul of) the old invalid "Moses" when he asks him to look into the heavens and sees him smiling (68); and Carrie Kate urges Father John to speak about the sin of the white man, feeling she is about to learn a truth she can live by ever after (116). As Kabnis—or the "dictie" in Toomer?—would put it, these are "nigger soul[s]" who are "getting drunk on a preacher's words" (114) or, like the African ancestor of Barlo the jackleg, they are "[d]runk with rum, / Feasting on strange cassava, / Yielding to new words and a weak palabra" ("Conversion," 28). It is true that their relief is frail and often short-lived, but their souls nevertheless know how to find the words that feed their hopes and restore their identities, be they dreamers' souls or believers' souls, while Kabnis remains "[s]uspended a few feet above the soil whose touch would resurrect him" (98), like a modern Antaeus.

Yet the nature of this call-and-response exchange is not altogether clear in *Cane*. The common point between Esther's story and Father John's solemn condemnation of the whites is the theme of making the Bible lie. Dreaming is neither shaped nor told in terms of truth, whereas preaching cannot be otherwise, even when it deals with visions. (This is precisely what Kabnis rejects, just as he tries to deny the existence of "soul" and "sin,"[15] because the simple fact of dealing with beauty and horror is already too much for him, as Lewis justly analyzes.) Hence the inevitable confrontation between the messianic hope of black Christian folk and the cruelty of a world marked by slavery, which refuses to consider souls otherwise than in black or white.

This confrontation is rooted in the impossibility for the white or nearly white characters to understand the nature of the ecstatic escape reached in church by the believers: "Listening to them at church didnt tell you anything," Bob Stone reflects in "Blood-Burning Moon" (33) as he tries to define what he knows in fact about the blacks living next to him. Likewise, but in a derogatory manner, Kabnis wonders about the essence of Father John's soul: "Your soul. Ha. Nigger soul. A gin soul that gets drunk on a preacher's words. An screams. An shouts. God Almighty, how I hate that shoutin. Where's th beauty in that? . . . Aint surprisin th white folks hate y so" (114).

These beautiful "preacher's words," inexplicably effective and soothing to the churchgoers, drowning the Southern country under "a holy avalanche" ("Kabnis," 111), are fit for the ultimate other, the "Nigger," who cannot be met on wholly loving terms by those dreaming minds struggling painfully against their attraction to black beauty—such as the narrator's condemnation of Avey's "laziness," Bona's puzzlement when she first realizes she loves Paul ("He is a harvest moon. He is an autumn leaf. He is a nigger. Bona! But dont all the dorm girls say so? And dont you, when you are sane, say so?"; 72), or Bob Stone's confusion as he tries to define his feeling for Louisa ("She was lovely—in her way. Nigger way. What way was that? Damned if he knew. . . . Beautiful nigger gal. Why nigger? Why not, just gal? No, it was because she was nigger that he went to her. Sweet . . . "; 33, 34). For the dreaming poets, teachers, and philosophers of the book—who are desperately trying to kill the weakness or the passion within themselves and find their own words to reach beauty by controlling the ramblings of their minds—this magic of spiritual call-and-response, aesthetically based on the pleasure of taking in the other's words, is a dry grain in the mouth, in which they find no taste, in spite of their hunger.[16] Their "fear to call" is inseparable from their refusal to respond to these other words and visions as the "weak" souls do; but here, more than the fear of alienation, it is the intolerable prospect of becoming one with the lowly, credulous souls that is at the root of their revolt against the power of preaching: "The old man sinks back into his stony silence. Carrie is wet-eyed. Kabnis, contemptuous" (117).

Cane poetically dramatizes the problem of the limits imposed upon words and visions by the reality and setting of the South through the insistent presence of the fringe of pines. This image is fraught with a sense of imprisonment mingled with heavenly visions of glory: "Push back the fringe of pines upon new horizons," the narrator exhorts himself in "Fern" (18), and in "Becky" (8) the whispering or shouting fringe of pines weighs on the country like an omen. In "Georgia Dusk" (15), the pine trees become guitars whose strumming rains down luminous needles, bringing their fringe down to earth like a blessing; their "sacred whisper" accompanies the "resinous and soft" songs of the pompous caravan of black pagan-Christian high priests, bringing "dreams of Christ to dusky cane-lipped throngs."

In "Fern," the pine trees are linked with dusk again, but their presence evokes a vision of reconciliation and hope when the story of Kabnis (and hence the book) ends at dawn: "Outside, the sun arises from its cradle in the tree-tops of the forest. Shadows of pines are dreams the sun shakes from its eyes" (117). Within the poetic system of echoes or mirror effects in *Cane*, this construct can be read as an appeasing inversion of images of evil and alienation, such as the ill omen of the full moon ("Blood-Burning Moon"), the hostile walls or houses closing on beings ("Box Seat"), or the ambiguous image of the half-moon as "a white child that sleeps upon the tree-tops of the forest," cradled by the night as by a black mother, but certain to fall "when the bough bends," at the beginning of "Kabnis" (84). More interestingly, the picture of dawn as a godly awakening[17] could very well be a preacher's image: in "The Creation," the first of his seven Negro sermons in verse, James Weldon Johnson, inspired by old-time preaching, wrote: God "batted his eyes, and the lightning flashed."[18]

The constant closeness between the "low-hanging heavens" (31) and the fringe of pines in *Cane* might well point to a dream of another form of communication and exchange, reuniting dreamscapes and preacher's words, speech and physical touch: "O pines, whisper to Jesus; tell Him to come and press sweet Jesus-lips against their [Becky's two sons'] lips and eyes. . . . Pines shout to Jesus!" (8). In this new form of call-and-response between the poet and the other, between body and soul, the painful limits of verbal communion and eye contact (lips and eyes) seem to be forgotten, or healed, by the marvelous power of touch.

In between dreams of beauty and incantations to a healing Christ, elasticity appears as one of the key concepts of the book as bare feet almost float above the earth or glide on a bed of golden pine needles,[19] cotton bales,[20] fresh blades of grass,[21] or fallen leaves.[22] As in "Calling Jesus," where the woman is given back her furry-soft, doglike soul at night as she lies asleep "upon clean hay cut in her dreams," "cradled in dream-fluted cane," this ideal of a pleasurable lightness[23] and elasticity leads both poet and reader to a recovery of the unity between body and soul—a physical, direct sense of fullness that was denied in other environments where people, seeming to fit in the world, only "clicked into" receptacles that encaged them and weighed them down.[24]

The image of the fringe of pines, as used by Toomer in this type of elastic pattern of call-and-response with his reader, offers a striking parallel with an image found in a funeral sermon related in the Works Progress Administration (WPA) collection in which the preacher looks over a pine forest while describing the dead man's soul climbing Jacob's ladder up to heaven:

> [Brother Wash] was buried on top of de hill, in de pines just north of Woodward. Uncle Pompey preached de funeral. White folks was dere. Marse Williams was dere, and his nephew, de Attorney General of Arizona. Uncle Pompey took his text 'bout Paul and Silas layin' in jail and dat it was not 'ternally against a church member to go to jail. Him dwell on de life of labor and bravery, in tacklin' kickin' hosses and mules. How him sharpen de dull plow points and make de corn and cotton grow, to feed and clothe de hungry and naked. *He look up thru de pine tree tops* and say: "I see Jacob's ladder. Brother Wash is climbin' dat ladder. Him is half way up. Ah! Brudders and sisters, pray, while I preach dat he enter in them pearly gates. I see dem gates open. Brother Wash done reach the topmost rung in dat ladder. Let us sing wid a shout, dat blessed hymn, 'Dere is a Fountain Filled Wid Blood.' " Wid de first verse de women got to hollerin' and wid de second, Uncle Pompey say: "De dyin' thief I see him dere to welcome Brother Wash in paradise. Thank God! Brother Wash done washed as white as snow and landed safe forever more" (my emphasis).[25]

Perhaps here the sermon joins hands with the poet's dream: the successful escape of the endangered soul, climbing the treetops like a celestial ladder, takes place under the joint signs of salvation, elastic unity of body and soul, and vital communication with the other human beings, defined as brothers and sisters beyond the limits of a song. In this scene from the old black South, the seer-preacher and the singers share the same vision of glory, a dream they will to happen for the dead man's sake, as witnesses to his long hoped-for liberation from slavery.

The common point between dreaming and preaching in *Cane* is the association they create between deep longing and subtly linked images or obsessions. The mechanisms of dreams and sermons are the same as those of the book: a series of calls and irregular responses between images, words, gestures, and symbols of beauty or truth.

Perhaps the intent is the same also: dulling the pain to make it sweet and beautiful, despite the persisting hunger and dissatisfaction of the lonely soul that fears to call: "I beat my palms, still soft, against the stubble of my harvesting. (You beat your soft palms, too.) My pain is sweet. . . . It will not bring me knowledge of my hunger" ("Harvest Song," 71). Beauty cannot save the world,[26] but, like preaching and dreaming, it may rock it to sleep or acceptance of a soft, at times gravelike, cradle until inspiration changes again. Whether they be happy dreams of finding Jesus in escape, nightmares, or expressions of hope or contempt, "things are so immediate in Georgia" ("Kabnis," 86) that the poet sometimes has to twist them to knit them together—but not too close.

Notes

Page numbers refer to Jean Toomer, *Cane* (New York: Norton, 1988).

1. In this case, Lewis might be more of a well-wisher (like the narrator in "Fern") than a dreamer disconnected from the actual dispositions of the other protagonist in the exchange. In other scenes, he is more akin to a preacher figure, insofar as he can find the right words to communicate his message. As for Carrie Kate, we only know that she "fearlessly" loves into Lewis's "Christ-eyes," which does not tell how much she shares in his vision of her life to come. Like Kabnis in part 3 and Stella in part 5 of "Kabnis," she is the one character in the scene who feels that Lewis's eyes speak a truth about herself, hidden until then but meant for both of them. Probably these short exchanges of visions can happen only because the various seekers meet an actual seer—which would be an interesting counterpoint to the Fern/narrator pair, if we remember that Fern's eyes "sought nothing" (16).
2. The introduction of Lewis by the narrative voice suggests this connection between Kabnis and Lewis, although the former is not supposed to be conscious of it: "[Lewis] is what a stronger Kabnis might have been, and in an odd faint way resembles him. As he steps towards the others, he seems to be issuing sharply from a vivid dream" (97). But whose vivid dream? Kabnis's? Carrie Kate's? Or Toomer's dream of his own self?
3. Paul himself, though one of the most lucid seers in *Cane,* can only see himself through the eyes of other people sensing his difference and appears to himself "cloudy, but real" (77)—as if seen through a glass pane?—whereas white faces around him are endowed with "glow and immediacy" in the same vision.
4. Morrison, *Bluest Eye*, 163.

5. Here, the dreamt and actual visions conflate in the lover's eyes, joining past thoughts with present contemplation. But his wonderment at it will not stop his mind from escaping the loved one: "From force of habit, I suppose, I held Fern in my arms—that is, without at first noticing it. Then my mind came back to her" (19). And at this point, he finds himself and God held in her eyes and is moved by the sight of her, but still cannot comprehend her feelings.
6. "Her eyes hardly see the people to whom she gives change. . . . She rests listlessly against the counter, too weary to sit down" ("Esther," 25); "Esther listlessly forgets that she is near white, and that her father is the richest colored man in town. . . . She learns their names. She forgets them" (24).
7. "The body of the world is bull-necked. A dream is a soft face that fits uncertainly upon it. . . . God, if I could develop that in words" ("Kabnis," 83).
8. "Now that the sun has set and I am chilled, I fear to call" ("Harvest Song," 71).
9. In the case of Lewis at the end of section 5 in "Kabnis" ("The glowing within him subsides. It is followed by a dead chill"; 112); this chill points to his painful impotence as a messianic figure rather than an opacity that would keep him from seeing himself. The immediacy here is that of his real surroundings, people and setting, that "descend upon him" with such intensity that he has to leave the scene, being at the same time "completely cut out" and in the center of it. He can neither offer himself nor respond to this silent call of pain.
10. This meaning could be more akin to Dorris's "simple" wish of being loved and given "kids, and a home, and everything" (55) than the fact, once again imposed from outside, of being left alone like Becky and Esther or "becoming a virgin" like Fern (16), even if this discarding is rephrased as "being above them."
11. The immediate puritanical assimilation of the dream to a sin shows how pleasurable this vision of herself as a mother was for Esther; it drives the reader toward the very equation between "dream" and "pleasure" that Paul takes for granted when he speaks of the "pleasure . . . of love or dream" (77).
12. Toomer insists on defining dream as a thing of the mind, apparently as the artistic side of it: "[King Barlo] left his image indelibly upon the mind of Esther. He became the starting point of the only living patterns that her mind was to know" (23); "Mind pulls him upward into dream" ("Theater," 55). But the will can wrench the mind from the attraction exerted by dream and sensuality: "He wills thought to rid his mind of passion" ("Theater," 53); "She wants her mind to be like that. Solid, contained, and blank as a sheet of darkened ice" ("Esther," 26). Or is it the "dictie" speaking in John, Muriel, and Esther (and in Toomer himself?), who refuses to accept the "nigger" within the self?
13. John expresses this strange survival instinct of dreamers' minds when he tells himself, even before singling out Dorris on the stage: "Her I'd love I'd leave before she knew that I was with her. Her? Which?" (53).
14. "John's melancholy is a deep thing that seals all senses but his eyes, and makes him whole" (55); "Their stares, giving him to himself, filled something long empty within him, and were like green blades sprouting in his consciousness. There was fullness, and strength and peace about it all" ("Bona and Paul," 77). In both cases, a sense of wholeness is found in the mind's solitary escape into dream, which makes each lover-dreamer invisible to the loved one or radically cuts him out from the group. Thus, being saved or given back to themselves, they are lost to the others.
15. "Soul. Soul hell. There aint such a thing" (84); "It was only a preacher's sin they knew in those old days, an that wasnt sin at all. Mind me, the only sin is whats done against th soul. Th whole world is a conspiracy t sin, especially in America, an against me. I'm th victim of their sin. I'm what sin is" (116).
16. "And I hunger. I crack a grain. It has no taste to it. My throat is dry" ("Harvest

Song," 71); "Love is a dry grain in my mouth unless it is wet with kisses" (Paul, in "Bona and Paul," 76).

17. "The countryside dogs barked and roosters crowed as if heralding a weird dawn or some ungodly awakening" ("Blood-Burning Moon," 31). As Bob Stone runs toward Tom and Louisa, "[r]oosters crowed, heralding the bloodshot eyes of southern awakening" (35).
18. Johnson, *God's Trombones*, 18.
19. "Pine-needles are smooth and sweet. They are elastic to the feet of rabbits" ("Karintha," 4); "A spray of pine-needles, / Dipped in western horizon gold, / Fell onto a path. / . . . Rabbits knew not of their falling, / Nor did the forest catch aflame" ("Nullo," 20).
20. "Cotton bales are the fleecy way / Weary sinner's bare feet trod, / Softly, softly to the throne of God" ("Cotton Song," 11); "Some one . . . eoho Jesus . . . soft as the bare feet of Christ moving across bales of southern cotton, will steal in and cover it [her soul] that it need not shiver" ("Calling Jesus," 58).
21. "Robins spring about the lawn all day. They leave their footprints in the grass. I imagine the grass at night smells sweet and fresh because of them" ("Avey," 47–48).
22. "There are no trees in the alley. But his feet feel as though they step on autumn leaves whose rustle has been pressed out of them by the passing of a million satin slippers. . . . She barely touches his arm. They glide off with footfalls softened on the leaves, the old leaves powdered by a million satin slippers" ("Theater," 55).
23. Bona's words, Paul feels, lack this pleasurable touch of bare contact, because they are lost on him: "Her words have no feel to them. One sees them. They are pink petals that fall upon velvet cloth" (76). In the same way, Paul, who goes out with her "to gather petals" in the Crimson Gardens and to finally know her, describes his former thoughts as "matches thrown into a dark window" (80).
24. "Muriel comes in, shakes hands, and then clicks into a high-armed seat under the orange glow of a floor-lamp. . . . Muriel's chair is close and stiff about her. The house, the rows of houses locked about her chair. . . . Each one [of the spectators] is a bolt that shoots into a slot, and is locked there" ("Box Seat," 61, 63, 64); "Rhobert wears a house, like a monstrous diver's helmet, on his head. . . . He is way down. He is sinking. His house is a dead thing that weights him down" ("Rhobert," 42).
25. My emphasis. Rawick, *American Slave*, 179–180.
26. In 1937, the French surrealist poet André Breton ended his book *L'amour fou* with the prophecy: "LA BEAUTÉ SAUVERA LE MONDE."

"Karintha"

MONICA MICHLIN

A Textual Analysis

As a liminary text, "Karintha," the first sketch in Jean Toomer's *Cane*, necessarily calls attention to the way it introduces the many themes and stylistic effects of the work, which, in its splintered aspect, relies heavily upon the echoes created by the stories and their motifs to form a coherent whole. The pun on this last word—"whole" or "hole"—actually structures this initial story, which revolves around a blank in the text, a foregrounded ellipsis. What is the status of this blank: absence, loss, or mimetic aborting of the text? The term "blank" itself raises questions in a story that is fundamentally a redefinition of blackness: what vision of blackness does Karintha have—one that is full and strong or one that is weak and self-defeating, aborted or deformed, in some way stillborn, or mutilated? The connection between the missing center and the polyphonous structure and between Karintha's silence and the multiplication of voices also seems to herald the double movement that is present in all of *Cane:* on the one hand, its broken syntax, its frustrating lack of narrative continuity, its use of elision, ellipsis, symbolism, innuendo, and heavy metaphorization and, on the other hand, its constant accretion of voices, pieces, poems, and sketches. It appears that the discordant symphony of voices that arise page after page in "Karintha" ultimately serves to negate the wishful lyricism and celebration of the book's epigraph as the narrative voice keeps differing from itself (from prose to poetry, from archaic to modernist styles, from lyrical to staccato bitterness) in Toomer's effort to differ from past writing on blackness and to differ from both black and white.

The first point that draws the reader's attention in the sketch is the song that immediately follows the title. The lack of introduction to this lyric is ambiguous: does the song read as a "referential" reality preexistent to the literary text, which served the writer as a source of inspiration for his story, or does Toomer want to emphasize that in literary terms, to describe Karintha, he could only use a literally, not metaphorically, musical voice? At a first reading, one sees the song as aiming mainly at a naive local-color effect, with the immediate inscription of the anonymous and collective voice of black folk song, whereas at the second, one reads the same song as a deliberate inscription of the black heritage and of a modern use of the primitive for purely literary effect. Indeed, the song sets the tone and key of the story not just in its theme but in its writing by announcing the register of the narrative voice itself, a voice of parataxis, of metaphor, of simile, of indirection. The italicization of the song underlines the different status of the two voices and points to the juxtaposition of various voices with no transition whatsoever.

The song itself is a celebration of a beautiful black woman—black being suggested through the use of the term "dusk" and the image of the setting sun, and beauty, through the apostrophe "O can't you see it," which draws attention to the fact that the reader cannot literally see the praised skin and yet is being made aware of the desire this beauty evokes ("O" could be, in this context, the sound of absolute longing). This song of desire is surprising for two reasons. The first is that it does not name the woman and does not clearly say that the woman is black. So far, the reader has only seen the color "purple of the dusk" in the epigraph, and in the entire sketch the only time the adjective "black" appears is when Karintha is compared to a "black bird that flashes in light"—but she is also said to be "as innocently lovely as a November cotton flower," and such flowers are white. The image of black skin being like dusk seems essential to the rewriting of the color "black" that Toomer was attempting in *Cane*. As many critics have pointed out, the title of the book itself is a reflection of the attempt to escape the black-white vocabulary of race and ethnicity. How does this function, and does it succeed?

"Karintha" already heralds in some ways the black perspective that authors like Toni Morrison have imposed since: within the black community, it is obvious that the song is about a black woman, so that we are immersed in a black reading in which a priori everyone is black, unless otherwise specified. This interpretation makes "Karintha" a subversive black story, because it implies a reversal in the contract with the (mainly white) readers as to which is the color of reference and which the color of "otherness." However, the rest of *Cane* shows that the black-centeredness is not that absolute. The fact that the vocabulary of the landscape and of nature is used to circumvent the abstract function of color in racial definition is a constant feature of the book, but instead of blackness being used as the natural color of reference, it becomes a part of the book's (white) primitivistic strategies. In "Bona and Paul," Bona (who is white) describes Paul (who is black) in these terms: "He is a harvest moon. He is an autumn leaf. He is a nigger" (72). Despite the fact that "Bona and Paul" is a story that attempts to redefine blackness beyond the white gaze, this white gaze of "naturalization," however metaphorical, of the black body, with all of its potential ambiguity (black is hot and primitive; white is cold and abstract), is never quite overcome. There is one strong moment in which Paul, who is "passing" but never acknowledges this to himself, when suddenly confronted by the hostility in the white gaze, envisions his blackness as full, as a difference that makes him more real than white people; the latter are described as "wonderfully flushed and beautiful," but also as "carbon bubbles" or as "a purple fluid, carbon-charged, that effervesces" (75). This description, which redefines white skin as fragile and transparent in its coloring ("purple fluid") is a subversive racial reversal: the initial reason for the bubble image is that Paul's white friend is "bubbling over" with joy, but the image obviously shifts into that of a death wish (what if the bubble should burst?). This moment when Paul thinks of his blackness as more real than the effervescent whiteness is an essential moment in early twentieth-century African American literature, because Toomer tried *not* to accept the image Henry Louis Gates Jr. has since determined to be fundamental to white representations of blackness: black equals absence, black equals invisible. Toomer was trying to evade voicing the anger of the "invisible" black man, who needs to challenge the white gaze that negates him—the voice Ralph Ellison immortalized a generation later. Toomer attempts, through Paul, to calmly reverse the (un)reality of black and white—much in the way Toni Morrison does at the beginning of *Sula* when Shadrack, the black veteran, sees his blackness as the one solid and reassuring reality in a world turned chaotic by war and post-traumatic stress. In "Bona and Paul," the stratagem Toomer uses when he suddenly redefines black as *full* in the eyes of a character who is "passing" does not work because Paul is necessarily caught in a vicious circle of contradiction, denial, and overcompensation. Having suddenly discovered that his difference is not attractive to the white eye,[1] he supposedly feels renewed; the white stares are "giving him to himself, fill[ing] something long empty within him" (76), without causing pain: "There was a fullness, and strength and peace about it all" (77). The notions of fullness and strength that could possibly result from the assertion of the self in this conflict with the racist gaze are undermined by the impossible assertion of peace (a kind of magical transformation within a "realistic" text), something that the following paragraphs of the text deny, as Paul becomes extremely agitated watching the white faces around him. The bad faith in this reluctance to voice conflict between black and white—both literally and metaphorically: the color used in describing Paul's inner consciousness is *green*[2]—and the desire to pull a blanket of weak, wishful thinking over the moment of truth make this text a strained epiphany reflecting Toomer's own contradictions and denials.

This is not immediately apparent in "Karintha" only because, from the first line of the narrative, the conflict that the story centers on is sexual, not racial. As the narrator integrates the song from the epigraph into his tale—"Men had always wanted her, this Karintha, even as a child, Karintha carrying beauty, perfect as dusk when the sun goes down"—he decodes the song of praise into one of sexual domination and reification. The syntax of the sentence makes Karintha an object, not a subject, of what should be *her* story, and the deictic "this" disguises the ambiguity of praise/object/censure as the deliberate use of a "loose," spoken style. The ominous aspect of "even as a child," which points to the paedophilic aspect of the men, both young and old, as they are described in their games with her in strictly parallel sentences, is reinforced by the vocabulary of bestiality when we are told that the young men are "counting time" to "mate" with Karintha. The narrative voice censures this by saying they "should have been dancing with their grown-up girls," but the moral aspect of the modal auxiliary is contradicted by the ambiguity of the term "grown-up girls," which is meant to designate their adult girlfriends but seems to extend the "child abuser" aspect of the men's desire to all women. This is reinforced by the narrative voice's intrusive judgment: "This interest of the male, who wishes to ripen a growing thing too soon, could mean no good to her." The use of "male," like that of "mate," points to the predatorlike aspect of the men, and the term "thing" once again turns Karintha into an object. Even if one takes it to be an organic image, the reduction of the human to the organic is disturbing, although it is part of Toomer's half primitivistic, half mystical stategy to use the same words ("a growing thing") for Karintha's body, her soul, and later (implicitly) for the unwanted baby.[3]

The connection between the song and the narrative is not merely that of a decorative device to make the story more picturesque, more realistic, more grounded in local color and local voices, even though this is part of the song's obvious function. Within the overall structure of the story the song literally embodies the theme: Karintha, who *carries* beauty, then *carries* a child; the song itself functions as a burden, since it serves as the musical chorus of the story (occurring three times in two pages). It is also the burden (almost a curse) placed on Karintha, since it seems to define and narrow down Karintha's life, like a sinister version of the "oracular" celebrated in the epigraph to *Cane*. It seems to herald the voice of gossip one finds just two paragraphs later ("Already, rumors were out about her") that seems to seal Karintha's fate when she is only twelve: her sexual initiation happens immediately after the appearance of this voice. Before the age of twelve, Karintha is the incarnation of freedom, of flight and pure movement ("a bit of vivid color"; "a black bird that flashes in light"; "a whir"; a "sudden darting"); these images find a symbolic summarization in the sentence: "Karintha, at twelve, was a wild flash that told the other folks just what it was to live." The sentence combines the active mode—Karintha is the subject of the sentence; she is an ideal of vitality—and the dehumanizing use of "that" instead of "who" in the image of the flash, the ambiguity of the flash that "tells," and the allusion to a speaking body instead of a speaking voice. This ambiguity—do women need a voice if their body speaks?—is one of the primitivistic ambiguities of the sketches of part 1. In "Carma," one finds the same use of the "chorus of the cane" (as a song about Carma, or as Carma's song), which replaces Carma's actual voice, much in the way the text replaces the description of an anonymous woman singing in the background ("From far away, a sad strong song," 12), with a "corporeal" song, literally embodied, devocalized: "She does not sing; her body is a song." This allows the text, in its own vocalization, to reflexively appropriate these sensual images for itself, as Toomer strives to turn his voice into a body and reactivates the dead metaphor of "the body of the text," a body that dances and sings; on the plane of representation and of distribution of voice, however, this quest for the control of voice turns all the protagonists' voices into background voices, sometimes overlapping with, but always superseded, by the deliberately "primitive," controlling narrative.

This is never more obvious than in "Karintha": Karintha's voice is effectively silenced from beginning to end, and when the narrator describes her singing, as a child, it is to criticize her voice and justify its suppression in the text. The fact that Karintha's voice is placed against the background of peaceful and harmonious sounds and voices sustained by the use of assonance ("dusk," "hush," "supper") and the onomatopoetic use of "s," suggesting soft whispering, as well as the fact that her voice is described in contrasting consonance ("pitched," "shrill," "itching") point to an aesthetic flaw. On the one hand, this serves to underline the contrast between the domestic tableau and pastoral harmony of the local women's "supper-getting-ready songs" and Karintha's wild behavior and child status. On the other, the fact that the narrator stresses that no one thought of silencing Karintha and that he, implicitly, does, is a political irony of the text. By employing the lyrical primitivism of the neologism "supper-getting-ready songs," the narrative voice points to the way its own voice is infused with the language of the simple rural black folk of Georgia and to the way it molds its language to its theme, but it also signals its alignment with these voices of the hidden, lyrical chorus, rather than a desire to let Karintha's shrill voice arise. The rhapsodic aspect of the voice is thus reinforced at Karintha's expense. The use of literary primitivism (in the vocabulary, in the use of parataxis, and in the deliberate simplifying of description) to make things "immediate" to the reader is also evident, in all of its potential ambiguity, in the description of Georgia homes when the voice says: "Homes in Georgia are most often built on the two-room plan. In one, you cook and eat, in the other you sleep, and there love goes on" (4). It is obvious that the homes described are those of the poor people of Georgia (black or white), and not those of rich white landowners. Here again, one discerns the voice's reluctance to present things as they are sociologically and politically; inherent in the contract with a black reader, within a major innovative black text, was not to speak words such as "black" and "poor" but to infuse a quiet dignity into what at the time was the norm of life for black people almost everywhere in the United States: to be black overwhelmingly meant to be rural and poor. By presenting these houses as the norm in Georgia, by deliberately selecting the term "loving" rather than "sexuality," and by refusing to describe in realistic terms the utter poverty of black sharecroppers or sawmill workers and the extreme promiscuity created by such living conditions, Toomer appears to be sidestepping the vocabulary of naturalistic, sentimental, or moralizing literary discourses. On the other hand, this can also be seen as the construction—through the selection of a simple narrative style and a deliberately nonanalytical approach—of a pastoral, idealized rural Georgia, a style that reflects the notion that "things are so immediate in Georgia" (86). At the conclusion of the leading character's long monologue in the first scene of "Kabnis," in which he erratically evokes the utter poverty of the poor blacks in the hills surrounding him ("unwashed niggers," "stinking outhouse") and the racial violence they are submitted to, Kabnis ruminates, before doing a total about-face in which he wishes all to be peaceful in an extreme example of wishful thinking and self-hypnosis:

> He forces himself to narrow to a cabin silhouetted on a knoll about a mile away. Peace. Negroes within it are content. They farm. They sing. They love. They sleep. Kabnis wonders if perhaps they can feel him. If perhaps he gives them bad dreams. Things are so immediate in Georgia. ("Kabnis," 86)

This is reminiscent of "Karintha" not only in combining parataxis, minimalism, and primitivism, but also in combining focalization and the performative assertion of "peace": the voice creates the immediacy and rural harmony that it knows is a fiction. Kabnis exposes the temptation that the narrative voice deflects in "Karintha" through the use of irony: that of presenting social determinism as compatible with the pastoral mode and of asserting that peace and harmony are coherent with the violence of existence when one is black and poor.

The dissonance of voices, or the dissonance within the narrative voice, in "Karintha" indeed points to the illusion contained in any assertion of harmony, as when the narrator explains Karintha's early sexual initiation: "One could but imitate one's parents, for to follow them was the way of God." This naive use of the expression "God's will"—as if the narrative voice merely relayed the half pagan, half religious voices of Georgia without criticizing this apparent contentment—can be read both as a signifying and as a critique of fatalism in which the cycle of poverty and lack of choice in deciding one's destiny is only thinly disguised by religious platitudes. In the same way, the deliberate selection of vague phrases such as "she played 'home' with a small boy," "that started the whole thing," "she has been married many times," to show that from the moment Karintha becomes a woman she loses her initial freedom and becomes a sexual object, can be understood on one level as the voice's shying away from cruder terms out of hypocrisy or the fear of censorship; but it seems much more probable that the narrator chooses these expressions to side-step all moralistic judgment. This motivation becomes clear when one reads interpretations such as that of W.E.B. Du Bois, who, in praising the forthright mention of sex in *Cane*, summarizes Karintha as "an innocent prostitute" (170). The problem in using this epithet is that the adjective "innocent" cannot quite erase the contemptuous connotations attached to the term "prostitute." What the narrative voice suspends in not calling Karintha a prostitute is not reality but judgment: it exposes the dynamics of the creation of prostitution by the fact that even when Karintha was a child, both young and old men perversely desired her, and that it is their obsession of "count[ing] time," then money (both expressions being purposefully put on the same plane) to possess Karintha that in turn alienates her.

From the moment Karintha is sexually initiated, the tense of the story, with the new burden, changes: "Karintha is a woman." This sentence, repeated twice, then becomes: "But Karintha is a woman, and she has had a child." The permanence of being a woman, the burden of it ("Karintha is a woman. She who carries beauty"), the fact that it means to bear children suddenly upsets what seemed to be Karintha's absolute power above all men ("Karintha smiles, and indulges them when she is in the mood for it. She has contempt for them") and her role as a femme fatale who reduces men to puppets ("Young men run stills to make her money. Young men go to the big cities and run on the road. Young men go away to college. They all want to bring her money"). The core of the story is here in the use of the past perfect tense ("has had a child") before it turns to an elliptical description of the baby's death. The phrase "a child fell out of her womb" is clearly a way to obscure whether what happened was stillbirth, abortion, or infanticide. The "bed of pine-needles in the forest" on which the child falls is meant to signify either that nature is kinder to the child than society or, more subversively, that death is as natural as birth and that abortion or infanticide are as natural as childbearing. The fact that what happens in the forest is taboo is suggested by the breaking down of the linear narrative, as the text now progresses through association of ideas, simultaneously laying the ground for a web of imagery that will recur in "Nullo" (the association of the pine needles, the rabbits, the fire, and nothingness) and in "Kabnis." The softness of the pine needles under the rabbits' feet seems to aggregate several meanings: the fact that Karintha walks softly toward the sawdust pile after the death of the baby; the sexual connotation of rabbits as compulsive breeders; the ironic notion of luck (rabbits' feet); and the ironic recasting of the pastoral imagery of the initial paragraphs to suggest violence (especially since rabbits often destroy some of their own litter). The sawdust pile connected to the sawmill evoked in the second paragraph of the story now becomes the funeral pile (or pyre) for the unburied baby through the ambiguous use of the pronoun "one": "It is a year before one completely burns." This announces the deadly lullaby in "Kabnis" that connects the bearing and the burning of babies: "Burn, bear black children / Till poor rivers bring / Rest, and sweet glory / In Camp Ground" (83, 87, 105). Too many readers pass judgment on Karintha (many students find themselves using words such as "sinner"), disregarding the careful construction of the story in such a way that judgment only falls on the community in general—Karintha is clearly a victim herself, identified with the child she bears, through the image in which the narrator describes as a "growing thing ripened too soon." Besides, small details such as the "pyramidal" sawdust pile must not be overlooked in a sketch that is so poor in adjectives; it seems to act not only as a coded pun on "pyre" but, before the openly African imagery in "Georgia Dusk," as a reminder of other funeral rites that were perhaps those of black people in the land before Georgia.

African American syncretism of Christian imagery and the belief in ghosts are evident in the scene in which the smoke from the sawdust pile "curls up and hangs in odd wraiths about the trees, curls up, and spreads itself out over the valley": clearly, this is the image of the baby or fetus as it haunts the valley. The pun on "wraith" (ghost) must not mask, however, another, more reflexively artistic, pun on the connection between death, the hole in the story and in Karintha's body, and the new weaving of voices. To compensate for the collective guilt over the unburied baby—expressed through the concrete imagery of the ashes, symbol of guilt and atonement ("the smoke was so heavy you tasted it in water")—"someone ma[kes] up a song." The significance of the song, quoted in direct speech in the sketch, seems on the one hand to inscribe black rural culture in a literary text—Toomer gives literary status to all such songs, beyond the body of "recognized" spirituals—and to indirectly explain that all such apparently innocuous songs are full of unspeakable tragedy and black "soul." The simple lyrics ("Smoke is on the hills. Rise up. / Smoke is on the hills, O rise / And take my soul to Jesus") become the voice of the baby, of the dead, the mute voices missing from the text; or the voice of the entire black community begging for deliverance and death. If this seems an excessive interpretation, reading "Becky," in which the same prayer to Jesus comes true when Becky is buried alive, or "Song of the Son," in which the poetic voice only inherits its voice by capturing the swan song of the Old Negro ("Pour O pour that parting soul in song"), once again associated with the smoke spreading across the valley, makes it quite unavoidable. The web of imagery in "Karintha" cannot be read (retrospectively) except as heralding the images that recur in all of part 1; and the conclusion of "Georgia Dusk" and its imagery of voices rising ("the chorus of the cane / Is caroling a vesper to the stars") call to mind the chorus in "Karintha," particularly the last lines of the poem:

> O singers, resinous and soft your songs
> Above the sacred whisper of the pines,
> Give virgin lips to cornfield concubines,
> Bring dreams of Christ to dusky cane-lipped throngs.
> ("Georgia Dusk," 15)

The somewhat stilted vocabulary and imagery (compensated for by the musicality of the poem) seem to find their justification in the rehabilitation of the "prostitute" into the more biblical "concubine," who is performatively, through this song and this "chorus of the cane," being given "virgin lips." "Chorus of the cane" reflects the literary voice itself as much as it means the imagined chorus of black people who are figured in the image of the Georgia dusk. The same paradox appears in "Karintha": the image of her innocence ("innocently lovely as a November cotton flower") is also that of her silencing, since "virgin lips" may mean virgin of speech.

The other main effect created by the song for the dead baby is the structural oxymoron introduced into the story by the imagery of the soul rising, in contrast to the initial song for Karintha and its image of the setting sun. The narrative voice now takes up its leitmotif ("Karintha is a woman") to distance itself from both those who judge Karintha and those who have unwittingly destroyed her ("Men do not know that the soul of her was a growing thing ripened too soon"). Parataxis and suspension marks become even more transparently crucial to the meaning of the sketch as the voice implies that the men who have tried to buy Karintha shall literally have spent their lives in vain ("They will bring their money; they will die not having found it out"). The tragic ending brings the story almost back to its beginning in something of a loop that is just imperfect enough to suggest that the voice has drawn an arc from the song of praise to the epitaph and has shifted from the celebration of the beautiful woman to the idea that beauty in a woman of Karintha's social condition means death at twenty; for it is only now, belatedly, that we are told Karintha's age ("Karintha at twenty, carrying beauty, perfect as dusk when the sun goes down"). The funeral eulogy for Karintha then starts with the suspended sigh: "Karintha . . . " Only then does the narrative voice conclude the story by taking up the initial song; but this time it introduces suspension marks before the words "When the sun goes down," which reflexively puncture the line of the text, as if the sun were disappearing from the horizon or as if Karintha were dying and the song for the dead baby were also a song for her. This suspension of voice is the ultimate effect in the long series of punctures, holes, and absences in the text (Karintha's life between the ages of twelve and twenty, her life afterward, the death of the baby). The last line of the sketch, as it suspends the voice in the final murmur "Goes down . . . ," seems to herald an ending such as that of Toni Morrison's *Beloved* ("This is not a story to pass on. . . . / Beloved") in its combination of epitaph, spiritual, and a last (verbal) kiss. Karintha seems to be the narrative voice's beloved, as if this voice alone were a worthy lover of the woman whose body has been used and whose soul has gone unnoticed and who died too young.

Beyond the character Karintha, the symbolism of this initial text seems to be that of the dying Old Negro Toomer believed he was capturing in this text; the note of mourning thus becomes that of the nascent book. But what is the significance of placing one's book under the sign of beauty that turns into death and under the auspices of aborted life and broken voices? The most likely answer is that Toomer meant part 1 as a swan song of (and for) rural black folk; this inaugural text on black rural life was also to be the last of its kind, and so the life/death oxymoron was essential to the narrative voice. Beyond this, however, it seems that Toomer was haunted by the fear of personal and artistic failure, which led him to produce what one could call an aborting and aborted text. The line between what is visibly controlled and what may be subconscious is rather thin. The reflexive use of the imagery of smoke in this initial sketch announces the deliberately "unreadable" quality of the book, with the first description of smoke—"At sunset, when there was no wind, and the pine-smoke from over by the sawmill hugged the earth, and you couldnt see more than a few feet in front"—acting as the emblematic image of the text; ellipsis and parataxis make the forest scene literally "illegible," and the reader can move only one sentence (or a few feet) at a time, "piecing together" what must have happened.

In addition to this form of controlled literary teasing, the deep-seated anxiety Toomer felt in relation to his work and to his theme seems to show in the selection of Karintha's name. Beyond a possible variation on the name "Corinthians" or an African name, it can be read as an anagram of Toomer's real first name (Nathan): Carry Nathe. A strong reason for making this hypothesis is that the last part of *Cane* ends with a character who is clearly a virgin and whose name is abbreviated into "Carrie K." Toomer seems to have placed his book under the sign of stillbirth, abortion, infanticide, and virgin birth, masochistically calling upon this first muse or inset figure to "Carry Nathe" (and to abort him) and to the last feminine-maternal figure, Carrie K., to carry *Cane,* the book, out to the reader (but *Cane* too is aborted into the initial letter "K"). The interpretation of authorial anxiety illustrated by this pun is further supported by the fact that the "K" in "Carrie K." can simultaneously stand for Kabnis, the character, who pictures himself as an aborted poet and as a literal and literary fetus:

> Th form thats burned int my soul is some twisted awful thing that crept in from a dream, a godam nightmare, an wont stay still unless I feed it. An it lives on words. Not beautiful words. God Almighty no. Misshapen, split-gut, tortured, twisted words. . . . I wish t God some lynchin white man ud stick his knife through it an pin it to a tree. ("Kabnis," 111)

This text combines much of the imagery in "Karintha" in its image of the twisted fetus, which calls up that of the pregnant mother ("split-gut" seems to be a hypallage, indicating what the monstrous fetus is doing to the mother), in its telescoping of the soul, the body, and the growth within the body, and in its mirroring of author figure and character (Toomer wrote to Waldo Frank: "And Kabnis is *Me*"; 151).

The identification of these images in "Kabnis" clarifies the implicit connection in "Karintha" between the obsessions with pregnancy, death, and beauty. The constant connection between death and blackness, between death and song, between missing centers and the multiplication of voices to compensate for the "parting soul" or the mutilated body, seems to be the core of the initial sketch. The beauty of its lyricism is already endangered, or threatened from the inside, by the staccato rush of parataxis and repetition and by the use of truncated song. Indeed, the moment when Karintha turns into a woman is marked by a mutilated version of the initial song. Apparently this serves to illustrate in the linear development of the story the acceleration and movement of desire ("young men counted faster") as Karintha becomes an acceptable sexual object, socially speaking. But the very fact that the voice mirrors the young men's desire, even as it condemns it, reveals the contradictions within Toomer's liminary sketch. The voice of desire in the omniscient narrative voice does not seem fundamentally different from the old men's or the young men's desire—although this voice stresses that Karintha is soul as well as body, it does not represent this: Karintha is as absent within the text as the dead baby—an underlined absence, a gaping hole. The voice itself mutilates and "aborts" its creation.

The desire to represent black identity as tortured, because of the impossible equivalence of word and reality, of self and society, of inner identity and voice, of blackness and fullness seems to be at the core not only of "Karintha," but at the core of *Cane*. Toomer built his text not on a controlled alternation of prose and poetry, styles, and assertive polyphony but on a series of aborted texts that show the impossiblity of a self-authenticating voice; those voices that are most self-assertive in the text are also the most neurotic, as Dan's voice in "Box Seat" and Kabnis's voice in "Kabnis." Only Halsey and Layman in "Kabnis" represent a strong black voice in black dialect. Mutilation and death are inscribed in the themes of the book: the story "Rhobert" ends on the imagery of burial, already announced by Karintha's "going down"; Becky is buried alive; Father John is a near mute who lives in the Hole. All are variations on the absent center, on the unintelligible voice, on the voice buried alive, on the past that is impossible to confront, on the birth that kills. All are mirror images of Toomer's own conflicts in dealing with his blackness and of the voice in the text in dealing with the cane. Perhaps cane is the fundamental image: it is sweet inside, but only after it has been voided and hollowed out, can it make music. The rhapsodic element in *Cane* cannot be separated from the central void in the text, the tear between all of its parts, the constant abortion of voice, or its stillbirth. It is in this context that one can reread the constant elisions and contractions of punctuation in the book—not merely as a modernist form of minimalism but as the contractions that precede the book's bleeding out of itself, purple like blood, oracular like death, as it "goes down" from its very first page.

Notes

1. This is completely unrealistic, given Paul's age and the fact that he is aware enough of the difficulty of being the other in a white society to be "passing" (as white); it can be contrasted with the scene in Toni Morrison's *The Bluest Eye* when Pecola, the little black protagonist, sees that the white gaze negates her, that the white grocer's eyes glaze when they settle on her—but Pecola is a child, and this is one of her first encounters with white hostility.
2. The white stares "were like green blades sprouting in his consciousness" (77). The writer might have used the word "blade" to evoke the cut, the pain, of a razor blade. But this image seems to be borrowed from Whitman's *Leaves of Grass* and "Song of Myself"; it appears in the form of an epiphany (calm, cool, and pastoral, although mutilated) in "Box Seat" where Dan Moore appears "as cool as a green stem that has just shed its flower" (69). It is tempting to connect the image in "Bona and Paul" to the statement Toomer made to Sherwood Anderson about his trip to Georgia, which engendered *Cane:* "My seed was planted in myself down there. Roots have grown and strengthened" (148). In this poem, the impossible images of self-fertilization, of black being "seeded" painlessly by white, and of spontaneous growth create the same ambiguities of identity and racial and psychological consciousness as the fictional texts in *Cane*.
3. These body/soul confusions are at the heart of such later pieces as "Calling Jesus" (58) or "Prayer" (70) in *Cane,* but in "Karintha," given the emphasis on sexuality, this amalgamation is more disturbing and ideologically dangerous because the identification of black people with animal sexuality is constant in the racist white gaze.

References

Chase, Patricia. "The Women in Cane." *CLA Journal* 14, 3 (March 1971): 259–273.

Clark, Michael. "Frustrated Redemption: Jean Toomer's Women in *Cane*, Part One." *CLA Journal* 22, 4 (June 1979): 319–334.

Dutch, William L. "Three Enigmas: Karintha, Becky, and Carma." In *Jean Toomer: A Critical Evaluation*, ed. Therman O'Daniel, 265–268. Washington, D.C.: Howard University Press, 1988.

Kerman, Cynthia Earl, and Richard Eldridge. *The Lives of Jean Toomer: A Hunger for Wholeness*. Baton Rouge: Louisiana State University Press, 1987.

McKay, Nellie Y. *Jean Toomer, Artist: A Study of His Literary Life and Work, 1894–1936*. Chapel Hill: University of North Carolina Press, 1984.

O'Daniel, Therman, ed. *Jean Toomer: A Critical Evaluation*. Washington, D.C.: Howard University Press, 1988.

Toomer, Jean. *Cane*. New York: Boni and Liveright, 1923.

Toomer, Jean. *Cane*. Ed. Darwin T. Turner. New York: Norton, 1988.

Dramatic and Musical Structures in "Harvest Song" and "Kabnis"

GENEVIÈVE FABRE

IT SEEMS IRONICAL that, at a time when minds were set on ideas of rebirth and awakening, Toomer called *Cane*—a work that opened a new innovative and modernist era—his "swan song," ironical also that Toomer, who was considered one of the new and most promising stars, disappeared so quickly from the Harlem literary scene.[1] When the book came out, it was hailed mostly by whites who had read parts of *Cane* in *Broom*, *The Double Dealer*, or *The Little Review*. Waldo Frank, who had traveled with him to Georgia and wrote the foreword to this first edition, Gorham Munson, Alfred Kreymborg, Robert Littell, Paul Rosenfeld, who wrote enthusiastic reviews, and Sherwood Anderson, who had been corresponding with Toomer, all thought highly of Toomer's exceptional gifts as a writer. Among black critics the book received milder praise, and few were those who tried to assess its originality beyond cursory and impressionistic remarks.[2] W.E.B. Du Bois and William Stanley Braithwaite however hailed him in their reviews in *Crisis*. Years later, Alain Locke was to stress Toomer's ability to soar "above the plane of propaganda and apologetics to a self-sufficient presentation of Negro life in its own idiom," giving it "a proud and self-revealing evaluation."[3] Most critics were just eager to present the book as an example of the idealistic and assertive affirmation of race that was to characterize the renaissance. Claude Barnett, the editor of the Associated Negro Press, had a brief exchange of letters with Toomer, who seems not to have appreciated the terms in which he assessed his work: "My style, my esthetic, is nothing more or less than my attempt to fashion my substance into a work of art."

Cane eludes description and categories and can be seen as both a part of, and apart from, the renaissance. Published before the guidelines for New Negro writing were set in Locke's seminal anthology, it is more of a forerunner than a direct emanation of the movement. In tune with certain concerns—social, moral and esthetic, or philosophical—of the time, it developed in directions that were dictated less by tradition, prescription, or fashion than by Toomer's inner convictions and exigencies, and these often went against the grain of the spirit of the era or were inspired by experiences—personal, literary, and professional—that took Toomer away from Harlem.

The book was born of two major experiences: Toomer's encounters with literature and with the South and "the souls of black folk."[4] After having experimented with a variety of trainings and activities, Toomer, following his paternal uncle's inclination for reading, discovered a new passion for books: Dostoevski, Baudelaire, Freud, Frost and the imagists, Hart Crane, Waldo Frank (the author of *Our America*), and Sherwood Anderson were among his favorite authors and awakened his vocation. After giving most of his time to writing, he suddenly felt that "he had in his hands the tools for his creation" (Turner, *Wayward,* 53–58). The attention he received from magazines like the *Double Dealer* and *Broom* confirmed him in his determination to become a writer. A visit to the South with Waldo Frank, who later published *Holiday*,[5] and a stay in Georgia where he had a position in a school further inspired him to write *Cane*: "There was a valley, the valley of cane, with smoke wreaths during the day and mist at night. The folk spirit was walking to die on the modern desert; that spirit was so beautiful, its death was so tragic. This was the feeling that I put in *Cane*" (Turner, *Wayward,* 58).

Toomer always connected his artistic growth with his Georgia experience; he spoke lyrically and metaphorically about it as a springing to life and repeatedly paid tribute to the folk spirit. The creation of *Cane*, he wrote, "is like a leaf that will unfold, fade, die, fall, decay and nourish me." In the same metaphorical mood, a mood that is to be found in many pages of *Cane*, he wrote to Anderson: "My seed was planted in the cane-and-cotton fields and in the souls of black and white people in the small southern town. My seed was planted in myself down there"(Turner, *Cane,* 148). Reversing the path that many took, seeking the "city of refuge" and embracing the future they saw opening on the horizon, Toomer returned to the land of his ancestors, to the land and soil, and embraced its fading culture.

"There is nothing about these pieces of the buoyant expression of a new race," he said about some pages that came nearest to the "Old Negro" (Turner, *Cane,* 151). In spite of his optimistic statements when he described his artistic involvement in the writing of *Cane*, a close reading of the work suggests that the experience must have been rather excruciating and perplexing; the work revealed greater complexities and contradictions than he was willing to admit in his enthusiastic reports to his friends. The book speaks insistently, through its images and metaphors, of the gap between what was sought and longed for and what had actually been reached and achieved. Toomer's communion with the South and his Negro heritage was fraught with ambivalent feelings, with uncertainty about the future of the race, about what literature or art could do, with a sense of unfulfilled hopes and ambitions and of partial failure. It is perhaps these tensions, to which he managed to give controlled artistic expression, that make for the unique character of *Cane*.

Two pieces may best illustrate the diversity of moods and modes, strains and voices to be found in *Cane* and the careful composition that pits them against one another or weaves them together: "Harvest Song" and "Kabnis."

In his description of the movement that informed *Cane* in his December 1922 letter to Waldo Frank, Toomer said that "from the point of view of the spiritual entity behind the work," after an awakening the curve plunges into "Kabnis". . . ends in "Harvest Song" (Turner, *Cane*, 152).

"Harvest Song"—an antithesis to the more hopeful "Song of the Son"—can be read as a prelude to "Kabnis" and an artistically pertinent ending to Toomer's swan song. Blending fear and anger, aspirations, and a sense of lack of accomplishment, it gives the lie to what one might read into its title. The time of the day—sundown and dusk—and of the year—the end of the harvest season—is conducive to reflection; after a day's work, the "reaper," in an implicit analogy with Toomer's own harvesting during his traveling season in the South, looks back on what he has accomplished and onward to what the future has in store for him. The voice that is heard through the poem is different from the new black voices one would expect to hear at the onset of the renaissance. Although the word "hunger," used as a verb and substantive and in many variations as a sort of inner rhyme and burden in this poem, may express desire, expectation, and anticipation, it also means deprivation, dearth, exhaustion, and weariness. The reaper-poet is shown here as having partly lost the acuity of his senses ("blades are dulled"), on which so much of the perception of the living world depends. "Chilled," "fatigued," "dry," "dulled," "blind," and "deaf": all these words seem to spell his fate and seal it in dusk and caking dust. The season is over, and yet the harvest has not been up to the reaper's expectations; his longing for knowledge—the grain—and for companionship is unfulfilled. Unfulfilled too is the promise expressed in "Cotton Song." The song will not be the work song and the call-and-response that could help sustain energy during the harvest between distant reapers. This is an unfinished song, and, more dramatically, the "singer" seems unable to respond to any call or offering from his fellow workers: "I fear I could not taste it."

The positive and poetic quality of dusk, so strikingly present at certain moments in *Cane*, seems lost here, even if some sweetness or softness still endures. But this unborn song is nevertheless a song, a blues from a solitary reaper, and the chant of all the other harvesters who, unseen, unheard, brothers or strangers, all share his condition and predicament.

If the harvest-reaper motif could serve as a metaphor for what the New Negro movement hungered to be, this song certainly did not fit the mood that prevailed when parties were organized in New York to celebrate the new era. Toomer's reaper is a poor prototype for the New Negro. Although the hunger for knowledge was vividly expressed in the poem, the fear of that hunger and the fear of sterility were never so clearly voiced. Yet the blues-song-poem, with all its tensions and uncertainties, is not only Toomer's parting song—when his own harvest is perhaps left unfinished and he realizes that "you can't go home again"—it also epitomizes the situation of any poet, whose mission is never totally accomplished. While experimenting with that particular musical form, the work song, Toomer also paid tribute to that part of the rural and folk heritage that did not receive much attention from the poets of Harlem and to the workers of the soil who nurtured tradition and were only left with the stubble since, as the popular song goes, "the white folks get the corn, the niggers get the stalk."

"And Kabnis is me," wrote Toomer when he spoke enthusiastically of his writing to his friend and travel companion, Waldo Frank, to whom he dedicated this third section of *Cane*. "Kabnis sprang up almost in a day, now it seems to me. . . . There [in Georgia] for the first time I saw the Negro, not a pseudo-urbanized and vulgarized, a semi-americanized product, but the Negro peasant, strong with the tang of fields and soil. It was there that I first heard the folk-songs rolling up the valley at twilight, heard them as spontaneous and narrative utterances.They filled me with gold, and tints of an eternal purple. Love? Man, they gave birth to a whole new life. . . . I am certain I would get more inner satisfaction from a free narrative form. . . . When I say 'Kabnis,' nothing inside me says 'complete, finished'" (Turner, *Cane*, 151).

Toomer's reports on his writing contain many clues for our reading of his text: the meaning folk songs had to him, the importance of their integration in the narrative structure, the emphasis on a free narrative form and on visual as well as aural images, the symbolic scheme of colors, and the opposition between the urban and rural Negro. One is struck also by the way the experience is described as a rebirth, in a mood that is in keeping with the renaissance discourse. Yet this text makes no reference to the strains and tangles that are very much present in "Kabnis"—a text that does not have the clarity of purpose, the illuminating simplicity that parts of the letter seem to suggest. In the little town of Sempter, the true peasant is seen only fleetingly; "Kabnis" offers a gallery of portraits that represent a whole range of characters in a setting that is already spoiled by the assault of "civilization" and where the effects of semiurbanization and Americanization can be felt. There is no mention in the letter of the critical gaze Toomer fixed on Northerners and Southerners and on their failure to communicate, on the inadequacies and inefficiencies of his central character, the would-be educator, poet, and singer. We have no indication either of why he chose to give to the title figure a puzzling mixture of poetic and burlesque traits.[6] The letter makes no mention of the mock-epic, grotesque, comic, and fantastic elements so frequent in "Kabnis" or of the use of irony and parody. Finally, the mood that dominates the text is more ambiguous and disquieting and poetically complex than what we would anticipate from Toomer's statements to Frank.

The following remarks will focus on two aspects in "Kabnis": dramatic form and songs.[7] Like other writers of the renaissance, Toomer was attracted to the theater and played with the idea of creating, not a folk drama as Hughes and Hurston did with *Mule Bone* and other productions, but a new idiom that would introduce a greater diversity of perspective and voices and those elements that his lyrical narrative and his poetical or realistic descriptions could not accommodate. The potentialities that the dramatic mode offered and that are explored in *Balo* or *Natalie Mann* and in many pages of *Cane* interested him both as a frame for this longer piece and as a metaphor to represent more fully a situation, a dilemma, or contradictory emotions, feelings, and ideas.[8] The mode also allowed for a greater distance—both critical and ironic—to his subject, the "Kabnis is me," and to the description of his own divided self and ambiguous response to the whole experience, to race and violence in the South, and to the dialectical tension between the beauty and the ugliness he encountered. Conflicts and contradictory impulses could thus be dramatized, and the tragedy of it all could be relieved by comic interludes.

Like Hurston, Toomer was fascinated with the language of the "folk" who lived in these rural communities, the way they dealt with the slave heritage of indirectness, double dealing, and disguise, with the whole range of expressive modes he found in the vernacular —jokes that Hurston called "lies," maxims, proverbs and sayings, witticisms, and the propensity for metaphor.[9] Toomer could experiment more freely with all these forms in his dialogue, integrate them in the new idiom he was striving to create, in homage to the richness and diversity of folk culture. Contrasting them with the more polished, intellectual language of the aspiring Southern elite or the Northern literati, he was able to dramatize the gap, the lack of understanding and communication when Kabnis is unable to take a joke or when his companions make fun of his lyrical flights or of his philosophical-metaphysical divagations. Toomer's talent for satire—which shows his closeness to other writers of the renaissance: George Schuyler (*Black No More*), Wallace Thurman (*The Blacker the Berry*), or Jessie Fauset (*Comedy, American Style* and *Plum Bun*)—could expose pretentiousness, pomposity, and inflation; it could even offer a sort of self-parody of his own poetic lyricism by introducing sudden antitheses or ironic comments by the narrator or one of the characters. Toomer could more freely express his objection to the religious language of some preachers, to the self-righteousness of moralists and "sin bogies of respectable southern colored folk," or to the rhetoric of his times, blending in a grotesque fashion the message of a Booker T. Washington with that of the New Negro. He did this in a masterly way by taking as a target Kabnis's worst enemy, Hanby, and turning him into a burlesque figure. Hanby's tirade in section three can be read as a brilliant parody of the prevailing discourse on the progress of the race.

In "Kabnis," more than in other pieces, Toomer was eager to find a way of discussing certain serious issues and ideas that he took very much to heart. These found expression in the dialogues with Lewis and with the representative figures of the small Georgia town and in Kabnis's conversation with himself, but the narrator treats them in a playful or grotesque mode that illuminates them in an unusual fashion. Toomer exposed them to more critical appraisal by having them discussed in the most preposterous moments or situations or by having them uttered as absolute truths or dangerous truisms or jokes by ludicrous or mock-heroic characters. His later writings which treated these matters more directly and seriously, were not as successful aesthetically. Although the grotesque has been carefully studied by some critics, like Fritz Gysin, the satiric and humorous veins have not always received the attention they deserve.

It is also interesting to look at Toomer's use of descriptions as stage directions or the use of stage directions as descriptions: given with precision and objectivity, in a neutral tone, in terse, short sentences, they offer a wealth of realistic details and notations that immediately assume symbolic or metaphoric dimensions. Objects, lights and colors, the moment of the day, the position of the characters in space or in relation to one another, their motions and gestures are meticulously described and suggest feelings or inner thoughts. One is struck also by their cinematic quality, and perhaps as directions they would be more appropriate in a film script than in a play. The descriptive passages alternate with poetic phrasing and more enigmatic statements that create a mysterious and elusive atmosphere and are often offered in sharp contrast to the dialogue that follows. Whether they portray interior scenes, faces, or the landscape, these "directions" are elaborate compositions, vividly visualized, musically treated, evoking Toomer's close connection in his writing with the pictorial arts and music of his time.

The rich and creative way in which Toomer plays with the idea and concept of theater/drama could be further developed by looking at his use of performance, theatricality, and role playing and shifting, not only in "Kabnis" but throughout *Cane*. A close look at two moments in "Kabnis" may illustrate Toomer's use of vocabulary, motifs, and imagery in order to enhance the dramatic irony.

In the opening scene, Kabnis, in a sort of monologue akin to, yet different from, the stream of consciousness method, has a long dialogue with an invisible companion, whose identity remains mysterious. This "sweetheart" could be one of the women whose presence he longs for, or he may have used the term ironically to designate a whole array of possible interlocutors with whom he will be confronted in his fits of anger and madness: the undesirable creatures that haunt his cabin—a hen, a stray dog—or himself, the "other" Kabnis, his double, or some deaf and mute irresponsible god in a Godforsaken country, or perhaps some incarnations of his fears and fantasies. This imaginary dialogue, staging Kabnis's divided self and inner tensions is tragicomic; Kabnis's solitary confinement in the "mud hole" is real, and so are his confusion and his hunger for companionship and communication; the scene anticipates other moments when desperate calls for attention will only meet sarcasm, silence, or indifference. Not really heard by his fellow companions, even in hours of joyful conviviality, Kabnis himself often will not listen or not hear what the others have to say, rejecting them or fearing to be rejected. The calls get no response. This opening also presents Kabnis as a rather comical and ludicrous figure, who fears harmless and familiar animals that are part of the daily lives of Southern rural blacks; it prepares us for all the inadequacies and deficiencies that other episodes will reveal. This rather trivial drama and comic interlude, which ends with Kabnis's wringing off the chicken's head because its insolent cackling is driving him mad, foreshadows other instances of insanity that will demand more tragic sacrificial victims.

The gruesome lynching stories that will be told to Kabnis to kill his excessive innocence and force him to face the real "face" of the South later throw a different light on the initial scene. The killing of the hen seems like a parody of lynching, performed with the same casualness—in the South the life of a "nigger" does not count more than that of a hen—with the same determination and destructive violence, the same self-righteousness and insanity. Ironically

Kabnis is animated with the same anger and fear as the lynchers. Unconsciously, he reenacts a ritual of violence that is being perpetuated on his people (a people whom, in another moment of insanity, he will reject as his ancestors). The scene that in a more prosaic vein reminds us that blacks often vented their anger and frustrations on animals closest to them, has other, more tragic or ironic, implications. On one level, the overly soft Kabnis playfully trains himself to become a "square face" to confront the world, "and the body of the world is bullnecked" (153). His mock fight with the hen is part of his initiation into a violent and "ugly" world. His grotesque cursing of the hen heralds the curses to come, directed at all those who irritate him, shouters and preachers, and ultimately at God himself, his maker. On another level, the sacrifice of the hen introduces him as actor and accomplice into a world of violence and designates him as one of its next possible victims. Not only will a fear-ridden Kabnis imagine that he is the next prey of men hunters, but he will, in a self-destructive, suicidal impulse, wish to lynch his own soul: "I want t feed th soul . . . wish t God some lynchin white man ud stick his knife through it an pin it to a tree. An pin it to a tree. You hear me?"(224–225). The lynching image becomes a fit metaphor for his love and hatred of the "nigger" soul, and the language of violence is perhaps the only possible response to the pain he could read in the eyes of his people and to the hell that is evoked in their songs: "You know what hell is cause youve been there. Its a feelin an its ragin in my soul in a way that'll pop out of me an run you through, an scorch y, an burn an rip your soul" (232). In many ways, Toomer anticipates the violence to be found in the theater of the 1960s, most notably in LeRoi Jones's Revolutionary Theater. One of Kabnis's major confrontations as a teacher educated in the North and a poet whose ambition is to "become the face of the South" ("How my lips would sing for it, my songs being the lips of its soul"; 158) is perhaps his grappling with words, the silent words on the lips of a muted people, the words on the lips of white folks, black or yellow niggers. "Been shapin words t fit my soul"—this phrase is repeated like a burden in a song, with many variations: "I've been shapin words after a design that branded here. Those words I was tellin y about, they won't fit int th mold thats branded on m soul." Part of the growth of Kabnis will be the recognition that the "beautiful an golden" words that he looked for to translate the beauty "his eyes had seen" in the Georgia landscape—to paraphrase a well-known spiritual—would not suffice to embrace the whole experience: "Th form thats burned int my soul is some twisted awful thing that crept in from a dream, a godam nightmare, an wont stay still unless I feed it. And it lives on words. Not beautiful words. Misshapen, split-gut, tortured, twisted words" (223–224), as twisted as the mind and soul of the one who utters them.

Toomer's choice of the dramatic form enabled him to stage all these confrontations, between the dream and the nightmare, the beauty and the ugliness, the excitement and the pain. In his word-shaping activity, Kabnis is also confronted with other artists, like Halsey, who has been carving things out of blocks of wood or with the liquor maker who is doing with a still what Kabnis tries to do with words (184). It is significant that Kabnis, at the end of the play in Halsey's workshop, resorts to a craft he "was good at th day he ducked from the cradle" (223). The descendant of a family of orators, who likes rhetorical outbursts, inflation, and exaggerations, has to learn his trade more modestly.

Kabnis's coming to grips with words is also effectively conveyed through the staging of his encounters with the various characters who, in some way, impersonate the discourse to be found in the South or force him to find an appropriate response through his own use of language to the enigma or challenge they offer.

Whether the dramatis personae are friends or foes, models or foils, doubles or antagonists—and most are both at the same time—they force Kabnis to dialogue with a part of himself that he has been unwilling to acknowledge or to see some aspect of the world he would rather be blind to. Kabnis's drama and the stages of his consciousness are illuminated through a multiplicity of scenes and settings that deserve careful attention. One of the most theatrical moments is perhaps when Toomer turns Kabnis into a real actor and stage director to perform a mock-heroic piece that is both a self-parody and a pastiche of a theater form (an implicit allusion to the minstrel tradition?) and seems best suited to Kabnis's personality and propensity for inflation and exaggeration. The theater serves also as metaphor for all the role-playing and shifting, for the masquerading, masking, and unmasking and disguise that are important motifs in *Cane:* it enabled Toomer to deal in both a playful and serious way with autobiographical material he treated very differently in his more straightforward autobiographical writings.

The staging of the last scenes of *Cane* contributes to enhance the mystery of the ending as it plays on sharp contrasts between settings: dusk and dawn, physical movements or words and moods, attitudes and emotions. The long delayed confrontation between Kabnis and the Old Man, the father image that the "bastard son" longed to find and was repeatedly denied, takes place in the Hole, another hole where Kabnis fears to be entrapped: it is suddenly transformed from a convivial merrymaking space where Halsey and his friends try to forget the frustrations of their lives into a dark and gloomy underground retreat where a solitary old figure seems to be awaiting death. The scene, highly visualized, can be read as the climax of "Kabnis" and as the son's parting song to a declining era.

To Kabnis's more dramatically inclined disposition, the immobility and apparent resignation of the mute, deaf, and blind old man is too remote from the "theatrics" he has imagined for the death of a parting soul (he would rather see it pinned to a tree). Just as the serenity of a Georgia landscape is too oppressing for him, so is the silence that surrounds the Old Man, and Kabnis tries to break it through his own gullibility, sarcasms, and curses. His verbal assault on Father John is like another (parodic) reenactment of the lynching ritual and accumulates all the terms used to insult "no count niggers." Kabnis's harangue is another way of rejecting what the Old Man represents—another denial—yet somehow they both share the same concern for the soul and the same insight: "The only sin is whats done against the soul. Th whole world is a conspiracy t sin" (236); and "O th sin th white folks 'mitted when they made the Bible lie" (237). The mock solemnity with which Kabnis acts, his exaggerated ceremonious gestures, his grotesque costuming in a gaudy robe he trips over help to play down the gravity of the situation. Because of his excessive physical, verbal, and emotional behavior, Kabnis cannot be taken any more seriously than the "old black fakir," "mumbling sin and death." Yet both characters, under whatever mask or disguise they appear, proffer part of that knowledge and truth that they hunger for. It is, significantly, Carrie K., the silent witness to the scene, who will gently soothe Kabnis and stop his masquerade. But, deprived of his rhetorical tools and of his robe, Kabnis, called back from his sleepless night or from his dream, must resume his new role as an apprentice to Halsey.

His ascent from the hole is not any more glorious than his descent. As he stumbles over a "bucket" of dead coals (an ironic allusion to Booker T. Washington's famous metaphor?) and "trudges upstairs," with "eyes downcast and swollen" (238), he seems again like a "scarecrow replica" of himself and is excluded from the final scene.

The ending of "Kabnis" is deliberately problematic. Toomer often stated that he had no solution or resolution to offer, and he probably rightly sensed that the ambiguities that pervade *Cane* should not be dispelled. Lewis's questions about Father John, "Black Vulcan? . . . A mute John the Baptist of a new religion—or a tongue-tied shadow of an old," are left unanswered. Kabnis's future as he goes back to the blacksmith's shop is uncertain, just as the accomplishment of his ambitious mission is deferred and his ability to embody the face of the South or the dream of a new age is questioned. This arrogant descendant of a family of orators, the butt of many jokes, still has to learn a lesson in language and has not learned to carve new words. His Northern education and concern for esthetics have "twisted" his mind and leave him unable to cope with the reality of the South. Yet we are made to think that his poetic sensibility may redeem and save him, and that the birth song that takes shape at the end of the play may anticipate his rebirth. The irony with which Toomer treated this "portrait of the artist"—Kabnis drawn as antihero or would-be poet—enabled him to deal more lightheartedly and with humorous distance with earnest matters: his sense of incompleteness when he finished *Cane*, his dissatisfaction with language, his irritation with constricting racial categories, and his hope in a new emerging identity (an identity that he tried to define through aesthetic and ethical interrogations) in an essay he may have proposed for publication in the *New Negro;* the piece was later titled "The Negro Emergent" (Jones, *Selected Essays*, 47–54).

The message, if any, is conveyed poetically in the ending, in a few lines where the narrator allows himself to use the golden words he temporarily denied Kabnis and through two picture images that are vividly visualized in two short, ambiguous paragraphs, still shrouded in mystery. One has often been described as a Nativity scene. The other is both sunrise and birth song and contains echoes of some of the most lyrical passages in *Cane*. Yet both combine effectively images of tomb and womb, of death and rebirth, imprisonment and escape, dream and reality, less to emphasize their opposition than perhaps to suggest a transitional age and a new composition that might be aptly called "dusk of dawn."

The dramatic form in "Kabnis" is further enhanced by the musical structure and the use of songs. Antiphonal in function and structure, the songs interspersed through the play interrupt or prolong the narrative and the dialogue; they serve as counterpoint, climax or anticlimax, or comment on the action and its dramatis personae; they themselves offer variations of rhyme and rhythm, of burden and chorus lines and stanzas, of moods and tones that reappear insistently and become part of the texture of the play. They often introduce, through the call-and-response pattern and the alternation of solo voice and chorus, a dramatic dialogue between the "singer"—the narrator or the central character—and the community of listeners whom he seems to summon, addressing them with an urgent request. Imperative or injunctive, the song also frames a statement or a question about a situation presented in a few phrases as a picture and an enigma, as a challenge to both mind and senses. Providing elements to frame some answer that may be expressed rhetorically as new unanswerable questions, it demands an immediate response.

Because in "Kabnis" the songs appear at crucial dramatic moments, the call is extended to the characters, who are summoned to respond, or it is a response and a comment on their situation. The songs relieve or reenforce the dramatic tension, illuminate the situation or enhance its confusion or mystery;

they also encode complementary information or instructions and suggest communal relationship and spirit. They often have a narrative function: they present in a few concise terms a story or a significant, often intensely dramatic, moment in a person's life; these stories are more like vignettes in the structure of *Cane* and provide contrasts or echoes to the main story. They create a sudden irruption, a break in the narrative sequence, and at the same time serve as transitions and expansions. This interplay between songs and text is rendered even more complex by the repetition within "Kabnis" of the same song. In each reiteration, the song assumes a different meaning and intensity and in turn gives new meaning and intensity to Kabnis's "drama." Thus repeated, the song becomes irritating or haunting and cannot be dispelled. It insistently offers more images for Kabnis to deal with, and its semantic ambiguity increases the confusion. Yet as it creates an emotion and shapes an idea, it suggests keys to a deeper understanding of the "face of the South," for the rhythmical and spiritual exploration of its "soul." Repetitions within the song—phonetic and semantic—provide poetic continuities and reenforce the meaning. They also create a spell, a form of incantation, and function musically. Each song, at the same time unique and part of a collective utterance, is a call and response to other songs and echoes other calls and responses in the text. It acts as a burden whose musicality heightens the drama and challenges the imagination.

The songs, with their troubling simplicity and subtlety, play an important role in *Cane*, perhaps because Toomer sensed that this expressive form, so pervasive in the area he was visiting, was the very core of the folk culture he was suddenly confronted with. In many passages of his correspondence or his autobiographical writings, he has described his encounter with the music of black folk, which he saw as an expression of their feelings, an effort to control their emotions, a response to their experience in an attempt to transcend it. Poetically compelling, the songs were also rooted in the soil and in the community. Sensually, physically, and vibrantly present in the daily lives of the people, and with their ramifications in the past, they were solidly anchored in structures and institutions, in work and church activities; they were the mold in which the souls were shaped, offering both frame and patterns that could channel and discipline their outpourings. They resorted to devices borrowed from a diversity of traditions—of indirectness, double dealing, mask and disguise, imagery and metaphoric phrasing combined with intricate rhythmic, melodic, and harmonic variations. Improvisational, they were innovative and bore testimony to the intense creativity and dynamism of the culture. At the same time as he was overwhelmed by the music he heard in the fields, the shacks and the churches, Toomer saw it as a tragic and desperate effort to sustain a mood and tone that seemed about to disappear—an expression that was ridiculed and disparaged by some and might not be able to sustain the energy it so powerfully displayed: "A family of back country Negroes had only recently moved into a shack not too far away. They sang. And this was the first time I'd ever heard the folk-songs and spirituals. They were rich and sad, and joyous and beautiful. But I learned that Negroes of the town objected to them. They called them "shouting." They had victrolas and player-pianos. So, I realized with deep regret that the spirituals, meeting ridicule, would be certain to die out. . . . The folk spirit was walking to die on the modern desert" (Turner, *Wayward*, 123).

Like many of his contemporaries in the 1910s and 1920s, after Du Bois and Rosamond and James Weldon Johnson, before Locke, who theorized his view of the music, and like Hughes and Hurston, among many others, Toomer was fascinated with the music. His concerns were different from Locke, who wanted both to preserve the folk spirit and give it loftier forms,[10] and he was alarmed by the distortions and displacements he perceived in the new music he was beginning to hear in the small towns and cities (the second section of *Cane*, which significantly has only one song and in which the call seems unsuccessful in getting a response, is full of victrola records and sounds that are replacing the human voice). *Cane* is both celebration and dirge: it captures the vivid poignancy and beauty of the singing and, as a "parting song," it registers the signs of its dying away, and the tension between the two intensifies the drama. As a writer and poet, and very much like Hughes and other later writers like Ellison, Toomer was convinced that literature had much to learn from music, and he set out to explore all these potentialities. The whole text is full of references, explicit or implicit, to the musical culture and infused with musical motives, themes, ideas, and imagery. The songs in "Kabnis" are experiments in the poetics of music and the implications it may have for the creation of a new idiom. Toomer also delved into a deeper meaning of the songs, their capacity to convey and encapsulate the reality of experience, what he called "actuality" as opposed to vision.

It is interesting to look at the way the songs are inserted in "Kabnis," at what moment in the sequence of events, what time of day, for which listeners; at the purpose they serve, the resonance they give or receive from other parts of the text, the echoes they contain from other sections of *Cane*, their connection or sharp contrast with other poetic or dramatic utterances; at the extent to which the evocation of behavior or landscape alters them or how, conversely, they may introduce some sudden or progressive change in mood and tone, in sayings, behavior, emotions, or landscape.

We shall limit our remarks to the way these songs reverberate in Kabnis's consciousness. If we consider Kabnis's many contradictory roles—as protagonist in the drama but also as an outsider and spectatorial presence, as a "reaper" who has come from the North and shares some of the prejudices of city-bred people, as a poet who wishes to become the "lips of the south" but can be blind and deaf, as a person gifted with real insight, yet unable to deal with the whole of experience—we are made to feel that he will not be an active and creative participant in the drama. "Harvest Song" aptly describes the ambivalence of the reaper as someone who hungers for knowledge and wishes to frame a song and who fears that hunger. It anticipates Kabnis's failures as a spectatorial conscience—he is less receptive and perceptive than his double and fellow Northerner, Lewis—and as an unwilling and reluctant listener and a potential singer (the song will never come through his dry throat, and his confused utterings and his too intellectualized pronouncements will not meet with a response from indifferent listeners).

The first song occurs at dusk, in the opening scene, after a brief description of Kabnis's cabin and, like many songs, is introduced by a realistic and lyrical evocation of setting and mood. Whispered by night winds—vagrant poets, a mirror to Kabnis's own ramblings—through black cracks in yellow walls, the weird song seems like an ironic response to the fantastic setting of the cabin and to Kabnis's attempt at settling down to a solitary and studious evening. The song is an intrusion, breaking the delusive quietness of the scene, and foreshadows many other disturbances to come. Kabnis is as unwilling to listen as he is to admit that there is more to learn from the songs than from books.

The song introduces him bluntly to the stark realities of the rural South. Verbs are at the same time injunctions—from God or from a white voice?—and statements about how things are. The "poor" rivers contrast sharply with the deep rivers of the spirituals and of Hughes's famous poem "I Have Known Rivers." There is also not much to reap from the red dust "of slave fields, dried, scattered." The enigmatic line "Burn, bear black children" anticipates at the same time images and horrid tales of violent destruction by fire and images of nurturing and fertility associated with the black (earth) mother of the later poems. In "white man's land" the only solace and escape offered to poor niggers will be the promise of "rest and sweet glory in Camp Ground." The irony of the last two lines, Toomer's incisive comment on the missionary work among Southern Negroes, will be further expanded through images of unnatural death and afterlife rest. The portentous ambiguities and silences of the song are more than Kabnis can bear to hear and he promptly dismisses the message, seeking release in a semicomic dialogue with his "sweetheart."

The second song, introduced by a lyrical passage that emphasizes the contrast between Kabnis's ludicrous but violent fight with the hen and the deceptive serenity of the Georgia night, encodes another complex message. It alternates lyrics from a lullaby with a description of a tableau: a black mother and a white child. This new scene from which black children are absent is loaded with historical memories of intimate connections between the two races and of the black mother's many functions and sacred power. It is also one of Toomer's numerous comments on the arbitrariness of the color line, the "chalk line" of clear divisions between black and white, that are offered throughout *Cane* as other elaborations on the same theme (the dramatized variation—white woman/black child presented in "Becky" or, in Layman's words: "An only two dividins. An even they aint permanent categories. They sometimes mixes um up when it comes to lynching" (172). Kabnis can identify with both the black and white children of the song: like the "half-moon" he is "half" and "neither black or white, yet both." The brown mulatto, who likes to think of himself as part of a Southern and Northern elite, is confronted with his "nigger soul" and becomes a bastardized son of the South. Kabnis is a symphony of colors and, like a chameleon, shifts from one to the other—brown or yellow or white, he can become as black as any "nigger."

The humming of the black mother in the song is ominous: "cradle will fall and down will come baby" may be nonsensical words in a croon song; they may also be prophetic of other falls to come, literally and figuratively—falls from treetops, from dreams and expectations; prophetic also of the power the Black Mother, who can kill or heal, can have over the fate of both white and black children. The cradle image contrasts with the nightmarish setting that the cabin is for Kabnis: in his mudhole, he finds neither protection nor serenity. As irritated by the song as he is by the cackling of the hen, he goes back to his mock fight and completes his mission as a "hen-neck-wringer." Yet the words, images, and sounds seem to penetrate into his consciousness, forcing him to acknowledge fragments of his identity—as both white and black, as a motherless child in search of a cradle, as an "earth child," before he sees himself as the bastard son of his maker: "God is a profligate red-nosed man about town. Bastardy; me. A bastard son has a right to curse his maker. God . . . " (161). The grotesque figure of God is offered as an antithesis to the swaying black mother of the song. The lyric also announces Kabnis's encounters with several impersonations of the black mother, Stella or Carrie K., and his confrontations with her disfiguration and violent destruction.

Ironically, it not the lullaby that soothes him but the song of the chilling night winds. The repetition of the first song at the end of the second section in "Kabnis" is like a burden; enigmatic, it contains all the contradictions and tensions between white man's land and "nigger" life and the intimations of an uncertain future and certain death in an existence ruled by white will and law.

The hearing of the next song is prepared by a series of scenes that elaborate on the Camp Ground image: the gathering of Negroes around the church puts into action "the path that leads into Christian land," while another gathering in Halsey's shop unexpectedly becomes the setting for a storytelling session in which gruesome stories of cruel death and violent lynching will be told. The spiral of a buzzard above the church tower becomes as ominous as the court tower where "white minds, with indolent assumption, juggle justice and a nigger" (163) or as the moon in "Blood-Burning Moon": overshadowing Halsey's convivial meeting, it brings a "gathering heaviness" into the house. When Layman starts his tales of lynching, suddenly breaking the silence that follows such barbarous acts ("Thems things you neither does a thing or talks about if you want to stay around this away, Professor"; 173), he does so in a neutral and low-keyed voice, not unlike the soft whispering winds when they sing weirdly through the ceiling cracks (210), and is accompanied by the insistent, chanting monotone from the church. His stories are stark comments on some truths Negroes have learned to live by, illustrating sayings, maxims, or truisms: "Ain't supposed to die a natural death" or "A nigger's baby ain't supposed to live." Reminiscent of the blood-burning madness, they describe ways of going up "to rest and glory." In view of these stories, the spiritual "One More Sinner Is Acoming Home" assumes a different meaning when one knows who defines the "sin" and what kind of chastisement awaits the sinner.

If the dramatic tension is controlled in the telling, it bursts out with sudden violence in the yelling from a shouter, to recede again when the choir sings an old spiritual. While the woman's frantic cries are the immediate response to the climax in each story and an encouragement for the teller to become more daring in recalling his memories, the singing from the congregation—the chorus responding to her solo voice—is more subdued. Kabnis's reaction, his strong identification with the shouter ("Her voice is almost perfectly attuned to the nervous key of Kabnis"), his own physical response ("Fear flows inside him; it fills him up. He bloats"; 179) are as excessive as the sister's, yet he is unable to transmute the flow of emotions into song. His "I hate this yelling "—his more intellectualized reaction—exemplifies the objection many Negroes had against high-pitched notes in church singing. The parallel Toomer so artfully establishes between the drama in the church and the crescendo of the storytelling session in Halsey's home enables him to reach a deeper layer in his exploration of folk culture. This parallel is all the more effective as Kabnis's inability to cope with the face of the South is contrasted with the way the community manages to control its pain and anger. Everything in the singing in the church and in the telling in the home is carefully orchestrated, here by the preacher, there by the teller. The community, represented by both the congregation of churchgoers and by the "laymen" in two highly symbolic places, is demonstrating its capacity to find ways of dealing collectively with the experience and to create expressive forms, verbal or musical, that, in a sort of ritualistic reenactment, can help break the silence and salvage the memory.

Church choir and chorus from valley, treetops, and fields alternate in a call-and-response pattern, each set in different keys, and occasionally a solo voice rises. The music is described in vivid visual terms as it invades land and sky in a symphony of colors, sounds, and smells: "Like tallow flames, songs jet up" (192); and "An old woman fetches out her song, an th winds seem like th Lord made them fer t fetch an carry the smell o pine an cane"(220). Images of "tongues" of flame and blood burning cannot be dispelled, just as images from "Portrait in Georgia" are conjured up here: the pervading whiteness in house walls, winds, and moonlit nights, the "ashen and still countryside" (180) evoke the image of the earlier song poem, "white as the ash of black flesh after flame" (50). The music, heard intermittently in between long silences and an unearthly hush, is insistent and overpowering, more gripping than Kabnis's solitary verbal explosions. Human voices and whispers from the wind merge in a common chant. Nature and people join to create a song that is first like a dirge, then becomes a birth song.

As the drama unfolds after several crescendos and the play proceeds to its ending, a gradual transformation from womb/night song to birth/day song takes place, and it is perhaps in this metamorphosis that the musical message of *Cane* lies, adding another enigma to Kabnis's consciousness, enjoining him to participate in the general chorus ("nigger, sing") or to create his own solo song.

When the first song is repeated in section 5, it is less grim, and the emphasis seems to be less on the destruction of body and soul than on fertility and the possibility of life's triumph over death. The few lines that open the section and introduce the "womb-song" effect this shift in meaning. The highly visualized incantatory and haunting picture of the pregnant Negress ("Night, soft belly of a pregnant Negress, throbs evenly against the torso of the South"; 208), the impersonations of the night and the South, the powerful serenity of the woman—the picture evokes African sculpture and finds echoes in the "African princesses" or in the descriptions of Carrie K., "lovely in the fresh energy; in the calm and confidence and nascent maternity which rise from the purpose of her present mission" (233)—all set the scene for the womb song that in turn heralds the "birth-song" on which the play and the book end.

Songs in "Kabnis" as in the other parts of *Cane* perform many functions: poetic, lyrical, and musical, dramatic and narrative. They weave a complex web of images that combine pictures, smells, and sounds and, in their multilayered dimensions, blend literalness and metaphor, memory and prophecy, ugliness and beauty. On one level, they tell ruthless stories, harsh, unrelenting facts that create the "actuality" that Toomer encountered when he visited the South; he insisted, in one of his accounts, that what Waldo Frank called a "vision" that would have protected him was, in fact, an actuality strongly related to reality (Turner, *Cane*, 143). The facts are offered as fragments of that reality, "the face of the South," to nurture the reaper's hunger for, and fear of, knowledge. On another level, the songs, "carolling softly souls of slavery," are also "petals of dusk" (153) that the poet-reapers in *Cane*—personae like Paul and Kabnis—set out to gather; yet ironically none seems to be able to complete the harvest. If we return to "Harvest Song" as a kind of metaphor of Kabnis's unsung song and incomplete harvest, we read "Kabnis" as precisely an attempt at collecting scattered fragments that could compose the unborn song, a song that a more mature, "new" Kabnis might one day create, at last realizing an ardent wish and long deferred dreams and promises.

Notes

This is a shorter and revised version of an essay on "Kabnis" published in Françoise Clary and Claude Julien, eds., *Jean Toomer's Cane* (Paris: Ellipses, 1997).

1. References are to Jean Toomer, *Cane* (New York: Harper and Row, 1979). References to Toomer's autobiographical writings are, unless indicated otherwise, to Darwin T. Turner, ed., *The Wayward and the Seeking: A Collection of Writings by Jean Toomer* (Washington, D.C.: Howard University Press, 1980), or to Darwin T. Turner, ed., *"Cane": The Authoritative Text, Background, Criticism* (New York: Norton, 1988). References to Toomer's essays are in Robert B. Jones, ed., *Jean Toomer: Selected Essays in Literary Criticism* (Knoxville: University of Tennessee Press, 1996). The most comprehensive bibliography is Robert Jones, "Jean Toomer: An Annotated Checklist of Criticism," *Resources for American Literary Studies* 12 (November 1995): 68–121. It provides a fairly complete list of books and articles on *Cane* published until 1995.
2. For a more detailed study of the response of contemporary writers to *Cane*, see Turner, *Cane*, 147–57; Toomer's correspondence with Sherwood Anderson, Waldo Frank, and his publisher, Liveright; and "Toomer's Art," 157–162.
3. Alain Locke, "From *Native Son* to *Invisible Man*: A Review of the Literature for 1952," *Phylon* 14, 1 (March 1953): 34–44.
4. Toomer has written at some length about the genesis of *Cane*, his trip to Georgia, and his spiritual growth, both in his letters and such autobiographical writings as

"Earth Being," "Incredible Journey," "Outline of an Autobiography," and "On Being an American" (see Turner, *Wayward*, section 1, 116–127, and Turner, *Cane*, 140–148).

5. Toomer wrote several critical pieces on Waldo Frank's books (see note 6). He mentions the fact that he wrote *Cane* before Frank completed *Holiday* (Turner, *Wayward*, 25). One should also note that, on several occasions, Toomer spelled *Cane* as "Cain" (Turner, *Cane*, 127).
6. One is tempted to see in both Kabnis and Lewis an ironic self-portrait in disguise. This essay does not deal with the intricate, mirrorlike relationship between Lewis and Kabnis as competing and complementary characters.
7. In "On Being an American," Toomer also mentions that his grandfather, who was an important figure in his life, "died on the day after [he] had finished the first draft of 'Kabnis,'" the long, semidramatic closing piece of *Cane*. Did this death lead to significant changes in "Kabnis"? "Kabnis" is dedicated to Waldo Frank, whose complex relationship with Toomer has been analyzed by Toomer's biographers. Also see Toomer's "The Critic of Waldo Frank: Criticism, an Art Form" (Jones, *Selected Essays*, 24–31) and his "Waldo Frank's Holiday," *Dial* 75 (October 1923): 383–386.
8. On Toomer's drama, see Turner, *Wayward*, section 4, 243–410, which includes *Natalie Mann* (completed in 1922) and *The Sacred Factory: A Religious Drama of Today*. "Karintha" was written as part of *Natalie Mann*. This shows how the writing of pieces to be included in *Cane* was interwoven with Toomer's experiments in drama. Of all his plays, only *Balo* was produced, by the Howard University Dramatic Society. One should note that *Natalie Mann* and "Kabnis" were written shortly after the success of *Three Plays for a Negro Theater* by Ridgely Torrence (1917) and of *Shuffle Along* (1921). In the early 1920s, Toomer's ambition was to create a theater that would focus on the black culture and condition—an ambition later shared by Langston Hughes and Zora Neale Hurston, who, however, were more concerned with creating a dramatic Negro folk idiom.
9. Hurston treated the Negro folk idiom very differently in her anthropological works, as well as in her fiction and plays.
10. Although the importance of music in black life was recognized, many folk forms were seen as a threat to higher culture, and professional concert training and productions were encouraged. Alain Locke, who was proud to recall the folk origins of the very tradition that was then considered classic in European music, argued for a more systematic exploration of the resources of Negro music but insisted upon a broader concept and a more serious appreciation of its distinctiveness. The music after the heart of the Harlem Renaissance was to be produced much later in symphony form and concert halls with compositions like *Creole Rhapsody* (1931) and *Symphony in Black* (1934).

Black Modernism?

The Early Poetry of Jean Toomer and Claude McKay

WOLFGANG KARRER

IF WE TAKE Pierre Bourdieu's theory of cultural fields seriously—and I mean to do so in what follows—then modernism occupies a particular position in the literary field of the twenties, and—here Bourdieu's theory somehow has limitations of its own—this position is taken in different national fields at the same time (29–73). What complicates the matter is that modernism in the United States brings together authors from different ethnic subcultures in the same field: Jewish American, Anglo-American, African American, to name the most important groups. The critical and social separation of these groups has resulted in different categorizations for modernism and the Harlem Renaissance. And only recently these differences are breaking down.

Why do we think about Toomer and McKay in terms of the Harlem Renaissance and not in terms of international modernism? Why do we say black modernism but not white modernism? Do we have to downplay Gurdjieff or Marx to highlight spirituals or Booker T. Washington? If Gertrude Stein, Sherwood Anderson, or Tristan Tzara indulge in modernist primitivism, how do their approaches to African or African American art and music differ from that of Toomer?

I shall elaborate on my reading, starting with George Hutchinson. He considers modernism a cultural field where black and white artists struggle for positions, in Europe as well as in the United States, where "writing black" or "writing white" means what others call a "racial formation" (Omi and Winant) and where black artists and writers struggle in this formation under a distinct disadvantage.

I shall try to show how Toomer and McKay broke into literary publishing and how the retrospective grouping with the New Negro group around Alain Locke and the Harlem Renaissance distorts and simplifies their early trajectories in the literary field (Bourdieu, 276 n. 44).

To briefly recall earlier argumentations revolving around these two writers: The failure/success debate of the Harlem Renaissance and the debate whether McKay used outmoded forms like the sonnet or blackened these forms (Baker, 85) mask ideological debates about a racial formation. The cubism debate about the poems in *Cane* implies an affiliation of Toomer outside Harlem (Bush and Mitchell). I shall try to show that McKay and Toomer take far more complex positions even in their early poetry and that their ambiguities on race are reactions to various pressures from an early modernist field.

Modernism

American poetry between 1900 and 1920 was at a low point. It was the age of fiction, and the early modernist poets worked against overwhelming forces in the literary market. The romantic tradition had largely exhausted itself, and realism of the domestic and local-color varieties dominated the poetic field. Titles such as *Kentucky Poems*, *North of Boston*, *Spoon River Anthology* or *The House of a Hundred Lights*, *The Book of Joyous Children*, *The Mother and the Father* by writers such as Cawein, Frost, and Masters (Ludwig and Nault, 129–149) told the readers what to expect. These titles used keywords establishing poetic claims in a literary field that was largely dominated by the novel. At the same time, other poets tried to discover new forms through various revivals of older times. Their attempt is comparable to that of the historical novel. The sheer number of classicist, Gothic, and Renaissance titles that came out during these twenty years is simply surprising. To name just a few: *Pan: A Choric Idyl; Artemis to Acteon; Personae; Helen of Troy; Hymen;* or, on the Gothic side: *Sword Blades and Poppy Seeds; Merlin; Lancelot; Black Armour;* or, more relevant to our authors, the Renaissance: *Medley and Palestrine; Sonnets and Poems; Canzoni; Renascence; The Sonnets and Ballads of Cavalcanti.* The Gothic was a worn-out romantic tradition, as were titles dealing with simple nature: birds, flowers, or sunsets. Early modernists like Ezra Pound or Hilda Doolittle worked themselves out of an imitative classicist or Renaissance tradition into modernism. All these returns were in themselves a type of "renaissancism": to bring about a new flowering of poetry through the mastering of older forms and their modern deformation.

African American poetry between 1900 and 1920 remained fixed in local color or domestic conventions. Dunbar tried to repeat his success in *Lyrics of Lowly Life* (1896) in *Lyrics of Love and Laughter* (1903) and *Lyrics of*

Sunshine and Shadow (1905); Brathwaite copied him in *Lyrics of Life and Love* (1904) and added a domestic variant with *The House of Falling Leaves* (1908). The innovations came from Du Bois: in *The Souls of Black Folk* (1903) and *Darkwater* (1920) he not only mixed poetry and prose but related them in new and intricate patterns.

These were the options around 1920 for McKay and Toomer: they could align themselves with the romantic school by using Gothic or nature titles, they could remain with domestic or local color realism, or they could participate in the classical or Renaissance revival. McKay chose local color in both his collections: *Spring in New Hampshire* (1920) sounds like Robert Frost, and *North of Boston* and *Harlem Shadows* (1922) sound like a combination of the local-color school, as in Sandburg's *Chicago Poems*, with Dunbar: "Shadows" or "Dark" are signifying titles in the African American tradition. *Cane* simply subverts the romantic paradigm: cane is hardly a romantic plant, it is a word with many meanings, subtly implying an agricultural region and slavery, among other things.

There were other choices besides poetry and affiliation with certain poetic traditions. Modernism in Europe was not simply neoclassicist as in the case of Hilda Doolittle or T. S. Eliot or neo-Renaissance as the early Pound. Modernism included primitivism and exoticism. Especially artists and writers in Paris, Berlin, and London, the centers of colonial power, were inspired by colonial exhibits, mainly from Africa. African arts and literature inspired a large number of German and French avant-garde writers to return to simpler, more expressive forms called "primitive." Joachim Schultz has compiled a dictionary of primitivist terms and techniques widely used by European avant-garde artists who dealt in primitivism or exoticism. Some of them are relevant to McKay and Toomer, although we do not know exactly how much they recognized European primitivism or their American equivalents like Lindsay's *The Congo* (1915). Here are some of the terms listed and analyzed in Schultze's dictionary: animal, banjo, dance, dark, fetish, jazz, jungle, laughter, mask, naive, negro, night, religion, woman. These symbols also appear in modern art, as in Picasso's *Demoiselles d'Avignon* (1906). Gottfried Benn writes *Negerbraut* (1912), Sigmund Freud writes *Totem und Tabu* in the same year, Apollinaire's *Zone* appears in 1913, Carl Einstein publishes *Negerplastik* in 1915, Cabaret Voltaire in Zurich organizes *danses nègres* in 1917, and the following year Tzara composes *Note sur la poésie nègre* (Schultz, 17).

The techniques to express primitive force were sound poems, a nonsense analogue to African poetry, and the so-called telegram style: the reduction of syntax to formulaic expressions linked without conjunctions or punctuation. Toomer experimented with both, sound poems and telegram style, McKay did not. McKay's elaborate syntax in his sonnets must be read as a firm rejection of primitivism. Both, Toomer and McKay, must have been aware of the primitivist and exoticist tendencies of modernism, as they were available in the United States as well through the Boas school of anthropology. Black modernism had to react to such pressures, but it was not simply a question of the taint of white modernism by primitivism and exoticism (Hutchinson, 19–20). Nor could it simply reject modernism as too bohemian or avant-garde as Du Bois demanded (167).

Field and Trajectory

There were other, even more pressing, things to consider: where to get published. Before 1924, young black poets had a choice between the *Crisis*, liberal white periodicals like the *Nation* or the *New Republic*, or radical socialist bohemia, represented by the *Masses* and its successors, the *Liberator* and the *Modern Quarterly*. A fourth choice was Randolph's *Messenger* or Mencken's *American Mercury* (Hutchinson, 289), both printing iconoclastic satire. The choice was a political one between conservative and liberal or left positions that were either moderate or radical. The founding of *Opportunity* in 1924 added a more conservative platform for young writers. Other options lay outside New York and did not significantly affect the Harlem Renaissance.

McKay enters the literary field through a white patron in Jamaica who introduces his dialect poems as "the charmingly naive love-songs" representing "the thoughts and feelings of a Jamaican peasant of pure black blood" (Cooper, 5, 9). His unpublished sonnet on Booker T. Washington of 1916 shows already a clear break with the dialect tradition, masking resistance very much like some of Dunbar's earlier poems. It is interesting to compare McKay's Washington poem with Dunbar's sonnet on Frederick Douglass. Both are cast in the heroic mold, poetic monuments to black political leaders. A year later McKay publishes "The Harlem Dancer" in *Seven Arts*, a modernist socialist periodical. The editor and founder, James Oppenheim, objects to the outmoded form of the sonnet. McKay insists and complains to Joel Spingarn of the National Association for the Advancement of Colored People (NAACP). In 1918, McKay joins the Wobblies (Industrial Workers of the World) and the working class. He finds it hard to publish his radical sonnets—editors like Oppenheim demand more racial subjects—and he submits "Harlem Shadows" and four other poems with an introduction entitled "A Negro Poet Writes" to Frank Harris's *Pearson's Magazine*. In 1919 he meets Max Eastman, who publishes his work in the *Liberator*. After the London interlude, where he publishes in the *Worker's Dreadnought* and the *Cambridge Magazine* and, with help from *Cambridge*, brings out his first collection, *Spring in New Hampshire*, he returns to New York, where he joins the *Liberator* as coeditor and helps Toomer to publish some of his first poems. With the help of Joel Spingarn McKay manages to get another poetry collection published at Harcourt and Brace. It is the first important poetry collection by an African American since Dunbar's *Complete Poems* in 1913 and Fenton Johnson's *Songs of the Soil* in 1916. It brings conservative acclaim and is later considered to be a milestone for the Harlem Renaissance (Tillery, 29–64).

McKay's trajectory in the literary field is clearly left-wing. It avoids and disagrees with the uplift ideology of the *Crisis* and the NAACP until 1924; on the other hand, it resists the pressure of modernist editors like Oppenheim or Eastman to write in a more contemporary form. McKay seems to have experimented with free verse, but he never published any poems in free verse. Ironically, the *Crisis* and its literary editor, Jessie Fauset, tried to dissuade their poets from free verse. McKay was caught in a dilemma: on the one hand his poems were kept in Hoover's FBI files as incriminating evidence, and on the other hand his poems were criticized for their formal conservatism.

Today, we often get to read McKay through his *Selected Poems* of 1953. For *Harlem Shadows* (1922) and *Spring in New Hampshire* (1920) you have to go to the rare-book department in big libraries. Accounts of their contents are contradictory or vague, sometimes plainly wrong. *Harlem Shadows* contains seventy-four poems, no less, and is not a reprint of *Spring in New Hampshire*. *Selected Poems* eliminates most of the political poems, and *Harlem Shadows* selects only twenty-three poems from *Spring in New Hampshire*. Both collections omit many of the radical poems that were published in the *Liberator*.

McKay's preface to *Harlem Shadows*, "Author's Word," following the introduction by Max Eastman, reveals some of the pressures of the literary field McKay feels himself exposed to. After mentioning his British schooling and dialect poems in Jamaica and the native song tradition of rhyme and metrical stanzas he declares:

> Consequently, although very conscious of the new criticisms and trends in poetry, to which I am keenly responsive and receptive, I have adhered to such of the older traditions as I find adequate for my most lawless and revolutionary passions and modes. I have not used patterns, images and words that would stamp me a classicist nor a modernist. . . . I have never studied poetics, but the forms I have used I am convinced are the ones I can work in with the highest degree of spontaneity and freedom. I have chosen my melodies and rhythms by instinct, and I have favored words and figures which flow smoothly and harmoniously into my compositions. And in all my moods I have

> striven to achieve directness, truthfulness and naturalness of expression instead of enameled originality. I have not hesitated to use words which are old, and in some circles considered poetically overworked and dead, when I thought I could make them glow alive by new manipulation. (xx)

This is a clearly premodernist position: feelings are poured into forms, and "smoothly" and "harmoniously" are hardly modernist concepts. Only the possible discord between traditional form and revolutionary passions point at the strain of this position. The representation of the revolutionary passion in *Harlem Shadows* is even more equivocal. Disguise would be the word. After the Palmer raids, euphemistically called the "Red Scare," of 1919 and the consequent anticommunism and racism of the early twenties and because he accepted help from the NAACP to find a publisher, McKay had to defend himself as a conservative in form, not as a radical in thought. Many of his more outspoken poems from the *Liberator* and other radical periodicals are included neither in *Harlem Shadows* nor in the *Selected Poems* of 1953. Here are some of the titles: "The Dominant White," "A Capitalist at Dinner," "The Little Peoples," "Samson," "To Ethiopia," "Birds of Prey," and "To the Entrenched Classes." They have never been republished. McKay either thought of them as unworthy of being published in a collection or too topical, or he feared they would endanger the support for or the reception of his first American collection.

McKay's role as a "progressive" intellectual in Alain Locke's essay "The New Negro"(Gates and McKay, 960) is clearly to the left of James Weldon Johnson, and McKay's dire predictions of the decline of the United States hardly agreed with the boosterism of Harlem as the new Mecca. Locke, who refused to print the poem "Mulatto" by McKay, could call such a position only "defiance" or "cynicism." McKay had aligned himself with the *Crisis* in the conflict with the National Urban League and *Opportunity* about who would be included in the Harlem Renaissance (Hutchinson, 127).

Although the title *Harlem Shadows* seems to promise local color and regionalism, the title poem focuses on Harlem prostitutes and exploitation, and the exoticism of the "Harlem Dancer" is demonstrably absent or exists only in the consumer's eye. McKay's Harlem is working-class and beset by discrimination and exploitation. In Cooper's words, "He conveyed a startling bitter, and essentially modern, message of despair, alienation, and rebellion" (8). This view was hardly that of Alain Locke or the Urban League.

Toomer's trajectory was different in spite of some surprising similarities. It was Waldo Frank who accepted "Harlem Dancer" for *Seven Arts*, and it was Waldo Frank who helped Toomer to get into print (Gates and McKay, 982).

Toomer went through a phase of socialism between 1918 and 1920; he repeatedly tried to teach it to others. His first project after *Cane* was to write a collection of short stories on the communist influence on African Americans in Washington (Turner). But other than McKay he had little firsthand working-class experience, and his relations to literary periodicals were remote. Like McKay, Toomer was largely self-taught in literature, but he had an extended academic exposure to socialism, sociology, and psychology, and his literary studies were in modernist writers such as Sherwood Anderson, Waldo Frank, and the imagists. Internal evidence even points at Gertrude Stein for some of the prose experiments in *Cane* (Jones, 44). Toomer had already collected a trunk full of literary experiments before he returned from Georgia to begin the sketches that would ultimately become *Cane* (Turner, xv). It is significant that he reported his project to the *Liberator* while he published the first sketches in various periodicals. Of the poems, McKay, who was the editor, accepted "Georgia Dusk." *The Crisis* published "Song of the Son," *Nomad* printed "November Cotton Flower," and a New Orleans magazine published "Harvest Song" (Jones and Latimer, 258). Toomer's trajectory was clearly more modernist than socialist. The poems reflected various stages of formal experiments but hardly foreshadowed the complex achievement of *Cane*. It was hard work unifying these pieces, as Toomer reports in his letter:

> I've had the impulse to collect my sketches and poems under the title perhaps of *Cane*. Such pieces as K. C. A. ["Karintha," "Carma," "Avey"] and Kabnis (revised) coming under the subhead of Cane Stalks and Chorouses [*sic*]. Poems under leaves and Syrup Songs. Vignettes under leaf traceries in Washington. (Rusch, 11)

A little later he writes:

> Having as Sub-heads Cane Stalks and chorouses [*sic*] (Karintha, Fern, etc. and two longer pieces), leaves (poems), and Leaf Traciers [*sic*] in Washington, under which I shall group such Things as For M. W. and other sharp, brief vignettes . . . (12)

And again:

> I see the importance of form. The tree as a symbol comes to mind. A tree in summer. Trunk, branches, structure. Leaves the fillers-out, one might almost say the padding. The sap is carried in the trunk etc. From it the leaves get their sustenance, and from their arrangement comes their meaning, or at least leaves upon the ground do not make a tree. Etc. This symbol is wanting, of course, because a tree is stationary, because it has no progressions, no dynamic movements. A machine has these, but a machine is all form, it has no leaves. Its very

> abstraction is now the death of it. Perhaps it is the purpose of our age to fecundate it? But its flower, unlike growing things, will bud within the human spirit. . . . (22)

The stance here is clearly modernist. The organic analogy seems to belie this at first. The longer prose sketches are the trunks of *Cane*, the poems between the sketches their leaves, the short poetic lines inserted in the sketches (mainly at the beginning and end of each sketch) are the traceries of the leaves. But the rather regular, almost mechanic, alternation of poems and vignettes with sketches (two poems between each sketch and the next; two vignettes at the beginning and the end) point to another symbol: the machine. Both symbols overlap: Cane is organic and mechanical. More precisely, *Cane* is the interaction between both: "From their arrangement comes their meaning." This modernist principle of spatializing meaning as collage or montage determines not only the poems in *Cane* but also determines its double structure. *Cane* is not only "about" cane, it is not only built like a cane plant: it is meant to fecundate the machine that replaces it. The revolution is a spiritual one, and it happens in the mind of the readers of the new machine age. *Cane* is also a spiritual growth in the mind of the reader. Although this comes close to the circle concept that Toomer adopted later, it is not the same. The circle is mystic and comes from Gurdjieff and spiritism; cane comes from Georgia and a history of slaveholding. *Cane* thus contains pieces from different periods of experimentation, and the poems in particular reflect the temporary ideological orientations behind these experiments. To assume one spiritual entity behind *Cane*, as Toomer did later in his mandala quote (Rusch, 26–27), is to reduce *Cane* to Toomer's development behind the sketches. In this development "Bona and Paul" comes first—it dates back to his Chicago days—and "Harvest Song" last—it appeared in *Double Dealer* in December 1922. Instead of constructing a cyclic movement for *Cane*, as various critics have done, one comes closer to *Cane*'s conception by sticking to the principles of trunk-leaves-traceries and meaning-from-arrangement.

Poems such as "Her Lips Are Copper Wire," "Evening Song," and "Storm Ending" are imagist experiments from the trunk: they were written before Georgia, and whatever new meaning they acquire in *Cane* comes from their arrangement between the sketches and interaction with each other. They clearly belong to Toomer's aesthetic period (Jones, 3–20). The Georgia poems, some of which were published before *Cane*, belong to Toomer's ancestral-consciousness period and date roughly from September 1921 to December 1923 (Jones and Latimer, xiv). Of the poems first published in *Cane*, only "Cotton Song" and "Prayer" show a clearly spiritist vocabulary. The bulk of the leaves in *Cane* falls between the two phases, marking the earliest and latest texts assembled in *Cane*. A convincing case has been made for a cubist technique in some of them (Bush and Mitchell). But imagism, impressionism, and primitivism have also left their traces. Ideologically, aestheticism, the cultural nationalism of "Song of the Son," and the European spiritism of the later poems hardly make for a single spiritual entity behind the work. As I will try to show by examining one of the poems in *Cane*, we are on safer and more historic ground if we follow modernist principles of collage and apply the plant/machine analogy.

The Field in the Poems

I shall take Toomer's poem "Conversion" as an example and compare it later to "The Little Peoples" by McKay:

> African Guardian of Souls,
> Drunk with rum,
> Feasting on a strange cassava,
> Yielding to new words and a weak palabra
> Of a white-faced sardonic god—
> Grins, cries
> Amen,
> Shouts hosanna.
> (26)

The first thing that strikes the ear are the half rhymes in an otherwise unrhymed poem: *cassava*, *palabra*, *hosanna*. On second thought one realizes that they come from three different cultures—Native American *cassava* from Yucatan, Spanish *palabra* (word), and Hebrew *amen* (so be it) and *hosanna* (help me)—and reflect three stages of colonial experience: "strange cassava" indicates an African who is accustomed to other types of manioca and who has been exposed to Spanish and English Christianization. Another look reveals proud capitals for "African Guardian of Souls" and a lowercased "g" for "god." The African God Legba seems to have lost his strength by yielding to drink and Christianity. Religious conversion seems to have weakened the god, but why "sardonic," and what does "weak palabra" mean?

Readers of *Cane* know that poems like "Conversion" grow out of the stories like leaves out of tree trunks. Bell proposes that "Conversion" heightens King Barlo's parable in "Esther" (326), but if the African Guardian of Souls weakens under Christianity, does the poem not undermine King Barlo's parable of black power? The Christian term that makes Esther shrink from physical contact with Barlo is "sin": "conception with a drunken man must be mighty sin" (25). Is Barlo an African Guardian of Souls weakened by alcohol, and does Esther fail to see him as such?

The alcohol in the poem is rum, and rum is made from sugar cane. It is echoed in the parallel poem "Portrait in Georgia," which springs from "Blood-Burning Moon": "Breath—the last sweet scent of cane" (27). Breath here stands for rum. Syrup, sweetness, and rum stand for the product of cane, beginning with the motto of the text: "Oracular / Redolent of fermenting syrup." In other words, our reading of *Cane* is intended to be an intoxicating experience. Here is an ambivalence. A second word that ramifies throughout the text is "soul." It carries Christian, African American, and—by way of "Cotton Song" and "Prayer"—also spiritist connotations inspired by Gurdjieff. The African sense of "Guardian of Souls" has been converted to the Christian one. Is the African American concept of "soul" still present in the poem? Do *amen* and *hosanna* still mean "so be it" and "help me" or do they simply signify assimilation?

The word clusters in *Cane* are not restricted to one trunk or sketch as Rice has shown ("Repeated Images"; "Incomplete Circle"); they reach much further. "Conversion" develops its full power only if we read it as a companion piece to "Kabnis," which summarizes many of the foregoing patterns, very much as "The Dead" does for *Dubliners* or "Departure" for *Winesburg, Ohio*. After a night of drinking—whiskey, not rum—Kabnis lies prostrate before Father John in the hole; his long monologue can be understood as a cry for help. Father John obliges with a cryptic remark about the lies in the Bible. Kabnis who does not understand, calls him an "old black fakir" (116), the very words used to describe King Barlo when he tries to be a guardian of African American souls (20). Carrie doubles the ironies by answering Kabnis with: "Brother Ralph, is that your best Amen?" (116)

If we use "Conversion" as a key to "Kabnis," or rather if we construct meaning out of the arrangement of the two in the canebrake that is *Cane*, Brother John emerges as another African Guardian of Souls, and his rejection of Christianity does not reach Kabnis because of alcohol and the latter's concept of sin. "Sin" again is a keyword in "Kabnis," and Ralph Kabnis half believes in it (106). There is little doubt that the new word and weak *palabra* that the Spanish and English colonizers brought to Native and African Americans alike was "sin," or *pecado*. The preachers and teachers in "Kabnis" are weakened African guardians. "Conversion" is not a primitivist but a colonial parable of the weakening of the African American spirit through Christianization. Drinking mostly becomes an escape from sin or from fear of lynching in "Kabnis." In spite of all the degradation in the hole under Halsey's store, Stella and Cora emerge after a night of "weak" (108) and drunken sex as "two princesses in Africa going through the early-morning ablutions of their pagan prayers" (112).

In other words, African religion and vitality suffer under Christian colonization, and the ancient gods have become weak preachers and leaders of the African American communities. Certainly Kabnis is no spiritual leader for the black Georgia community; his soul is branded with the fear of lynching and cut off from the African spirit embodied in Father John. Lewis, who serves as a kind of foil to weak Kabnis, could become a leader, but he is too secretive. For a moment there seems to be a chance for a union with Carrie, but again she is stopped by the notion of sin: "The sin-bogies of respectable Southern folks clamor at her" (102), and the union between North and South, between Lewis and Carrie fails: "He wants to take her North with him What for?" (102). All we learn about Lewis is that he takes notes about lynchings in Sempter, and the case that is mentioned—a particularly gruesome case of a murder of a mother and the child in her womb—frightens and horrifies Ralph Kabnis; it is also a case that Claude McKay wrote a famous sonnet about, "The Lynching" (1920). Both Toomer and McKay took the account from an NAACP documentation on lynching in the South, and Lewis may either represent an NAACP worker or a socialist. Both would explain his secretiveness. Whatever his politics, his union with the South fails, just as that of Kabnis does. One can only speculate that the union of Kabnis's soul with the intellect of Lewis, the strength of Halsey in addition to the vitality of Father John, which survives in Carrie, Stella, and Cora, will bring about the dawn that at the end seems to replace the eternal dusk in the South. Here, too, the meaning would arise out of the interplay between the characters. Otherwise the birth song of the newly risen sun would meet only barren streets and sleepy windows that cannot be fecundated.

My second example, McKay's "The Little Peoples," was published in the *Liberator* in July 1919 and never reprinted. It is a protest against the failure of the Paris Peace Conference to take action in the decolonization of Africa:

> The little peoples of the troubled earth,
> The little nations that are weak and white;—
> For them the glory of another birth,
> For them the lifting of the veil of night.
> The big men of the world in concert met,
> Have sent forth in their power a new decree:
> Upon the old harsh wrongs the sun must set,
> Henceforth the little peoples must be free!
> But, we, the blacks, less than the trampled dust,
> Who walk the new ways with the old dim eyes,—

> We to the ancient gods of greed and lust
> Must still be offered up as sacrifice:
> Oh, we who deign to live but will not dare,
> The white world's burden must forever bear!
> (Donohue, 166)

This is a kind of poetic editorial, anger poured into the traditional form of a Petrarchan sonnet turning the thought with line nine. But the love sonnet becomes a hate sonnet; McKay inverts the form. Not just the form; McKay systematically inverts colonial diction and metaphors to serve his sarcastic indictment: Kipling's "White Man's Burden" becomes the white world perceived as a burden to the rest of the world, and the Austrian-Hungarian Hapsburg empire upon which "the sun never sets" becomes "upon the old harsh wrongs the sun must set." The setting of the sun seems to be the end of this empire. Quoting Du Bois—"the lifting of the veil of night"—not only extends decolonization to Georgia and *The Souls of Black Folk*, it also creates an ironic contrast between the imperial sunset and the veil of night. Political decolonization does not necessarily mean freedom from double consciousness. Neither does it guarantee a renaissance or "the glory of another birth." In a fourth sarcastic inversion, pointing at Africa and modernist primitivism, McKay identifies European and U.S. imperialism with human sacrifice: it sacrifices its colonial subjects to the ancient gods of greed and lust. Finally, the sarcastic contrast of little peoples with great men points at numbers: the Paris conference decides the fate of millions of people. And that undercuts the seeming resignation in the second-to-last line. International solidarity and daring—implied by the Georgia parallel—would be able to throw off the white world's burden. Echoes of the October Revolution? The "we" in the poem clearly sides with the so-called little peoples, probably another allusion to a contemporary phrase. (Today, "Kosovo" would be much clearer.)

McKay here parodies conventional form and diction to achieve a double vision: we are invited to read "weak and white" as "strong and black" to see the Paris conference as a primitive ritual of human sacrifice. The Africanism in the poem is quite different from King Barlo's vision of black power, but still relates to it.

The Cane Field

Toomer works with a modernist aesthetic of collage that owes as much to the mixture of prose and poems in the work of Du Bois as to similar experiments in those of Sherwood Anderson, Ernest Hemingway, and William Carlos Williams between 1919 and 1923. Toomer plays with modernist ideas of

Africanism, primitivism, and exoticism, but he carefully balances them with issues of cultural nationalism, such as the question of Northern leadership for the South and of internal cultural colonization. He even questions the political role of the black middle class both in the North and South and thus adds class-related problems to cultural nationalism. Some of the sketches and poems in *Cane* reveal contradictory positions, others create ambivalences. The forces active in the literary field—the aesthetic avant-garde, the socialist party, and the official position of the NAACP—are reflected in the tensions and contradictions in *Cane*. Toomer's hope to bring them together in the organic image of the sugar cane fertilizing the machine or in the spiritist image of the circle remains just that—a hope. *Cane* remains oracular, and it does not predict a role of leadership of the "Talented Tenth" or Harlem for the South. Nowhere does the union of male leadership and female vitality create offspring that will lead into a new future. As in *The Waste Land*, written in 1922, the voice of the wind and the spirituals carried by it remain unheard.

McKay suffers less from uncertainty and doubt. The question of leadership is not relevant to his poems; he writes from a working-class and socialist position. His poetry is either private or public, and in the public poems he is simply a spokesman for an international movement of socialists. He does not write primarily as an American, and he does not meditate on Harlem's role of leadership for the South. To him, The United States is an imperial power, and its patterns of racial discrimination can only be challenged by an international process of decolonization. He has little patience with the cultural nationalism of the Harlem intellectuals (Hutchinson, 157) and the struggles between the NAACP and the National Urban League to publish and define the "New Negro." He is careful to distinguish himself through allusions and omissions from the *Crisis* and later from the *Opportunity* poets. His Harlem is proletarian, the center of imperial power, and no Mecca for Southern or Caribbean migrants. Like Toomer's Washington, McKay's Harlem does not have much to offer to the rural masses. They also have to beware of not being sacrificed to the ancient gods of lust and greed, even in Harlem. Primitivism is a mask for colonialism. The sonnet may be another mask—but for rebellion. McKay would later find a subtler voice in the modern prose of *Home to Harlem* and *Banjo*.

Both Toomer and McKay remained outsiders to the Harlem Renaissance. Their early poetry shows the different pressures of a literary field that had not yet stabilized around Harlem. Both modernism and socialism had only a fleeting or marginal influence on developments after 1924. Local-color realism and protest sonnets would continue to be written after that date, but new beginnings were made with Nora Zeale Hurston's inversion of gender relations in the local-color tradition, the urban naturalism of Richard Wright, and the vernacular free-verse form of Langston Hughes. Toomer and McKay, in different ways, contested the racial formation of cultural nationalism that was to become the Harlem Renaissance, and both were retrospectively hailed as its forerunners or highlights, a position they had hardly asked for. Their texts ironically question—either by conversion or inversion—Harlem's claim in the twenties to be the cultural leader for the overwhelming majority of African Americans still living in the South.

Works Cited

Baker, Houston A., Jr. *Modernism and the Harlem Renaissance*. Chicago: University of Chicago Press, 1987.

Bell, Bernard. "A Key to the Poems in *Cane*." In *Jean Toomer: A Critical Evaluation*, ed. Therman B. O'Daniel, 321–328. Washington, D.C.: Howard University Press, 1988.

Bourdieu, Pierre. *The Field of Cultural Production: Essays on Art and Literature*. Ed. Randal Johnson. London: Polity Press, 1993.

Bush, Ann Marie, and Louis D. Mitchell. "Jean Toomer: A Cubist Poet." *BALF* 17, 3 (1983): 106–108.

Cooper, Wayne F., ed. *The Dialect Poems of Claude McKay*. 2 vols. in 1. Plainview, N.Y.: Books for Librarians Press, 1972.

Donohue, Charles Terrance. "The Making of a Black Poet: A Critical Biography of Claude McKay for the Years 1889–1922." Ph.D. diss., Temple University, 1972.

Gates, Henry Louis, Jr., and Nellie Y. McKay, eds. *The Norton Anthology of African American Literature*. New York: Norton, 1997.

Hutchinson, George B. *The Harlem Renaissance in Black and White*. Cambridge, Mass.: Belknap Press of Harvard University Press, 1993.

Jones, Robert B. *Jean Toomer and the Prison House of Thought: A Phenomenology of the Spirit*. Amherst: University of Massachusetts Press, 1993.

Jones, Robert B., and M. Toomer Latimer, eds. *The Collected Poems of Jean Toomer*. Chapel Hill: University of North Carolina Press, 1988.

Ludwig, Richard M., and Clifford A. Nault. *Annals of American Literature, 1602–1983*. New York: Oxford University Press, 1986.

McKay, Claude. *Harlem Shadows*. New York: Harcourt Brace, 1922.

Omi, Michael, and Howard Winant. *Racial Formation in the United States: From the 1960s to the 1980s*. New York: Routledge, 1986.

Rice, Herbert W. "Repeated Images in Part One of *Cane*." *BALF* 17, 3 (1983): 100–104.

———. "An Incomplete Circle: Repeated Images in Part II of *Cane*." *CLA Journal* 29, 4 (1985–1986): 442–461.

Rusch, Frederik L., ed. *A Jean Toomer Reader: Selected Unpublished Writings*. New York: Oxford University Press, 1993.

Schultz, Joachim. *Wild, Irre und Rein: Wörterbuch zum Primitivismus der literarischen Avantgarden in Deutschland und Frankreich zwischen 1900 und 1940*. Gießen, Germany: Anabas, 1995.

Tillery, Tyrone. *Claude McKay: A Black Poet's Struggle for Identity*. Amherst: University of Massachusetts Press, 1992.

Toomer, Jean. *Cane*. 1923. Reprint, New York: Liveright, 1975.

Turner, Darwin T. Introduction to *Cane*, by Jean Toomer. New York: Liveright, 1975.

Race and the Visual Arts in the Works of Jean Toomer and Georgia O'Keeffe

MARTHA JANE NADELL

Cane is, from one point of view, the record of a search for suitable literary forms.

Gorham Munson, *Destinations*

IN 1903, W.E.B. DU BOIS declared, "The problem of the Twentieth century is the problem of the color line" (xi). This statement, which appeared in his book *The Souls of Black Folk,* is perhaps the most famous articulation of the challenge that race posed to the United States at the beginning of the twentieth century. There is no doubt that the great and prescient Du Bois was on to something. In lifting the "veil," Du Bois was attempting to negotiate the boundaries that separated black and white.

For Jean Toomer, however, the problem was not the "line" but rather "color" itself. Toomer saw the American conflation of color and race as the greatest problem to overcome. His most celebrated work, *Cane,* is his effort to meet that challenge. In it, Toomer attempts to eradicate color as a demarcation of racial identity and to return literal colors to the realm of visual description.

Toomer's life and work have perplexed generations of critics and readers precisely because of the conundrum of color. What do we make of a man who lived on both sides of the color line but accepted neither?[1] What do we make of *Cane,* which defies genre categorization as fundamentally as Toomer wished to defy racial categorization?

Toomer's work addresses these questions, each of which stems from Toomer's dissatisfaction with racial and aesthetic classifications. *Cane* revolves around a subject that fascinated the writer: the inability of American racial discourse and of American literature to account for him in particular and for his understanding of race in general.[2] In reaction to the deficiency he detected in American notions of race, Toomer imagined a "new race in America"[3] that could be portrayed only by a new American literature. Toomer believed that he himself was the avatar of this new race. On the occasion of his marriage to Margery Latimer (a white woman), an event that prompted the national press to decry miscegenation, he asserted:

> There is a new race in America. I am a member of this new race. It is neither white nor black nor in-between. It is the American race, differing as much from white and black as white and black differ from each other. It is possible that there are Negro and Indian bloods in my descent along with English, Spanish, Welsh, Scotch, French, Dutch and German. This is common in America; and it is from these strains that the American race is being born. But the old divisions into white, black, brown, red, are outworn in this country. They have had their day. Now is the time of the birth of a new order, a new vision, a new ideal of man. I proclaim this new order. My marriage to Margery Latimer is the marriage of two Americans.[4]

Toomer wanted to combat what George Hutchinson aptly identifies as the American racial discourse's "belief in unified, coherent 'black' and 'white' American racial identities [that] depend formally and ethically upon the sacrifice of the identity that is both 'black' and 'white' " (227). He conceived of his new race as an American "ideal" that encompassed and yet transcended all racial categories, thereby moving beyond dualistic racial discourse.

Toomer thought that his new American race would be best portrayed by a literature that did not rely on classifications to describe individual identity, for these classifications, "the old division into white, black, brown, red," pivoted on and reinforced stereotypes of biological and social categories. As Sander Gilman writes, "Within the closed world they create, stereotypes can be studied as an idealized definition of the difference. The closed world of language, a system of reference, which creates the illusion of completeness and wholeness, carries and is carried by the need to stereotype. For stereotypes, like commonplaces, carry critical realms of associations with them, associations that form a subtext within the world of fiction."[5] *Cane* is Toomer's most powerful attack on the subtext of American racial stereotypes. It resists stereotypical depictions of African Americans in an unusual and daring manner; the text uses a variety of unusual visual descriptions of physical appearance to challenge prevailing conceptions of race.

In 1924, Toomer wrote to the painter Georgia O'Keeffe: "Have you come to the story 'Bona and Paul' in *Cane?* Impure and imperfect as it is, I feel that you and Stieglitz will catch its essential design as no others can. Most people cannot see this story because of the inhibitory baggage they bring with them.

When I say white they see a certain white man, when I say black they see a certain Negro. Just as they miss Stieglitz's intentions, achievements because they see clouds" (Rusch 1993, 280–281). In this letter, Toomer declares that his stories resemble photographer Alfred Stieglitz's *Equivalents*, a series of cloud photographs that the photographer produced in the 1920s. Stieglitz wanted the clouds to represent his emotions at the time he took each photograph, rather than portray clouds. Viewers could confuse, however, the ostensible subject of the photographs with the "intentions" of the photographer. Toomer imagined that his work suffered from the same misunderstandings. Readers could mistake his depictions of African Americans for "a certain Negro," that is, a representative type without individual, unique characteristics.

Toomer's remarks imply that the inadequacy of racial labels to depict the essence of individuality parallels the inadequacy of conventional literature and art to represent their real subjects. Toomer believed that the problem was the United States' obsession with defining individuals both by phenotypes and by the stereotypes attached to these phenotypes. He thought that literature that relied too heavily on words such as "white" or "black" was in danger of being misunderstood. The binary racial logic of the United States and the aesthetic logic of the time form the "inhibitory baggage" that does not allow readers full access, Toomer says, to his identity, his work, and his "essential design."

It is not surprising that Toomer thought that Stieglitz and O'Keeffe caught the "essential design" of *Cane* as no one else could. Although Toomer met Stieglitz and O'Keeffe shortly after *Cane*'s publication, the text uncannily uses the artists' visual methods. *Cane* is full of photographic images, painterly portrayals, and literary portraiture that together form a collage of African American life. These visual elements attempt to free physical appearance and personal identity from racial stereotypes. Race, Toomer hoped, would not be a sign of identity, and description would not be of service to the social categories and stereotypes of white and black. Toomer wanted race instead to be merely an ahistorical element of physical appearance that was devoid of social signification. Yet, *Cane* does acknowledge the competing reading of race as a social phenomenon with a violent history. Both the ahistorical formal notion of color and the historical, socially fraught conception of race remain in tension with each other throughout the text, thereby giving *Cane* its extraordinary power.

Written in bits and pieces during the first half of the 1920s, *Cane* was very much a response to a time in which racial and national identity were under contestation. The 1920 census had shifted definitions of "Negro" and "mulatto" from those of previous years;[6] 1924 saw both the Virginia Racial Purity

Act and the Alien Exclusion Act. "Scientific" texts about physiognomy presented racial types,[7] and artists of the Ashcan school painted stereotypical images of blacks.[8] Ideas about race were hardening along stereotypical lines.

In "The Negro Emergent," Toomer writes of his desire to see the United States "detaching the Negro from the social crust" that binds him. The "social crust" is the means by which the United States fixes its inhabitants in a limiting social system. Toomer declares, "For should there be set up an arbitrary figure of a Negro, composed of what another should have him be like, and the assertion made that he should model himself after it, this figure, though prompted by the highest interest, would nevertheless share the false and constricting nature of all superimposed images" (Rusch 1993, 92–93).

Cane is Toomer's effort to destroy the "false and constricting . . . superimposed images" of race. These "superimposed images," imposed externally and too often accepted internally, link racial labels with typifying social, political, and behavioral characteristics. *Cane* undermines the language that uses these stereotypes to describe identity. By offering descriptions that are visually based, *Cane* rejects words such as "white" and "black."

The first two sections of *Cane* are structurally similar. A series of prose vignettes interspersed with poetry depicts a variety of African American individuals and experiences. Both sections offer visual alternatives to "white" and "black." The vignettes "Karintha," "Esther," and "Theater" are especially concerned with these visual stand-ins. But *Cane*'s strength comes from its wrestling with the tension between visual portrayals that do not rely on society's racial codes and the social identifications that engender the violence and oppression African Americans suffer. Although Toomer may want depictions of physical appearance to be purely formal, ahistorical, and visual, he cannot neglect the history of African Americans as a group. The final sketch of each of the first two sections, "Blood-Burning Moon" and "Bona and Paul," brings this tension to a crisis point, ultimately without resolution.

The first section of *Cane* is set in the South. Each of its prose sketches revolves around a woman in the lush natural landscape of the South. Appearance and especially skin color are depicted by unusual natural images that are not firmly anchored in any specific color. Karintha's "skin is like dusk on the eastern horizon" (3). Esther's hair "looks like the dull silk on puny corn ears. Her face pales until it is the color of the gray dust that dances with dead cotton leaves" (25), and Louisa's "skin was the color of oak leaves on young trees in the fall" (30).

Although it is possible to imagine the color of leaves or the color of dusk, the descriptions reveal the ultimate failure of language to describe nuances of color in language. Even the gray of the dust is so contingent on the "dead cotton leaves" that it does not tell the reader anything literal about Esther's complexion. Instead of imparting a sense of specific color, the descriptions emphasize the impossibility of categorically fixing a person's complexion. The effect is to refuse the reader an easy understanding of skin color and an easy correlation of color and race.

The second section of *Cane* takes place in the North and portrays African Americans who have migrated there from the South. Toomer depicts ethnicity differently in this new environment where the language of jazz is the controlling device. "Seventh Street" sets up the location: "A crude-boned, soft-skinned wedge of nigger life breathing its loafer air, jazz songs and love, thrusting unconscious rhythmic, black reddish blood into the white and white-washed wood of Washington" (41).

In the vignettes of this section, Toomer detaches color adjectives from their racial connotations in two ways. First, he repeats the words "black," "red," and "white," thereby creating in the reader a sense of defamiliarization. Second, Toomer embraces hue, tone, and tint by using the many colors of the spectrum to describe physical appearance. Rather than emphasizing the imprecision of language in describing race (as in the lyrical, noncolorized images of the first section), these vignettes expand the conventional palette of color description.

Toomer calls attention to the difficulty of depicting individuals in terms of color in his essay "The Americans": "Moreover, it is a mistake to speak of blood as if it had various colors in the various races. All human blood is the same. When we use color adjectives what we really are referring to are skin pigments. This is one of our main troubles. We see a surface and assume it is a center. We see a color or a label or a picture and assume it is a person" (Rusch, 109).

Color, when connoting more than skin pigment, becomes society's understanding of racial identity, something multidimensional. Toomer wants racial description, if used at all, to be unidimensional, flat, just as the natural world, or rather the natural world as it is portrayed in the visual arts, may be composed of flat aspects. The problem that Toomer addresses, then, is how to return color adjectives to their most superficial, denotative meaning as far as race is concerned, to a value-free representation of skin pigment rather than a putative "center."

In "Theater," in the second section of *Cane*, Toomer uses color to paint a portrait of Dorris. The inclusion of so many colors emphasizes the visual nature of appearance rather than the social nature of identity: "Her hair, crisp-curled, is bobbed. Bushy, black hair bobbing about her lemon colored face. Her lips are curiously full, and very red. Her limbs in silk purple stockings are lovely" (53). The heightened focus on Dorris's face calls attention to this description as just that—a physical description that relies on color as color rather than on color as race.

Toomer's experiments with descriptions that are primarily visual are remarkably similar to O'Keeffe's experiments in painting. When, in 1924, Paul Rosenfeld wrote of the painter Georgia O'Keeffe that "no inherited rhetoric interposes between her feeling and her form of expression,"[9] he articulated the main reason for O'Keeffe's aesthetic appeal to Toomer. Both refused to confine their work to received ideas of what constituted their respective media, the "inherited rhetoric" of past generations of artists and writers. In their efforts to present individual "feeling" and "form[s] of expression," each strove for a precision of representation, a greater degree of "realism" than previously employed by writers and artists.

For Toomer and O'Keeffe, heightened precision of representation meant employing both "objectivity" and "abstraction."[10] "Objectivity" meant, for both, attention to what constituted "real" subject matter divorced from the "inhibitory baggage" of imposed labels; "abstraction," on the other hand, revolved around form, color, line, and texture. O'Keeffe's painting, in its attempts to balance subject matter and form, offers a stunning visual parallel to Toomer's work; just as he portrays individuals and color as elements of the visual world, she attempts to represent her subjects primarily as visual phenomena.

During the 1920s, when O'Keeffe and Toomer met, and the 1930s, when they had a brief affair, O'Keeffe was working on paintings of flowers and cities. The flower paintings emphasize color, form, and scale, thereby breaking with conventional representations of their subjects. In their unusual formal aspects, they deny the "old objectivity . . . the mechanical reproduction of the outside world which no longer satisfies" in favor of a "new objectivity," "the painter's representation of the complexity of his feeling before nature"(Peters, 130).[11] In O'Keeffe's work, this "new objectivity" becomes more abstract and, hence, more realistic than conventionally realistic work. Wassili Kandinsky, certainly an influence on O'Keeffe, wrote, "The new naturalism will not only be equivalent but even identified with abstraction" (Peters, 101).

O'Keeffe's flower paintings, such as *Canna—Red and Orange*, are magnified views of one or two blossoms. The paintings are large in scale and employ vibrant colors and an unobtrusive brushstroke. Although the subjects of the painting are recognizable as flowers, they seem abstract studies of color and shape. Thus, in focusing with extreme magnification, O'Keeffe simultaneously expresses a heightened realism as well as a heightened abstraction[12] (Peters, 44). In *Port of New York*, Rosenfeld describes this phenomenon: "In the definition of these flower-movements, these tremblingly unfurling corollas, what precision, what jewel-like firmness! The color of O'Keeffe has an edge that is like a line's. Here, for almost the first time one seems to see pigment used with the exquisite definiteness, the sharp essence, of linear markings. Much of her work has the precision of the most finely machine-cut products. No painting is purer" (202–203). O'Keeffe's precision in color is akin to Toomer's precision in description.

Toomer's visual descriptions, however, compete with the social connotations of appearance. *Cane* does not sustain an understanding of race as a purely visual phenomenon. In "Becky," in the first section of *Cane*, set in the South, description does not rely on the visual: "Becky was the white woman who had two Negro sons. She's dead; they've gone away. The pines whisper to Jesus" (7). Becky is never physically present in the sketch that bears her name; she resides in the imagination of the white and black populations that condemn her. "White" does not tell us what Becky looks like. Instead, it tell us about her social position and the understanding of race among the folk that populate the town.

In the second section of *Cane*, which is set in the North, "Box Seat" thematically explores the tension between color as a prison house of social identity and color as part of the dynamic visual atmosphere of the North. In presenting this tension, "Box Seat" reveals the essence of Toomer' concern: to criticize the social control of color, which is akin to racial labels. Toomer condemns the complicity of those individuals who accept the potential of color to be a bourgeois determinant of identity and behavior:

> Muriel, leading Bernice who is a cross between a washerwoman and a blue-blood lady, a washer-blue, a washer-lady, wanders down the right aisle to the lower front box. Muriel has on an orange dress. Its color would clash with the crimson box-draperies, its color would contradict the sweet rose smile her face is bathed in, should she take her coat off. She'll keep it on. Pale purple shadows rest on the planes of her cheeks. Deep purple comes from her thick-shocked hair. Orange of the dress goes well with these. Muriel presses her coat down from around her shoulders. Teachers are not supposed to have bobbed hair. (64)

The description of Bernice initially destabilizes any uniform understanding of color by highlighting its potential to represent social position. In moving from "blue-blood" to "washer-blue" the text focuses on the "blueness" of blue rather than on its social connection to "blue-blood." The text then sets up two competing modes of color description: the visual and the social. The bourgeois social controls of this story compete with the beauty of the "pale purple" and "orange." Muriel clearly sacrifices herself and the visual beauty of color to the social, though she attempts to straddle both worlds by placing her coat on her shoulders. The conflict of "Box Seat" is made apparent in color description; color as more than visual represents society's constructing a place in which the free play of identity cannot occur.

The tension between description as a means to offer a sense of the visual world and description as shorthand for social identity pervades both the first and second sections. Despite Toomer's efforts to deny the "inhibitory baggage" of social and historical definitions of race, they surface in "Blood-Burning Moon" and "Bona and Paul," the sketches that conclude the first and second sections of *Cane*, respectively.

"Blood-Burning Moon" depicts an interracial love triangle that ultimately ends in the violent death of a black man. Bob Stone, the white man in the sketch, competes with the black Tom Burwell for Louisa, an African American woman. Stone's articulation of his feelings for Louisa encapsulate the tension between physical appearance and racial labels: "She was lovely—in her way. Nigger way. What way was that? damned if he knew. Must know. He'd known her long enough. . . . Beautiful nigger gal. Why nigger? Why not, just gal? No, it was because she was nigger that he went to her. Sweet . . . " (34). Within the same few lines, Louisa goes from being "lovely, in her way" to lovely in her "Nigger way." But this way, which is so clearly associated with Louisa's social position, is what makes her attractive. "Lovely" is associated with her "skin [being] the color of oak leaves on young trees in the fall," but the "nigger way" competes. Just when the reader sheds the association of race with social categories, these categories are shored up by the population of the South, whose social status is predicated on racial hierarchy. The mode of racial description wins out and the story culminates in violence.

In "Bona and Paul," the Northern interracial story that parallels the Southern "Blood-Burning Moon," we see the culmination of the problems of color when fully identified with race. When the white Bona describes Paul, who we learn is African American, she describes him in terms that recall the first section. However, the racist label competes: "He is a harvest moon. He is an autumn leaf. He is a nigger. Bona! But don't all the dorm girls say so? And dont you, when you are sane, say so. Thats why I love—Oh nonsense" (72). The passage from "harvest moon" or "autumn leaf" to "nigger" echoes the movement of the text's first section; the white woman's gaze replicates the gaze of Bob Stone in "Blood-Burning Moon." Ironically, it is all of these ways of describing Paul that attracts Bona to him.

When Paul describes his white friend, Art, he employs color adjectives that attempt to fix Art's complexion:

> His face . . . is a healthy pink the blue of evening tins a purple pallor. . . . Art is a purple fluid, carbon-charged, that effervesces beside him. He loves Art. But is it not queer this pale purple facsimile of a red-blooded Norwegian friend of his? Perhaps for some reason, white skins are not supposed to live at night. . . . Bona didnt, even in the daytime. Bona, would she be pale? Impossible. Not that red glow. But the conviction did not set his emotion flowing. (75)

Paul, in a consciousness close to that of the narrator, turns his gaze on Art, his white friend. By using colors to describe whiteness as an element of the visual world in a way akin to his focus on blackness, Toomer essentially argues that all individuals, regardless of the socially ascribed racial designations of white and black, should be subject to a visual gaze. But within Paul's thoughts, we see his recognition that social and visual can be at odds with each other. In *Port of New York*, Rosenfeld writes about O'Keeffe in terms that can easily be applied to Toomer: "The struggle of the colorist is the struggle of the photographer; it is the grapple of foothold of media precisely, finely used and emotionally intensified against a world unwilling to read the language of the senses" (256).

Yet, Toomer's color adjectives not only indicate complexion and social position. They also refer to state of mind. Words like "pale" and "red" evoke unique interior characteristics rather than stereotypes. In doing this, Toomer undermines the associations of skin color with behavioral, intellectual, and emotional stereotypes. Toomer declares in a letter to Frank in 1922: "The only time I think 'Negro' is when I want a particular emotion which is associated with this name. As a usual thing, I actually do not see difference of color and contour. I see differences of life and experience, and often these lead me to physical coverings. But not always, and from the stand point of conventional criticism, not often enough. I'm very likely to be satisfied with a character whose body one knows nothing of" (Rusch 1993, 95).

Toomer rejects the "physical coverings" that are linked by "conventional" work to labels of social position, such as "Negro." These coverings, Toomer believes, have too many stereotypes attached to them. Rather, with "Negro" he wants to call attention to precisely the "life and experience" unique to individuals. Toomer questions the understanding of race that relies on bodily appearance to determine social identity.

By the conclusion of this story, Toomer's experiments fail him. The social readings of race win out despite Paul's attempts to redefine himself. Bona thinks of Paul that he is "Colored; cold. Wrong somewhere" (76), attributing his difference from her to his racial identity. Paul, too, recognizes that "people saw, not attractiveness in his dark skin, but difference" (76). It is a difference that stresses the social rather than the visual.

Toomer's most interesting attempt and failure to salvage color from the social world occurs at the conclusion of "Bona and Paul" when Bona and Paul hurriedly leave the Gardens, the restaurant in which they meet: "As the black man swings the door for them, his eyes are knowing. Too many couples have passed out, flushed and fidgety, for him not to know. The chill air is a shock to Paul. A strange thing happens. He sees the Gardens purple. And a spot is in the purple. The spot comes furiously toward him. Face of the black man. It leers" (79). At first, the doorman seems to condemn the interracial couple. But then Paul experiences a strange thing; he initially sees the doorman as a "spot" in the "purple" of the Gardens. From afar, the spot is part of the visual world. When Paul gets closer, the spot becomes the face of a "black man" that "leers." Unlike "purple," "black" is not denotative. Rather, "black" is connotative of race as a socially coded phenomenon. In the North, conventional social associations with race win out. Though Paul and the doorman shake hands at the conclusion, Bona has already left. The possibility of interacting as individuals, outside of social roles represented by color and race, is lost.

The visual is not confined to *Cane*'s prose vignettes. The text's poems employ visual devices as well. The first section of *Cane* contains three poems that had been collected in the *Modern Review* as "Three Portraits." The first two poems, "Face" and "Portrait in Georgia," employ something like the Petrarchan conceit. They compare the elements of a woman's face to a variety of objects or states. "Face" (10) begins by describing hair simply as "silver gray" like stars and brows as "recurved canoes." Although the poem begins conventionally, elements of "pain" intrude into the portrait as it catalogs the woman's countenance. The eyes produce a "mist of tears."

> And her channeled muscles
> are cluster grapes of sorrow
> purple in the evening sun
> nearly ripe for worms.

The comparisons shift from beautiful stars to rotting grapes, suggesting pain without naming it.

"Portrait in Georgia" (29) defines the "pain" to which "Face" alludes. The face in this poem is constituted by the racist violence in the South:

> Hair—braided chestnut, coiled like a lyncher's rope,
> eyes—fagots
> Lips—old scars, or the first red blisters,

Breath—the last sweet scent of cane,
And her slim body, white as the ash of black flesh after flame.

This poem is the scene of a brutal lynching. Southern racial violence dominates what could have been a conventional portrait poem. The "lyncher's rope," the "fagots" that burn the "black flesh" are images with which Toomer stresses how society's understanding of race has and will continue to produce unfathomable terror for African Americans. The visual images of "Face" become violent images in "Portrait in Georgia."

The poem is an extraordinary acknowledgement of the past of African Americans. Toomer recognizes that his desire for an ahistorical, free sense of the individual has a powerful enemy: the historical and present violence of the South. But if the two poems are so clearly about the social situation of the South, why does Toomer call them "portraits" and employ a woman's face as the central image? With the fragmentation of the poems and the list of the constituent parts of the face without cohesion that would make them into a unified whole, Toomer alludes to a type of modernist portrait that Stieglitz mastered, thereby attempting to diffuse some of the horror he portrays.

During the early 1920s, Stieglitz was engaged in one of his most famous projects, the portraits of O'Keeffe. Stieglitz photographed parts of her body, including her hands, face, breasts, and legs, making a series out of these fragmented body parts. This was a sort of American cubism, some have argued. Each part of O'Keeffe represented "her." However, within this impulse to depict the whole of a person's selves by means of a part, Stieglitz focused on the part as a thing in and of itself. Thus, the photograph of O'Keeffe's hands is as much about her as it is about her hands as hands and as a study in shape and design. The other effect of the composite portrait was that it represented O'Keeffe diachronically. Recognizing that individuals change across time and place, Stieglitz documented O'Keeffe as a mutable creature with many selves (Greenough, *Stieglitz*, 22).[13]

Yet, Toomer's fragmented portraits are different, and it is here that we see his fundamental departure from the almost pure formalism of Stieglitz and O'Keeffe. The poems demand an accounting for lynching, for burning. They take an ethical stance on the racial system of the South by explicitly attacking the violence depicted later in "Blood-Burning Moon."

It may seem odd to describe *Cane* in terms of photography and painting, especially because Stieglitz sometimes declared that photography and painting were opposites. In 1913 Maurice De Zayas writes in *Camera Work*, no. 41, in reference to Stieglitz: "Art is the expression of the conception of an idea. Photography is the plastic verification of fact."[14] De Zayas refers to Stieglitz's technique of trying to portray the forms of the natural and man-made world without focusing on subject matter.

It is clear though that Toomer's life parallels the lives of Stieglitz and O'Keeffe and that Toomer's work echoes the projects of both the artist and the photographer. Toomer, O'Keeffe, and Stieglitz all tried to represent their interior lives and attempted to achieve a specific kind of precision in representing themselves and their worlds. They each wrestled with an understanding of the interaction between social and completely personal identity. In *Port of New York* Rosenfeld writes, "The Stieglitz photographs lie at the point where the objective world and the subjective world converge. They are true alike to fact and to the inner sense of life" (270). Toomer too wanted *Cane* to express both his inner and outer lives.

Cane is primarily a personal expression. On January 10, 1924, in the first letter of a twenty-year correspondence, Toomer wrote to Stieglitz, "I am sending you a copy of Cane with these words: To Alfred Stieglitz's for whom an adequate inscription will be written in that book which is equal to me" (Toomer, Papers). Just as O'Keeffe expressed her inner thoughts and feeling in painting and Stieglitz expressed his thoughts and emotions in the *Equivalents,* Toomer believed that *Cane* was the concrete expression of his own experiences.

Toomer's sense that the text was "equivalent" to himself explains *Cane*'s use of many different literary and visual forms. Toomer wrote to Stieglitz on May 2, 1924, "And I've been thinking about you and O'Keeffe. But the thoughts have been patches, almost without words. All of my thoughts are this way" (Toomer, Papers). On February 20, 1924, he wrote, "Words, pure words, do not come from the motion that accompanies internal break-ups, inward re-buildings. I am broken glass, shifting now here, now there, to a new design." "Pure words" alone were not adequate to express the inner workings of his being. When Toomer asserted, "Nor can I reduce this experience to a medium" (Toomer, Papers), he articulated the central reason for his recourse to the visual.

In 1925, O'Keeffe painted a portrait of Toomer. She worked on this painting, entitled *Birch and Pine Trees—Pink,* after Toomer visited her and Stieglitz at Lake George.[15] Toomer did not know of the painting until a number of years later, during their affair. On February 8, 1934, O'Keeffe wrote to Toomer: "The feeling that a person gives me that I can not say in words comes in colors and shapes—I never told you—or anyone else—but there is a painting I made from something of you the first time you were here" (Toomer, Papers).

In this letter, O'Keeffe asserts that the formal elements of the portrait depict the emotions that Toomer inspired in her. The complex dance of color, heightened focus, and large scale reflect her thoughts on Toomer, not primarily of his social position (though the painting may refer obliquely to his complicated racial identity in its play of light and dark), but of the artist's personal, idiosyncratic feelings toward him. O'Keeffe wrote around that time, "I wish people were all trees and I think I could enjoy them then"(Peters, 88). Her work is what she imagines her subjects to be in relation to her; it is a study of both subject and form. *Birch and Pine Trees—Pink* does not depict the "look" of Toomer; it is primarily concerned with O'Keeffe's understanding of him.

During the mid-1920s, Stieglitz was working on the *Equivalents*, the series of cloud photographs that were meant to express what Stieglitz was feeling at the moment of their creation. The *Equivalents* operate on the same principles as O'Keeffe's paintings. These clouds, while recognizable as clouds, come to indicate much more than their subject matter. They represent Stieglitz's own conception of his emotions; neither the production nor the reception of the photographs was contingent upon external determinations, the photographer asserted. By focusing on the immediacy of personal reaction to natural phenomena and on the camera's ability to capture it, Stieglitz produced works that stress the richness of the aesthetic representation of individual difference, perception, emotion, and identity. Stieglitz asserted, "I detest superstitions that go against life, against truth, against the reality of experience, against the spontaneous living out of the sense of wonder—of fresh experience, freshly seen and communicated" (Norman, 54). These "superstitions" are the stuff of stereotypes, the barriers to a full understanding of individual and unique emotions. Work that does not rely on "superstitions" formed the core, he argued, of American art.[16] In other words, when Stieglitz photographed clouds, he photographed just that, clouds, which, for him, were the embodiment of his state of mind at the moment he took the photograph, just as they may embody something else for the viewer.

Although Stieglitz's *Equivalents* represent a moment and O'Keeffe's paintings are the product of a much longer process, Rosenfeld, in *Port of New York*, makes a connection between photography and painting that sheds light on Toomer's relationship with the two artists: "Modern color, supposed to be antiphotographic, is indeed the close ally of Stieglitz' photography. The colorist in his medium, like the photographer in his own, is seeking in the phrase of Paul Strand 'to use the expressivity of the objective world for the end of fashioning therewith subjective form'" (255).

By 1915, Stieglitz's photography had become freer of subject matter than it had in the past. He brought his camera close to objects so as to remove them from their surroundings. Both O'Keeffe and Toomer employed the same type of focus. This extreme concentration prompted De Zayas to write that Stieglitz has begun with the "elimination of the subject in represented Form to search for the pure expression of the object." (*Camera Work*, nos. 42–43 [1913]).[17] Stieglitz expressed this desire to divorce subject from form most clearly: "I have found that the use of clouds as subject-matter in my photographs has made people less aware of clouds *as clouds* in the picture. . . . The true meaning of the *Equivalents*, as I have called these photographs, (in reality all my photographs are equivalents), comes through directly, without any extraneous or distracting pictorial or representational factors coming between the person and the picture" (Dijkstra, *Hieroglyphics*, 102).

Toomer agreed when he wrote in *America and Alfred Stieglitz* some years later that Stieglitz caught the essence of the form of an object without any interference from contextual or mediated interpretations. Stieglitz could capture "the *treeness* of a tree . . . what bark is . . . what a leaf is . . . the *woodness* of wood . . . a telephone pole . . . the *stoneness* of stone . . . a city building . . . a New York skyscraper . . . a horse . . . a wagon . . . an old man . . . a cloud, the sun, unending place beyond . . . the *fleshness* of flesh . . . " (144). Hart Crane, who introduced Toomer to Stieglitz and Stieglitz's friends, felt the same way. When Crane saw Stieglitz's photograph *Apple and Gable*, he declared, "That is it. You've captured life" (Whelan, 442).

If we apply Toomer's and Crane's understanding of Stieglitz's representation of the "thingness" of an object to race, we find the strongest argument for Toomer's love of the visual in *Cane*. If race is a "thing" itself, tactile, visually apprehensible, responsive to the senses, in other words, simply color rather than a social phenomenon, then we may see a way out of the racial system of the United States. Toomer's letter to Stieglitz of January 10, 1924, early on in their correspondence, refers indirectly to this question: "This morning quite contrary to custom, I awoke early. For some reason my eyes were pulled to the window that frames a portion of the Woman's Day Court and adjoining prison. Usually, the buildings impinge, oppress, and bulk. Usually too the patch of sky between them is gray and leaden. But this morning as I looked, the patch was luminous, golden, crimson. And the somber masses seemed transfigured in this brightness. There came to me a vivid sense of your pure black. Last evening, the essence of it flushed me and for one moment I held a beauty as intense and clear as I've ever known" (Toomer, Papers). This transformation of the ordinary into the extraordinary, of the mundane material world into a remarkable aesthetic world, was equivalent, in Toomer's mind, with

Stieglitz's "pure black," an essence expressive of pure form and individual identity.

But what do we make of the phrase "pure black"? It demands an accounting for its racial politics. For Toomer, "pure black" is a direct expression of "truth," without the "superstitions" of the American racial discourse. "Pure black," then, is a color only, rather than a social fact, an expression without "superstition," an entrance into a purely visual world. In Stieglitz and O'Keeffe and in his art, then, Toomer found the possibility, but not the fulfillment, of a new vision of the world and the "somber masses" who populated it, a vision that would not be contingent upon social signification.

Looking back to those early years following *Cane*'s publication, Toomer found that the price of his admission to the life of a writer was the label "Negro": "Let me be called Negro. I was experiencing the life I wanted to experience" (Rusch, 102), he wrote later, seemingly accepting a designation that asserted his difference. Toomer, however, began to refuse this label early on: "When one day Liveright wanted me to push the Negro feature . . . I refused. He then wrote me to the effect that he did not see why I could not accept my race. This angered me, and I doubtless said something that angered him. Neither could I see why I should accept my race; but what I meant by my race and what he meant by my race were two different things" (Rusch, 102).

When Liveright asked Toomer to market himself as a "race writer," Toomer resisted the social designation. He wanted to slough off the label "Negro" at any cost, to become "an artist," to fashion himself as an "American" writer.

Toomer's interest in Stieglitz and O'Keeffe is directly related to his resistance to the label "Negro." Among Stieglitz and O'Keeffe and their coterie Toomer believed that he found a place that allowed him to be free of racial designation. In a 1932 essay, entitled "Fighting the Vice," Toomer describes how the New York scene in which he moved affected his understanding of himself as an artist. In the twenties, he writes, he found himself a "new life . . . in New York, with [Waldo] Frank, [Gorham] Munson, Hart Crane, Kenneth Burke, Paul Rosenfeld, and Stieglitz." Toomer was "in the life [he] wanted to be in, . . . absorbed in another world" that gave him some distance from those involved in the Harlem Renaissance (Rusch, 102). He had arrived.

> To "arrive" meant a great deal in those days of the early 20s. If you were doing anything worthwhile in any of the arts, and in the modern idiom, to arrive meant that you were welcomed, officially as it were, into the most remarkable up-swing yet to occur in our national

> culture. It meant that you found yourself not only with name and place in a local movement or "school" but with function in a regenerative life which transcended national boundaries and quickened people in every country of the post-war world. They were part of a living world of great promise. And in the world, if you so felt it, there was not only art but something of religion. (Kerman and Eldridge, 107)

In this circle, Toomer was not a "Negro" writer but rather an "American" who was formulating a new vision of America. Both the aesthetic and national programs of this group attracted him.

For Toomer, Stieglitz was the archetypal American artist. In their initial letters, exchanged every few days in 1924, Toomer and Stieglitz seem infatuated with each other. Toomer especially seems taken with his elder, who, according to Toomer, possessed both the creative genius and social stature that the young writer himself desired. Writing on the morning of January 10, 1924, after a previous night's meeting, Toomer declares that he found himself transfixed in a "strange deep place, in a quiet dignity," an emotional state in which he could not distinguish between "I and you," between himself and Stieglitz (Toomer, Papers). But, of course, Toomer cared very much what the "you" thought of him: Toomer began this letter twice before he sent the third, final version to Stieglitz. He began the letter in his journal and then wrote a rough version of it, from which he later made a final copy that he sent to Stieglitz. This self-consciousness is striking. Toomer desired acceptance and approval from Stieglitz, the grandfather of American modernism.

Toomer was interested in O'Keeffe because he saw parallels in their careers. O'Keeffe was labeled a woman painter as often and as easily as Toomer was labeled a Negro writer. Each rejected such tags as inaccurate, inappropriate, and limiting, for both felt that their work was representative of broadly human experiences, feeling, and beliefs.

Throughout her career, O'Keeffe was taken to be the quintessential female artist. Even Stieglitz accepted that interpretation. According to Peters, Stieglitz engendered an "instantly successful public invention of O'Keeffe": "the woman who embodied sexual freedom, spontaneity, and intuition; the unspoiled, unintellectual artist whose visually expressed emotions represented nothing less than universal truth." She was " 'the Great Child,' who was uncorrupted and unfettered by the past; the American who was an artistic law unto herself" (Peters, 71). Rosenfeld concurred; he declared that O'Keeffe "was being a woman and only secondarily an artist," and continued to assert that she painted "through the terms of a woman's body. For, there is no stroke laid by her brush, whatever it is she may paint, that is not curiously, arrestingly female in quality. . . . The essence of very womanhood permeates her pictures." Marsden Hartley asserted that "with Georgia O'Keeffe one . . . sees the world of woman turned inside out" (Eldridge, 79).

O'Keeffe detested these interpretations of her work. She resented being identified first as a woman and only subsequently as an artist (Peters, 131). In response, she thrust the responsibility for interpretation back onto her viewers, declaring that her art represented her, and that it was the pure expression of her own way of seeing: "I didn't like the interpretation of my other things. So I said to myself—I'll paint what I see—what the flower is to me but I'll paint it big and they will be surprised into taking time to look at it—I will make even busy New Yorkers take time to see what I see of flowers" (Eldridge, 82).

Her insistence that her work not be interpreted through the lens of her social and biological position, but rather on its own terms, as the product of an artist first, held a strong appeal for Toomer. He, like O'Keeffe, resented the invention of himself as the representative of his race by others. Instead, by conceiving of himself as more complex than a Negro writer and of *Cane* as work that participated in more than one medium, Toomer found a way to invent himself and to create the literature to portray his invention.

Notes

1. For more biographical information, see Kerman and Eldridge, *Lives*.
2. George Hutchinson addresses this issue very clearly: "The sense of entrapment in a racialist language founded specifically upon the denial of his own racial 'name' precipitated an intense realization of the general inadequacy of language to express 'truth.' Language always shaped by oppressive conventions and more profoundly by what Michel Foucault would later call the 'archive' of the 'cultural unconscious,' was a hindrance to spiritual development and self-redescription." Hutchinson, "Racial Discourse," 231.
3. Quoted in Rusch, *Toomer Reader*, 105.
4. Toomer wrote this in response to the outrage in the white press about his marriage to Margery Latimer. See Kerman and Eldridge, 202.
5. Sander Gilman, *Difference and Pathology: Stereotypes of Sexuality, Race, and Madness* (Ithaca, N.Y.: Cornell University Press, 1985), 28.
6. The 1910 and 1920 census contained instructions on how to report the "Negro" population of the United States. Enumerators, who were traveling the United States, were to report as "black" all persons who were "evidently full-blood negroes," and as "mulatto" all other persons having "some proportion or perceptible trace of negro blood." In 1910, the census reported a larger proportion of "mulattoes" compared to "negroes" than in 1920, a situation that was due, according to the later census, to the fact that Negro enumerators canvassed the black population and reported "mulatto" identity more accurately.

   In 1890, however, the census had a different definition of "black." At that time, the term "denoted all persons having three-fourths or more black blood; other persons with any proportion of Negro blood being classified as 'mulattoes,' 'quadroons,' or 'octaroons.'" In 1880 and 1900, no differentiation between black and mulatto was made in the black population, and in 1850 and 1860 the two terms were not defined.

The racial logic of the 1890 and the 1920 census are clear. Both relied on notions of "blood," or lines of descent, to define race and identity. However, the 1890 census relied on a heavily quantitative definition of race, calling attention to the specific admixture of "white" and "black" blood. Race in the 1890 census is clearly a matter of descent that is based upon a literal formula of identity. The 1910 and 1920 racial logic is somehow more remarkable. Although the census refers to "blood," it relies more on a qualitative definition of racial identity, an identity that, it assumes, can be read literally on the body. The enumerators determined who was black, mulatto, or Indian, whether or not they interviewed the individuals in question; the manner in which the enumerators made their determination rested on how they literally viewed their subjects. This racial logic is striking in that it bases definitions of demographic and, hence, social identity on aspects of the physical appearance of individuals that are contingent on the literal views of others. This conjunction of bodily appearance with social identity is at the heart of the determination of race. In this systematic understanding, race is first "what you look like" and then "who you are" socially.

7. This conception of race emerges in the discourse of physiognomy, the "science" of judging human character from appearance. The nineteenth century saw the publication of an abundance of books describing how to read character traits physically. In 1887, Joseph Simms, a medical doctor, for example, published *Physiognomy Illustrated or Nature's Revelations of Character: A description of the Mental, Moral, and Volitive Disposition of Mankind, as Manifested in Human Form and Countenance* (New York: Murray Hill). Texts such as this used a variety of physical characteristics to classify individuals into discrete populations. *The Races of Britain* by John Beddoe (Bristol, England: Arrowsmith), which was published in the United States, used tables of hair and eye color to distinguish among groups. The premise is clear: individuals can be classified into groups in which character traits are predicated on physical appearance.

   These "fictions of human science" used illustrations of "types" and caricatures to support claims of stereotypes, thus firmly arguing that physical characteristics were directly correlated to social condition. How then was race to be represented? In these texts, race became a way, not of individuating people, but of classifying them, always with attention to the connection between physical appearance and character or social place.

8. Among early-twentieth-century painters, race became a concern because they associated it with a particular social context. The painters of the Ashcan school, who were interested in "the shabby neighborhoods and seamy life of the urban lower classes," produced a variety of works that presented blacks in an urban context. Robert Henri, the leader of the school, "preached a down-to-earth realism, based on the objectivity of Dutch genre, the somber palette of Spanish tonal painting, and Manet's broad painterliness" and demanded "direct experience and an art based on the observation of life" (Rose, 23). However, Henri produced racist, stereotypical cartoons, and, as Jeffrey Stewart writes, "Stuart Davis produced stereotypical caricatures for the *Masses*, some of which his editor, Max Eastman, described as 'viciously anti-Negro' " (Stewart, 50).These works fail to address the individuality of their subjects, relying instead on a discourse of racial stereotypes founded on social codes rather than on individual difference.

9. Quoted in Sarah Whitaker Peters, *Becoming O'Keeffe: The Early Years* (Abbeville Press, 1991), 38.
10. See Peters, 129–132.
11. See De Zayas in *Camera Work*, nos. 42–43, especially "Photography," in Green, *Camera Work*, and Paul Strand, "Photography," *Seven Arts* (August 1917): 524–525.
12. As Sarah Whitaker Peters writes in *Becoming O'Keeffe*, "Some drawings are much more abstracted than others, but *none* is without concrete references. And they come across as almost aggressively personal, not least because of their large size" (44).
13. The structure of *Cane* is governed by this composite portrait technique as well. By including vignettes and poems that describe African American life in different places and time, *Cane* offers a vision of the multiplicity of African American life. Toomer's method denies any notions of typicality and uniformity in African American identity and experience.
14. "Photography," in Green, *Camera Work*, 263.
15. Stieglitz has a photograph of the same trees, entitled *Dancing Trees*. This photograph reveals, first, the close affiliation between O'Keeffe and Stieglitz and, second, their differences. Please see the longer version.
16. Stieglitz himself declared, "The moment dictates for me what I must do . . . I have no theory about what the moment should bring . . . I simply react to the moment. . . . I am the moment. This focus on the moment, on the spontaneous apprehension of the material world, prevents the visual from expressing anything but the immediacy of perception" (see Norman, 54).
17. "Photography and Artistic Photography," in Green, *Camera Work*, 279.

Works Cited

Dijkstra, Bram. *The Hieroglyphics of a New Speech*. Princeton, N.J.: Princeton University Press, 1969.

Du Bois, W.E.B. *The Souls of Black Folk*. New York: New American Library, 1969.

Eldridge, Charles C. *Georgia O'Keeffe*. New York: Harry Abrams, 1991.

Frank, Waldo, et al., eds. *America and Alfred Stieglitz*. New York: Doubleday, Doran, 1934.

Gilman, Sander. *Difference and Pathology:* Stereotype of Sexuality, Race, and Madness. Ithaca, N.Y. Cornell University Press, 1985.

Green, Jonathan, ed. *Camera Work: A Critical Anthology*. New York: Aperture, 1973.

Greenough, Sarah. *Alfred Stieglitz: Photography and Writing*. Washington, D.C.: National Gallery of Art,1991.

Hutchinson, George. "Jean Toomer and American Racial Discourse." *Texas Studies in American Language and Literature* 35, 2 (1993): 231.

Kerman, Cynthia Earl, and Richard Eldridge. *The Lives of Jean Toomer: A Hunger for Wholeness*. Baton Rouge: Louisiana State University Press, 1987.

Munson, Gorham. *Destinations: A Canvas of American Literature since 1900*. New York: Sears, 1928.

Norman, Dorothy. Introduction to *Alfred Stieglitz: An American Seer*. New York: Duell, Sloan, and Pierce, 1960.

Peters, Sarah Whitaker. *Becoming O'Keeffe*. New York: Abbeville Press, 1991.

Rose, Barbara. *Twentieth-Century American Painting*. New York: Rizzoli, 1986.

Rosenfeld, Paul. *Port of New York*. Chicago: University of Illinois Press, 1961.

Rusch, Frederik. *A Jean Toomer Reader: Selected Unpublished Writings*. New York: Oxford University Press, 1993.

Stewart, Jeffrey. *To Color America*. Washington, D.C.: Smithsonian Institution Press, 1989.
Toomer, Jean. *Cane*. New York: W. W. Norton, 1988.
———. Papers. Collection of American Literature, Yale University. Beinecke Rare Book and Manuscript Library, New Haven, Conn.
Whelan, Richard. *Alfred Stieglitz*. Boston: Little, Brown, 1995

Jean Toomer and Horace Liveright; or, A New Negro Gets "into the Swing of It"

MICHAEL SOTO

Noticed your full page ads in New Republic and Times Book Review. The literary fermentation that they are evidence of is almost incredible.

Jean Toomer to Horace Liveright

Liveright published Cane. . . . It was of no major importance that the book was circulating and becoming known as the work of a Negro author. In New York, with [Waldo] Frank, [Gorham] Munson, Hart Crane, Kenneth Burke, Paul Rosenfeld, and [Alfred] Stieglitz, I was in the life I wanted to be in. Let me be called Negro. I was experiencing the life I wanted to experience. Nevertheless when one day Liveright wanted me to push the Negro feature I refused.

Jean Toomer, "This May Be Said/The Inside Story"

Racial Discourse and the Literary Marketplace

The often asked question "Was the Harlem Renaissance a success?" tends to include another question as a subtext: "Did the Harlem Renaissance capitulate to a primitivist fad?" Usually, literary critical methodology determines the answer: those who privilege high literary expression find only a smattering of primitivism, easily overlooked, whereas those who take a cultural studies approach soon find themselves buried in the stuff. Thus, George Hutchinson, in *The Harlem Renaissance in Black and White* (1996), argues against the notion that "a sudden fascination of whites for the 'primitive' and 'exotic' caused profit seeking white editors at established firms to become interested in black contributors." A "crucial point to keep in mind when noting the 'explosion' of black literature often attributed to the 'vogue' of the New Negro," he warns, is that "writers and artists were generally in vogue, especially young ones. The publishing industry expanded and diversified, nourished by a rapidly growing market, the recent, massive waves of immigration, and a stimulating clash of ideologies."[1] Nathan Irvin Huggins, in *Harlem Renaissance* (1971), paints a picture with a less rosy hue: "It was a difficult thing for the Negro artist to maintain his racial and his artistic integrity under the aegis of the white patron. Yet, the Negro artist was necessarily dependent. He had no force or leverage within the publishing or critical establishment." Huggins recognizes the intractability of this issue, which dates back centuries, but also notes that patronage "is different when it is racial." He adds, "Without the help and friendship of white men and publishers, there probably would have been little production of commercial black art in the 1920s. But white guidance and encouragement probably prevented those few men and women of real talent from wrestling with their senses and plodding through to make those statements which the thrust of their lives and experience would force them to make."[2]

Hutchinson is right to point out that the Harlem Renaissance found its most solid publishing industry allies in new, less established firms—especially among figures like Benjamin Huebsch, Alfred Knopf, and Horace Liveright—and that these firms were engaged in expansive cultural nationalist projects. These so-called Young Jews (although Huebsch wasn't quite so young) would reinvent U.S. letters by opening up the field to previously neglected voices, including voices like their own. This does not mean, however, that primitivism or exoticism played no role in publishing decisions; in fact, the disfiguring pressure of a patron's interest in the primitive (a word inevitably used loosely) on occasion did stand in the way of "men and women of real talent," not to mention those of lesser literary worth. Langston Hughes's (and later David Levering Lewis's) assertion that the "Negro was in vogue" for a brief and dissatisfactory moment may have been heavy-handed in its treatment of white patronage, but the sentiment did not materialize out of thin air.

In examining the advertising campaign for the work of a central Harlem Renaissance figure like Jean Toomer, I would like to do some fence straddling, staking out a position between Hutchinson's defense and Huggins's indictment of the Harlem Renaissance's relationship with the rapidly evolving U.S. publishing industry; that is, I will address the issue from the territory between literary history and cultural studies. The advertising campaigns of Jazz Age publishers might be viewed as an early attempt to mediate between high and low, between an avant-garde intellectual elite and an educable philistine mass market. Conspiracy theories abound on both sides of the issue, but a fittingly subtle articulation of advertising's social role can be found in the work of the cultural historian T. J. Jackson Lears, whose *Fables of Abundance* (1994) sometimes lacks clarity of vision because the drama that unfolds within its pages remains a constant blur of competing social and psychological forces, including "longings for links with an actual or imagined past, or for communal connections in the present; professional aspirations, personal conflicts, idiosyncratic tastes." Lears argues that the "rhetoric and iconography of advertising [cannot] be reduced to a mere propaganda of commodities. There [are] too many variations and ambiguities arising from advertisers' own private needs and confusions."[3]

Individual advertisements transmit as many potential meanings as there are consumers, perhaps more. As Lears points out (following the British anthropologist Anthony Forge), the Abelam of New Guinea revered glossy advertisements for Spam luncheon meat as European counterparts to their *tambarans*, talismanic designs said to embody powerful ancestral spirits.[4] It goes without saying that the average European holds a different view of Spam ads. Within this open-ended spectrum of signification, though, it is possible to investigate how advertisements shape "communities of discourse," what the advertising historian Roland Marchand defines as "an integrative common language shared by an otherwise diverse audience." He proposes that "if the metaphors, syntactical patterns, and verbal and visual 'vocabularies' of our common language establish our parameters of thought and cut the furrows along which our ideas tend to flow, then advertising has played a significant role in establishing our frames of reference and perception."[5] The Boni and Liveright (B&L) advertising campaign for *Cane* (1923) envisions specific reading communities, as well as specific modes of reading. This advertising campaign also places *Cane*, and with it Toomer, within well-defined literary genealogies, including (but hardly limited to) the African American literary tradition he would resist for the rest of his life. What's more, B&L's assumptions about *Cane* and its author played a critical role in the book's early and ongoing reception—it cut the furrows along which *Cane* has been read, so to speak.

Getting "into the Swing of It"

Toomer met Waldo Frank at one of *Broom* editor Lola Ridge's Greenwich Village parties in late 1920, and as Toomer later recalled, he and Frank "went over and sat down on the grass and had a long talk. I felt immediately [Frank] would be a good friend of mine." But at the party Toomer also "felt [like] a hopeless novice,"[6] and some time elapsed before he summoned the courage to write Frank, a man who would give Toomer's career an important early lift. "In your 'Our America' I missed your not including the Negro," Toomer wrote in early 1922. He also sent along some poems and sketches, including early versions of work that found its way into *Cane*, which he described at the time as "attempts at an artistic record of Negro and mixed-blood America."[7] This association with Frank, conducted mostly by mail, would continue to flourish during the next several months as the two exchanged their views as well as their works in progress, and in September 1922 both men toured the South together, traveling in Jim Crow cars, passing as Negro professors, even posing as brothers.[8] From this experience Frank would write *Holiday* (1923), a novel mentioned primarily in association with Toomer these days, and of course Toomer would stitch together what became sections 1 and 3 of *Cane*—the book's Southern sketches and poems, and "Kabnis," a closet drama modeled after Toomer's stint as an assistant principal in Sparta, Georgia. Although Toomer had the idea of collecting his work under the title *Cane* at least as early as mid-1922,[9] Frank's frequent counsel and encouragement convinced Toomer to continue work on the manuscript, to which he added what became section 2, set in Chicago and Washington.

Then, in December 1922, Toomer sent the completed manuscript to Frank with a now famous letter in which he enigmatically compares *Cane*'s design to a circle: "Aesthetically, from the simple forms to complex ones, and back to simple forms. Regionally, from the South up into the North, and back into the South again" (JTP 3:83). In response, Frank suggested a few minor changes to "Bona and Paul" and "Box Seat," but otherwise offered little but praise for the manuscript, which he personally delivered to Liveright three days later. In the blink of an eye the book was accepted for publication, and on 2 January 1923 Liveright telegraphed Frank (who telegraphed Toomer that same day) with the good news (JTP 3:84). Within a week, Liveright sent Toomer the contract, although he later announced that its terms, including a $150 advance, rested upon two conditions: first, that minor revisions be made; second, that Frank provide the foreword.[10] "I deeply thank you for the acceptance," Toomer responded, "for the check, (but it comes in good!), and for the contract." Toomer felt that he had made it, that he was now a bona fide part of U.S. literature: "I am glad to be in the fold. There is no other like it. The American group with Waldo Frank, Gorham B Munson, TS Eliot—well, it simply cant [*sic*] be beaten" (JTP 1:16).

In order to secure a contract for *Cane*, however, Frank stressed Toomer's Negro ancestry to the publisher, and Liveright decided to make this information a key part of the subsequent marketing campaign. Frank asked Toomer if it was appropriate to introduce his Negro background in the foreword, to which Toomer replied that January, "Sure, feature Negro."[11] By late February 1923, Toomer completed the changes requested by Liveright and sent the revised manuscript, including the foreword written by Frank, to B&L. Liveright was pleased with the results, or at least he said so, and Toomer wrote back with obvious joy, "Your enthusiasm for CANE gives me a deep pleasure. And it also gives me an energy which I shall try to put to good purpose in the shaping of my next book." Toomer hoped to complete a collection similar to *Cane* in size and scope, but set entirely in Washington, and in which the "whole black and brown world heaving upward against, here and there mixing with the white" represents an "upward heaving . . . symbolic of the proletariat or world upheaval" (JTP 1:16). This design was hardly foreign to Liveright, who had, after all, already published John Reed and the first English translation of Trotsky during the height of the Red scare. But Toomer's enthusiasm, in spite of all that was going his way, would soon dissipate.

This is not to say that Toomer abandoned his writing career once he found a publisher for *Cane*. He continued to publish poems and sketches in little magazines like *Broom* and the *Modern Review*, he was on the editorial board of *S4N*, and he even submitted unsolicited manuscripts (such as "Values and Fictions" and "The Gallonwerps") to B&L and elsewhere. In May 1923, Toomer moved from Washington to New York, where he occupied the room in Gorham Munson's home recently vacated by Hart Crane. He soon found a small apartment of his own in Greenwich Village, between Sixth and Seventh Avenues, just down the street from the Washington Square bookshop run by Albert and Charles Boni and not too far from the famous B&L brownstone on West Forty-Eighth Street: "In New York, I stepped into the literary world. Frank, Gorham Munson, Kenneth Burke, Hart Crane, Matthew Josephson, Malcolm Cowley, Paul Rosenfeld, Van Wyck Brooks, Robert Littell—*Broom*, the *Dial*, the *New Republic* and many more. I lived on Gay Street and entered into the swing of it" (Toomer, *Wayward*, 126).

Early that summer, Toomer met Liveright for lunch. While the details of the meeting are unfortunately lacking, a few survive in Toomer's memoirs. Presumably they talked shop, but Liveright also brought up his early encounters with prejudice: "Once [Liveright] had said to me that he had run into prejudice in college, and asked if I had. I said, 'No.' That was that. Otherwise, the question of race had not come up even in a vague way" (Toomer, *Wayward*, 127). Toomer's recollection here is at least partially incorrect, for it turns out that Liveright never went to college; in fact, he dropped out of high school (where he did face constant anti-Semitism) to become a stock market clerk, librettist, and purveyor of "coon songs" on Tin Pan Alley.[12] As Toomer pondered the significance of Frank's foreword, he began to question the premise on which B&L had accepted *Cane*. His letters of early 1923 notwithstanding, Toomer's later feelings about this important introduction to the reading public were mixed: "On the one hand, it was a tribute and a send-off only as Waldo Frank could have written it, and my gratitude for his having gotten the book accepted rose to the surface and increased my gratitude for the present piece of work [the foreword] in so far as it affirmed me as a literary artist of great promise. On the other hand, in so far as the racial thing went, it was evasive, or in any case indefinite" (Toomer, *Wayward,* 125).

"Evasive" and "indefinite" hardly state the case. In the foreword, Frank writes, "A poet has arisen in that land who writes, not as a Southerner, not as a rebel against Southerners, not as a Negro, not as apologist or priest or critic: who writes as a *poet.*"[13] Given the racial climate at the time, when the Ku Klux Klan and lynchings were near their peak, Toomer's blackness could not be spelled out more clearly. Eighty years earlier, only a former slave would need to advertise that his autobiography was "written by himself," and in 1923 only a Negro from the South would or could claim *not* to write as a Southern Negro. One need only recall the racial calculus of Hughes's essay, "The Negro Artist and the Racial Mountain" (1926): "I want to be a poet—not a Negro poet" equals "I want to write like a white poet" equals "I would like to be a white poet" equals "I would like to be white."[14]

Toomer's suspicions that Frank pitched the book as "written by a Negro" were confirmed when Liveright asked Toomer to feature himself as such. Toomer insisted he was not a Negro. When asked to provide a biographical sketch for use by the publicity department, Toomer disappointed Liveright by sending a four-page personal history avoiding all direct mention of race: in Washington in 1910 "he for the first time experienced the rich sweet taste of dark skinned life" is as far as Toomer goes in the sketch (JTP 26:611). In a letter dated August 1923, Liveright charged Toomer with "dodging" his racial identity: "Mr. [Isador] Schneider gave me today the sketch of your life that you did. . . . In the first place, I think it is at least one page too long. Second, I feel that right at the very start there should be a note sounded about your colored blood. To my mind this is the real human interest value of your story and I don't see why you should dodge it" (JTP 1:16). Years later Toomer would write that this accusation "did nothing else than pull my cork" (Toomer, *Wayward,* 127). That September, meanwhile, Toomer shot back an often cited reply that reveals how the question of his racial identity had been rising to a boiling point all along: "My racial composition and my position in the world are realities which I alone may determine. Just what these are, I sketched for you the day I had lunch with you. . . . As a B and L author, I make the distinction between my fundamental position and the position which your publicity department may wish to establish for me in order that *Cane* reach as large a public as possible. In this connection I have told you, I have told Messrs

Figure 1. B&L "Fall 1923 Publications" list. *Publishers Weekly* (7 July 1923). *Courtesy of Harvard College Library.*

[B. G.] Tobey and Schneider to make use of whatever racial factors you wish. Feature Negro if you wish, but do not expect me to feature it in advertisements for you" (JTP 1:16). The book had already been published on 1 September 1923, and entered into copyright the following day. However, B&L established the public identities of Toomer and *Cane* well before this exchange between Toomer and Liveright ever took place.

Going Madison Avenue

As president and business manager of B&L, Liveright handled the firm's day-to-day business, overseeing both the sales department, directed by Julian Messner, and the publicity department, which was headed by the Bolshevik novelist and poet Isador Schneider.[15] Liveright originally planned to release *Cane* in August, and the title was first announced on 7 July 1923, in a *Publishers' Weekly* ad for the B&L "Fall 1923 Publications" list (fig. 1). As the most popular trade journal for publishers and retail booksellers during the 1920s, *Publishers' Weekly* functioned as an important venue for the top-down transmission of marketing strategy—it was how a New York publishing house communicated with a neighborhood bookshop in Peoria between sales visits—and in the era before publisher-subsidized returns and national retail chains the journal exerted considerable influence over how many books were ordered and which ones received prime billing in displays. Beneath the "August Titles" heading, the advertisement gives booksellers ideas for how they might pitch *Cane* to their customer base: "This book is a vaudeville out of the South. Its acts are sketches, short stories, one long drama and a few poems. Through them all one feels the primitive rhythm of the Negro soul." Also announced in the advertisement are a wide range of B&L titles, from a bestseller like Hendrik Van Loon's *The Story of the Bible* to one with greater staying power like the uncut edition of Theodore Dreiser's *The 'Genius.'* (The blurb for Frank's *Holiday* calls it "A new novel picturing the South of today written with poignancy and artistic brilliancy. Another proof that Waldo Frank is to be considered one of the leading forces in American fiction.")

This specific advertisement is not remarkable by itself, but it offers a glimpse into the marketing strategy B&L would deploy during the coming months. The book was released in September with an incongruous dust jacket design (fig. 2), a green-and-purple tropical jungle done in art deco style: the title, "Cane," flows across the jacket atop a river, behind which are the jagged outlines of a palm tree, the ocean, and in the distance mountains and billowing clouds. Inside the flap, the dust jacket copy repeats much of the language found in the *Publishers' Weekly* advertisement, and the vaudeville metaphor receives much more elaborate treatment:

> This book is a vaudeville out of the South. Its acts are sketches, short stories, one long drama and a few poems. The curtain rises (Part One) upon the folk life of Southern Negroes, their simple tragedies, their wistfulness, their waywardness, their superstitions, and their crude joy in life. Part Two is the more complex and modern brown life of Washington. Jazz rhythms all but supplant the folk tunes—one simple narrative weaves its plaintive way, and is almost lost amid the complications of the city. Part three (a single drama) Georgia again. But this is not a brief tale of peasant sorrow. It is a moving and sustained tragedy of spiritual suffering.
>
> There can be no cumulative and consistent movement and, of course, no central plot to such a book. But if it be accepted as a unit of spiritual experience, then one can find in Cane a beginning, a progression, a complication, and an end. It is too complex a volume to

Figure 2. Cane, first edition, dust jacket. *Courtesy of Yale Collection of American Literature, Beinecke Rare Book and Manuscript Library.*

> find its parallel in the Negro musical comedies so popular on Broadway. Cane is black vaudeville. It is black super-vaudeville out of the South.[16]

Although Toomer never compared the structure of the book to a vaudeville show, *Cane* does bear some resemblance to this highly popular, genre-bending vehicle. As Michael North points out, "vaudeville is 'out of the South' in that its sources are largely rural and black, but it is also 'out of the South' in that these forms have been transplanted into an urban setting and subjected to violent stretching and scrambling. . . . Vaudeville is also, most obviously, an oral form, but it is not for that reason a simple one."[17] However, vaudeville was not, as North goes on to argue, a metaphor for what Toomer was trying to accomplish in *Cane;* vaudeville's formulas and its oral expressiveness are comic masks that make no claims about the deeper significance of what remains hidden beneath. As the dust jacket notes, "It is too complex a volume to find its parallel in the Negro musical comedies so popular on Broadway" or, it might have added, in the South; that is, had anyone at B&L seen a Southern vaudeville show. B&L's references to the genre were little more than Madison Avenue shorthand for simple, pliant "darkies" already familiar to the average consumer thanks to icons like Cream of Wheat's Rastus or Quaker Oats' Aunt Jemima.

No text could successfully maneuver from "black super-vaudeville" on the one hand to "moving and sustained tragedy" on the other. This was precisely the point of those who attacked *Cane* early on for its vaudevillian affinities. In October 1923 the *Kansas City Star* followed the dust jacket's lead in a very brief description of the book as a "vaudeville out of the South," while that same month a *Boston Herald* reviewer wrote, " 'A book of vaudeville' is what Boni & Liveright call 'Cane' by Jean Toomer. It is black vaudeville at that—black super-vaudeville out of the heart of the South."[18] An anonymous *Springfield Republican* review of December 1923, entitled "Literary Vaudeville," went so far as to quote the dust jacket and foreword at some length:

> Fond of vaudeville? Vaudeville is what Jean Toomer's "Cane" (Boni & Liveright) is called by its publishers. "Its acts are sketches, short stories, one long drama, and a few poems." The entertainment before the intermission is concerned with the folk-life of the Southern Negro; that after the intermission, with the "brown life" of Washington. The drama is an "added attraction." Waldo Frank writes the foreword for the volume. . . . The reader not possessed of the key to ejaculatory expressionism and impressionism will find some of this vaudeville hard to follow. He may think that in some of it there is more of the showman than of the actor and his part.[19]

And a writer for the *New York Post* may have had the dust jacket in mind when he or she wrote in January 1924 that "Mr. Toomer is a negro who writes in the modern manner, a style of broken sentences and cacophonies of thought that remind one of the modern composers."

Toomer had something entirely different in mind, and his own review of

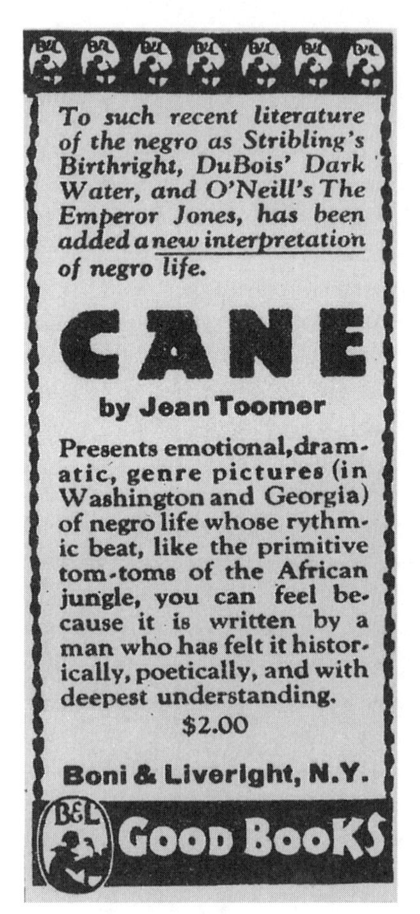

Figure 3. Cane advertisement. *New York Times Book Review* (16 September 1923). *Courtesy of Harvard College Library*

Cane, "The South in Literature," probably written in September 1923, dwells on the ironic relationship between a young man's cerebral passions and a "literary" form (vaudeville) incapable of rising to the occasion. "The outline of one story ['Box Seat'] must here suffice," Toomer writes. "A deeply sensitive young man offers his love to a woman who is prevented by conventional restrictions from accepting it. Later, while witnessing a vaudeville show, these very considerations (embodied in the audience) demand that she accept the coarser passion which an actor from the stage in mock-play tries to force on her. Much against her will, she does. The irony and unfairness of this episode whip the young fellow into a frenzy."[20] One has to wonder if this is literary criticism or autobiography.

These are not the only examples in which advertisements for *Cane* channeled the book's early reception along specific paths. On 16 September 1923 B&L ran an advertisement in the *New York Times Book Review* (fig. 3) that begins, "To such recent literature of the negro as Stribling's Birthright, Du Bois's Dark Water [*sic*], and O'Neill's The Emperor Jones, has been added a *new interpretation* of negro life." "Cane by Jean Toomer," the ad continues, "presents emotional, dramatic, genre pictures (in Washington and Georgia) of negro life whose rhythmic beat, like the primitive tom-toms of the African jungle, you can feel because it is written by a man who has felt it historically, poetically, and with deepest understanding." This nebulous "it," in other words, is felt and written by a Negro. Three weeks later, B&L ran another *New York Times Book Review* advertisement for *Cane* and several other titles on the fall 1923 list, repeating much of the same language (fig. 4). This time, the advertisement includes Toomer's photograph, as it does the photos of thirteen other authors on the B&L imprint, including such figures as Theodore Dreiser, Waldo Frank, Ben Hecht, and Edgar Lee Masters. The Dutch American historian and philosopher Hendrik Van Loon and the German American novelist Ludwig Lewisohn were just as well known at the time.[21] These advertisements were even more influential in framing early discussions of *Cane*.

Some examples of this influence are merely innocuous, such as the *Bookman* listing of *Cane* among the books received that fall: "There is something that resounds through these tragedies akin to the beat of an African tom tom at midnight in some Mississippi glade." In most other cases, a similar emphasis on primitive blackness reflects an implicitly negative value judgment, in which primitivist release entails a permanent surrender of the higher faculties. John Armstrong's *New York Tribune* review, which appeared in October, provides an interesting and not atypical example of what can be described as faint praise at best; patronization is probably more accurate. Armstrong argues that "it has always been felt that there are negroes in America with genuine poetic feeling, intellect, and discrimination approximating the standards of the more civilized whites. One has always known this and wondered, likewise, why they were never presented in our fiction. Seemingly until this book was written no one has had the courage or perhaps the inclination to seek out those real negroes and hold them up to view honestly." The review takes issue with the vaudeville metaphor deployed by B&L ("there is nothing of the theatrical, coon-strutting high-brown, none of the conventional dice-throwing, chicken-stealing nigger of musical comedy and burlesque"), and although Armstrong is generous in his praise of *Cane*'s novelty, its "discrimination," he is less so in his explanation for Toomer's success as a writer. Armstrong believes that Toomer possesses "a voice and a heart . . . that is synchronized with the aspirations, the hopes and the fears of the genuine darky," a "heavy, languorous" voice that "stuns the intelligence entirely, lulls it into torpor and compels it to recognize the authenticity of the racy negroes

THE NEW YORK TIMES BOOK REVIEW, OCTOBER 7, 1923 13

ADVERTISEMENT. ADVERTISEMENT.

The fingerprint identifies the individual

The B&L imprint identifies good books

B&L

Theodore Dreiser's **THE "GENIUS"**

This celebrated novel has just been reprinted unabridged from the original plates. It is the story of an artist and his love life. Considered by many critics to be Mr. Dreiser's most important work. *(All of his novels and plays now have the B&L imprint.)* ($3.00)

Waldo Frank's **HOLIDAY**

Waldo Frank's HOLIDAY is one single day of Southern drama. "No outline of the story can do justice to its dramatic qualities—its literary excellence—its gigantic systole and diastole in sympathy with human heartbeats. It is indeed of wonderful workmanship." *St. Louis Globe-Democrat.* ($2.00)

Ernita Lascelles' **THE SACRIFICIAL GOAT**

Is a brilliantly witty novel written around the character of one Moreby. The dialogue will suggest Shaw to so many "Times" readers that we beg you not to ask if Moreby is the great G.B.S. Perhaps he is. Perhaps he is not. "Miss Lascelles has achieved a first novel of extraordinary interest and importance." *(P. A. Kinsley in Philadelphia Record.)* ($2.00)

Ben Hecht's **THE FLORENTINE DAGGER**

A mystery tale where with shivering joy you will meet a nervous cavalier, and Floria—the lady of the dagger. "Behind the sensational happenings there is real tragedy. And the two things are connected in a manner so ingenious that the reader who suspects the real murder will gasp when he learns how it was actually committed." *Chicago Eve. Post.* ($2.00)

Jean Toomer's **CANE**

Presents emotional, dramatic pictures (in Washington and Georgia) of negro life whose beat, like the primitive tom toms of the African jungle, you can feel because it is written by a man who has felt it historically, poetically and with deepest understanding. *"It is a new and dramatic interpretation of negro life."* ($2.00)

W. P. Lawson's **LEM ALLEN**

A wild west tale that does not insult the intelligence. Plenty of straight two-handed shootings, cowboys, bandits, and old-time gambling episodes, to say nothing of a lovely girl AND LEM ALLEN HIMSELF. *A good man to meet in a book—a good man to meet anywhere.* ($2.00)

Hendrik Van Loon's **THE STORY OF THE BIBLE**

Undoubtedly the most important publishing event of 1923 is this new work by the author of The Story of Mankind.

To be published October 10th. ($5.00)

THE NUPTIAL FLIGHT by Edgar Lee Masters

Is an epic panorama of American life seen through three generations. An amazing study of woman in her role of the human Queen Bee. Another gallery of Americans as unforgettable as in Spoon River. The Philadelphia Record says, "THE NUPTIAL FLIGHT is easily the best American novel of the year." ($2.50)

DON JUAN by Ludwig Lewisohn

The tremendous audience which enjoyed Up Stream and which has awaited a novel from its author will find their expectations more than realized in DON JUAN. Here is a DON JUAN of 1923, free to adventure widely but bound by the convention of marriage. The book presents more than the problem of a mismated couple, for this Don Juan places the honor of his own heart upon an even higher pedestal than that traditionally occupied by woman. *(Publication date October 5th.)* ($2.50)

HIDDEN LIVES by Leonora Eyles

In Hidden Lives you meet a fanatical curate, and a modern young woman doctor. They fall in love. Helen gives herself to him less in emotion than to cure him of his delusions and repressions.

"As realistic, dramatic fiction it is tremendously effective. Helen is a new figure in fiction, the first fully grown up specimen of the really new woman." (N. Y. Herald.) ($2.50)

AFTER ALL by George F. Hummel

This novel of a progressive married life will focus your attention on Gus. Brenner's honest account of himself, an unveiling so fine and explicit that you will close the book at the end with a clarification of ideas and ideals. *"It is a pitiless analysis of marriage—a much better novel than for example Norris's "Brass."* N. Y. Herald. (8th edition—$2.00)

THE GIRL IN THE FOG by Joseph Gollomb

The first of the Red and Green Mystery Detective Series.

"The book is full of villains, and the king of them all, misshapen, with gorilla arms, puny legs, a catlike walk, unable to sleep unless he can hang monkey-like from cross beams, is one of the most infamous scoundrels this reviewer has met. *It is a mystery story not only unlike others, but better than others."* N.Y. Times. ($2.00)

STORIES OF THE FIRST AMERICAN ANIMALS by George Langford

"The American Jungle Book."

A collection of tales of the American jungle that existed ages ago, and the strange animals that lived in it. Children and grown-ups will thrill over these strange animal characters and their stories. *Illustrated with five 4 color pages by Ty Mahon and 37 black and white drawings by the author.* ($3.00)

HAUNCH, PAUNCH AND JOWL An Autobiography

The story of an immigrant boy who rose from gangster to judge of a high court. In the interim he was waiter, police court runner, lover, shyster lawyer, and strike-breaker. The author is unsparing of himself, and his people. He brings home to everyone what may be the bitterest of all tragedies—the tragedy of success. ($3.00)

THE MODERN LIBRARY

OF THE WORLD'S BEST MODERN CLASSICS

A forty page book with thumbnail portraits describing the authors and over 100 titles of this most famous of all libraries will be sent you on request. Modern Library volumes are obtainable at all bookstores at 95c per volume, each book bound in limp, flexible style, stamped and decorated with gold. When writing for this fascinating book about books ask for our other monographs.

B & L MONOGRAPHS

1. New Fall Catalog of all B & L Books.
2. Travels in Arabia Deserta (Doughty).
   "The greatest travel book of any time." *London Mercury.*
3. The Story of the Bible (Van Loon).
4. These United States.
   Each state is pictured by a literary son or daughter.
5. The Carra Edition of George Moore's work.

(Yours for the asking.)

BLACK OXEN has been the best selling novel in America since its publication in January.
FLAMING YOUTH has consistently climbed higher and higher on the best seller list during this same period.

BONI & LIVERIGHT GOOD BOOKS 61 WEST 48th ST. NEW YORK

Figure 4. B&L advertisement. *New York Times Book Review* (7 October 1923). *Courtesy of Harvard College Library.*

delineated."[22] An anonymous *Boston Transcript* review of December 1923 takes an even dimmer view of the book, once again partly inspired by the B&L advertising campaign. The review begins, not surprisingly, with an unfavorable comparison of the book and its gaudy dust jacket design: "It is a rather curious concoction. It tries to be impressionistic, and is bedeviled by a flaming green and purple moonrise in African jungle jacket, which is even worse than the worst of the volume." Not satisfied with judging a book by its cover, the reviewer describes *Cane* as "a daring overflow, for it presents the black race as we seldom represent it, mournful, loving beauty, and full of passion untutored and entirely unconnected with the brain."[23]

Perhaps most discomfiting to Toomer was the reaction of his closest friends and associates, many of whom, as North points out, mixed glowing praise with "a certain old-fashioned condescension."[24] Although the B&L advertising campaign did not directly condition most responses, they still reveal the existence of a small, but important, audience attentive to what Liveright called the "real human interest value" of Toomer's racial background. Commercial success would depend upon a trickle-down effect, as it were, from advertisement to reviewer to the reading public. Matthew Josephson, who published Toomer's work in *Broom*, considered Toomer's Negro background an asset, but this meant that his writing could be viewed as a success only narrowly, more for its unpolished vigor than for its formal accomplishment. Josephson writes in his October 1923 review for that journal: "At bottom Toomer is fiercely emotional, vigorous—and how often one has wailed at the lack of energy in contemporary writers—at times fearfully impolite, by standards of recent English schools. Perhaps it were better for Toomer to follow his five or six senses rather than search for cerebral super-forms."[25] Similarly, Robert Littell, in a *New Republic* review dated 26 December 1923, offers a peculiar argument on Toomer's behalf, describing him as a romantic visionary on the one hand and capable of little else on the other: "Cane does not remotely resemble any of the familiar, superficial views of the South on which we have been brought up. On the contrary, Mr. Toomer's view is unfamiliar and bafflingly subterranean, the vision of the poet far more than the account of things seen by a novelist—lyric, symbolic, oblique, seldom actual. . . . It isn't necessary to know exactly what [the book] means in order to find pleasure in reading it. Which is one way of defining poetry."[26] The following month, John McClure reviewed the writer, whom he had published in his *Double Dealer*. Again, the qualities most admired in Toomer and his work are precisely those thought to be lacking in "Caucasian" writers: " 'Cane' may be a landmark in American literary history because it represents the injection into our polite letters of the emotional ecstasy of the black man. Jean Toomer, a poet in whom many racial strains are mingled, owes to his Negro heritage the two salient characteristics of his work; ecstasy and music. . . . 'Cane,' I hope, is the fore-runner of work which will profoundly enrich American literature. Real ecstasy is the state of mind most seldom found among writers. The Negro has it, for he knows, as few Caucasians know, the love of God."[27] Here McClure more openly reveals the troubling logic behind the view that U.S. letters require an "injection" of "emotional ecstasy": the literature of the Negro is not "American" literature.[28]

The earliest review of *Cane* to appear in an African American literary journal was published in the December 1923 issue of *Opportunity*. Montgomery Gregory, a professor of drama at Howard University, wrote a glowing review in which he argues that "few books of recent years have greater significance for American letters than this 'first' work of a young Negro, the nephew of an acting reconstruction governor of Louisiana. Fate has played another of its freakish pranks in decreeing that southern life should be given its most notable artistic expression by the pen of a native son of Negro descent." Gregory goes on to explain how Toomer, as the descendent of P.B.S. Pinchback (Toomer's politician grandfather, not his uncle), has "sprung from the tangy soil of the South," combining "the inheritance of the old Negro with the spirit of the new Negro." As a result, Toomer represents Negro life as never before: "Verse, fiction, and drama are fused into a spiritual unity, an 'aesthetic equivalent' of the Southland." Even so, *Cane* "is not a book to be intellectually understood; it must be emotionally, aesthetically felt. One must approach it with all his five senses keenly alive if appreciation and enjoyment are to result." Significantly, though, Gregory does not attribute Toomer's success, or the reader's enjoyment, to racial exceptionalism. Gregory sees antecedents for Toomer in Paul Laurence Dunbar and René Maran, and contemporary analogues in Eugene O'Neill and "the grimly powerful work of the Russian dramatists."[29] W.E.B. Du Bois, in his *Crisis* review of *Cane*, similarly positions Toomer at the end of an African American literary tradition, this time as a representative of "The Younger Literary Movement." (Alain Locke reviewed Jessie Fauset's *There Is Confusion* under the same October 1924 title.) "There have been times when we writers of the older set," Du Bois explains, "have been afraid that the procession of those who seek to express the life of the American Negro was thinning and that none were coming forward to fill the footsteps of the fathers. Dunbar is dead; Chesnutt is silent; and Kelly Miller is mooning after false gods while Brawley and Woodson are writing history rather than literature." Into this void step Toomer, Fauset, and many more. Even when his review takes a slightly negative turn, Du Bois extends his range of reference beyond the African American tradition to suggest external parallels for Toomer's work. Du Bois writes, "Toomer does not impress me as one who knows his Georgia but he does know human beings; and, from the background which he has seen slightly and heard of all his life through the lips of others, he paints things that are true, not with Dutch exactness, but rather with an impressionist's sweep of color."[30]

In this manner Toomer found his way into *The New Negro* (1925) and into *Caroling Dusk* (1927), where, as Countee Cullen points out in the foreword, Toomer (among others) had "more to gain from the rich background of English and American poetry than from any nebulous atavistic yearnings toward an African inheritance."[31] Too often, critics fail to acknowledge the extent to which the Harlem Renaissance drew from myriad strands of U.S., European, and world culture. But if we pay head to the law of unintended consequences, if we regard the accidents of literary history as informing Toomer's and others' contributions to literary art, then a richer array of texts and contexts lend themselves to our understanding of Jazz Age cultural history. The remainder of this essay hopes to do just that by way (once more) of the B&L advertising campaign for *Cane*.

One Hundred Percent Americanism

The interested reader could turn to Liveright's two biographers, Walker Gilmer and Tom Dardis, for corroborating information, but Waldo Frank in 1926 set the tone for subsequent discussions of the publisher in his collection of biographical sketches, *Time Exposures* (published by B&L under the very Frankian pseudonym "Search-Light"). Frank's sketch of Liveright, a parody of nativist rhetoric entitled "One Hundred Per Cent American," covers all the important bases, which taken as a whole are almost an inversion of Ben Franklin's life story: the scrappy young HBL's journey from Philadelphia to New York; his early career on Wall Street; his love of the theater; the influence of his Modern Library; his ability to discover talent, even if he hadn't read the manuscript; his championing of the avant-garde and the heterodox; his famous run-ins with the censors; his infamous, liquor-laden brownstone on Forty-Eighth Street; and his knack for publicity (with a capital *P*). It is this latter aspect of Liveright and of B&L that gives Frank occasion to pause, to question the transformation inflicted upon the traditionally genteel publishing industry:

> When the book is ready, the trader is doubled by a circus barker. HBL can sponsor a book like a lover of Truth, and sell it like a patent medicine hawker. He has done more to put "life" into the literary market that any of his fellows. And . . . more's the pity . . . he is proud

> of it. For this "life" consists chiefly of undifferentiate adjectives of praise, lacking even the circus merit of alliteration. Of course, in this, Liveright is a child of the times. The complexity of reaching the scattered literate thousands, hidden in our hundred millions, is exasperating enough to make any one raise his voice. The trouble is that straightaway the other publishers raised their voices too. So that the "Book Page" has become a Bedlam—as noisy as the old Curb with which HBL used to be familiar. Even Paris is beginning to imitate the cacophonous ways of Liveright. He knows it's bad: but he enjoys the racket—precisely because he knows he started it.[32]

In Frank's analysis of the early-twentieth-century transformation of the book publishing industry, described by the publishing historian John Tebbel as the "Big Change," we get a hint of modernism's ambivalent relationship with modernity. As Lears points out, " 'modernism' . . . has often been rooted in hostility toward modernization, and in particular the modernizing tendencies within . . . bourgeois society,"[33] including the modernizing tendencies of the culture industry and Madison Avenue. We also see how Liveright's role in this transformation (or modernization) of U.S. culture qualifies him as "one hundred percent American." Like a circus ringleader, Liveright assembles the wards of Bedlam and pits them against those who speak for orthodoxy, against xenophobes who defined "one hundred percent Americanism" during the Great War. A tongue-in-cheek Frank notes how Liveright "sponsored half the advanced novelists who pollute our homes, half the radical thinkers who defile our customs, half the free verse poets who corrupt our English. He has defiantly come out for minorities in a land where the Majority is sacred. . . . He stands, first and last, for the Revolt of our misled youth against every proper tradition of the land."[34]

Liveright's "revolt" took shape in his impressive list, which gave U.S. readers inexpensive editions of modern European classics, the so-called Modern Library, which would serve as a model for countless other firms. The Modern Library popularized Dostoevski, Freud, Ibsen, Nietzsche, Pater, Strindberg, Wilde, and Yeats, among many others, before Liveright, desperate for cash, sold the prestigious backlist catalog to Bennet Cerf in 1925. (Cerf went on to found Random House with the Modern Library as the firm's backbone.) Liveright also sought out U.S. authors and landed several big ones, some of whom later got away: Anderson, Crane, Cummings, Doolittle, Dreiser, Faulkner, Hemingway, Loos, O'Neill, Parker, Pound—and of course Toomer. The B&L list reads very much like the one carried by the Masses Book Shop—a hodgepodge of texts on political radicalism, racial tolerance, and sexual liberty—

and in fact many of the editors and writers at the Masses Book Shop and its offshoots wound up on the B&L list or ended up working for B&L. (In addition to a Bolshevik like Schneider, the advertising department was also home for a while to the left-leaning Lillian Hellman.) B&L's famous trademark, a lone monk laboring with a quill over a writing table, prompted the longtime B&L employee Louis Kronenberger to remark that "never in publishing, and seldom anywhere else, has there been an atmosphere so unmonastic, so unstudious, so unsolitary as at Liveright's."[35]

The "accident" of Toomer's association with Liveright and B&L, then, provides another important context for the public meaning of *Cane*. As we have already seen, Toomer relished joining the "fold" of B&L writers like Gorham Munson and T. S. Eliot (whose *Waste Land* B&L brought to the United States in 1922), and advertisements for *Cane* often spell out exactly who constitutes this fold. Toomer belongs, for example, to a "negro life" tradition with T. S. Stribling and Yankees like Du Bois and O'Neill (fig. 3). Inclusion in a *Times Book Review* advertisement (fig. 4) with Dreiser and Masters, Lewisohn and Van Loon, provides yet another genealogy for Toomer, one broad enough to include all five writers. Additional advertisements for *Cane*, including one that ran in the September 1923 issue of the *Dial*, actually thematize Toomer's group affiliations. The *Dial* advertisement, which bears the title "A Few Informal Notes on New GOOD BOOKS from B&L," lists titles "chosen particularly for *Dial* readers" and pairs writers according to their regional identity. For instance, the advertisement mentions Dreiser and his "old friend" Masters (a "new friend" of B&L). It goes on to contrast this Midwestern duo with two Southern writers:

> On the other hand, HOLIDAY, WALDO FRANK's new novel, is one single day of Southern Drama. A day reflecting quiet contentment—quiet village life—the beauty of understanding between a white girl and a negro youth—sudden suspicion, and finally the storm of accumulated tragedy.
>
> The South is again pictured in a series of sketches, short stories and poems by JEAN TOOMER the author of CANE. A book whose tap roots run deep in the Southern soil, and whose music sways our emotions as only primitive desires can.

The advertisement proceeds to contrast the Southerners with the cosmopolitan "sophisticates" Ben Hecht and Djuna Barnes. Toomer's association with Frank had already been well established by their contemporary critics,[36] and B&L hoped to capitalize on the pairing. Presumably, Frank could bring Toomer to the same audience that made *Our America* (1919) a moderate financial success, and in turn Toomer could bring Frank to the growing market of African American readers.[37] For example, B&L placed an advertisement (fig. 5) in the *Survey Graphic* Harlem issue (March 1925), which Locke expanded into *The New Negro* later that year. The advertisement, which appears alongside Locke's bibliography "The Negro in Print," positions *Cane* beneath Fauset's *There Is Confusion* and Frank's *Holiday*. One could infer Toomer's and Fauset's racial identity from their inclusion in Locke's bibliography, but the advertisement itself makes no mention of race or of regional affiliation; commentary on all three is instead limited to favorable blurbs from published reviews.

Significantly, B&L established Toomer not just as a Negro or a Southern writer in its advertising campaign, although these elements have generated the most commentary. B&L also stressed Toomer's avant-gardism in order to appeal to an avant-garde elite. The October 1923 issue of *Broom* provides a fascinating example: in that journal B&L placed an advertisement (fig. 6) for *Cane* as well as Frank's *Holiday*, Barnes's *A Book*, and C. M. Doughty's *Travels in Arabia Deserta* (all published or reprinted in 1923). At the center of the page, the advertisement copy reads: "We fondly believe that wherever reading is regarded not as a duty but as a pleasant habit and one of the comforts of civilization, B&L books are well known. Q.E.D., BROOM readers know B&L books." B&L made several appeals to the refined taste of *Broom*'s limited circulation: of Doughty's *Travels* it says, "With the exception of 'Ulysses' by James Joyce, no book written in the last century has been so hard to get"; the advertisement describes *A Book* as "a book as individual as its creator."[38] And of *Cane* it says: "You have seen parts of this unusual book in BROOM and other portions probably in 'Little Review' and other unfashionable magazines. The book is really a stirring event in the year's literature." The irony here is almost palpable: that Toomer was so often published in "unfashionable" little magazines attests to his experimental bent, but it might also have predicted the book's thin sales. Much has been made of the fact that *Cane* sold fewer than 500 copies when first published (the actual number at the end of 1923 was 429). Given the lengths to which B&L went to promote *Cane*, including a large quantity of advertisements for a first-time author, the firm no doubt lost considerable money on the book.[39]

B&L had modest plans for Toomer and probably expected to take a loss on the unproven author, at least this first time around. By mid-1928, only 653 copies of *Cane* had been sold (JTP 26:610); nevertheless, B&L found it necessary to issue a second printing of *Cane* as early as March 1927.[40] This suggests that the initial print run for *Cane* was limited to 500 copies, well below the 1,500–plus copies a mid-size firm needed to sell to break even during the 1920s.[41] It is clear that Liveright never gave up on Toomer, on *Cane*, or on

African Clearings, by *Jean K. Mackenzie*. Houghton, Mifflin. Price $2.50.
The Quaint Companions, by *Leonard Merrick*. Dutton. Price $1.90.
God's Stepchildren, by *Sarah G. Millin*. Boni & Liveright. Price $2.00.
The Long Walk of Samba Diouf, by *Jerome and Jean Tharaud*. Duffield. Price $1.75.

Negro Culture

Afro-American Folksongs, by *H. E. Krehbiel*.
Songs and Talks from the Dark Continent, by *Natalie Burlin Curtis*. Schirmer. Price $4.00.
Negro Culture in West Africa, by *George W. Ellis*. Neale Publishing Co. Price $2.00.
Primitive Negro Sculpture, by *Paul Guillaume and T. Munro*. (on press) Barnes Foundation.
African Art Issue of Opportunity, May 1924.

Sharing increasing contact with the general world of letters, and speaking with a new cultural emphasis and breadth, Negro authors are collaborating in giving an artistically conceived version of Negro life and feeling to the world.

V—Negro Belles Lettres

Poetry

American Negro Poetry, *compiled by James Weldon Johnson*. Harcourt, Brace & Co. Price $1.75.
An Anthology of American Negro Verse, *compiled by N. I. White and C. A. Jackson*. Trinity College Press, Durham, N. C. Price $2.00.
Fifty Years and After, by *James Weldon Johnson*. Cornhill. Price $1.25.
The House of Falling Leaves, by *Wm. Stanley Braithwaite*. Luce. Price $1.00.
Sandy Gee and Other Poems, by *Wm. Stanley Braithwaite*.
The Heart of a Woman & Other Poems, by *Georgia Douglas Johnson*. Cornhill. Price $1.25.
Bronze, by *Georgia Douglas Johnson*.
Harlem Shadows, by *Claude McKaye*. Harcourt, Brace & Co. Price $1.35.
The Collected Poems of Paul Laurence Dunbar. Dodd Mead & Co. Price $2.50.

Drama

Rachel, by *Angelina Grimke*.

Fiction

Sport of the Gods, by *Paul Laurence Dunbar*. Dodd Mead. Price $1.50.
The Uncalled, by *Paul Laurence Dunbar*.
The Marrow of Tradition, by *Charles W. Chesnutt*. Houghton Mifflin. Price $1.50.
The House Behind the Cedars, by *Charles W. Chesnutt*. Houghton Mifflin. Price $1.50.
The Wife of His Youth and Other Stories, by *Charles W. Chesnutt*. Houghton Mifflin. Price $1.50.
The Conjure Woman, by *Charles W. Chesnutt*. Houghton Mifflin. Price $1.25.
The Quest of the Silver Fleece, by *W. E. B. Du Bois*. McClurg. Price $1.20.
Batouala, by *René Maran*. Seltzer. Price $1.25.
Cane, by *Jean Toomer*. Boni & Liveright.
There is Confusion, by *Jessie Fauset*. Boni & Liveright. Price $2.00.
The Fire in the Flint, by *Walter F. White*. Knopf. Price $2.50.

General

The Souls of Black Folk, by *W. E. B. Du Bois*. McClurg. Price $1.35.
Darkwater, by *W. E. B. Du Bois*. Harcourt, Brace. Price $2.25.
The Poetic Year, by *Wm. Stanley Braithwaite*. Small, Maynard. Price $2.00.
Up From Slavery, by *Booker T. Washington*. Houghton Mifflin.
Autobiography, *Frederick Douglass*.

A. L.

There Is Confusion

by Jessie Redmon Fauset

"A significant novel—in it the educated Negro becomes articulate."—*The N. Y. Evening Post.*

"The author of THERE IS CONFUSION can write. No one who reads this story can fail to recognize that fact. This book can be read with immense profit by white and black alike."—*The San Francisco Bulletin.*

"It is in these glimpses it gives, of a life about which the majority of white people know little or nothing, that the book is unusual and interesting."—*The N.Y. Times.*

$2.00

HOLIDAY

by Waldo Frank

". . . FIFTY years from now, Holiday will probably stand out in American literature as a new landmark . . ."—*The Survey.*

"As a work of art this book has few peers. As a real book, with a sincere motive, it is hardly to be approached."—*San Francisco Bulletin.*

"Waldo Frank is a genius."—*Syracuse Post Standard.*

"It is a book of powerful visualization and emotionalism." — *The Springfield Republican.*

$2.00

CANE

by Jean Toomer

"A distinct achievement, unlike anything of this sort done before. The book is indeed a spiritual chronicle of the Negro."—*N. Y. Tribune.*

"Here is a realist with an intense dramatic sense of the mystic, the unfathomable in life."—*Detroit Free Press.*

"He has his moments of sweeping power, and rarely loses a sense of moving tragedy or pathos. He does achieve striking effects and his style is peculiarly suited to the subject—the Negro on the plantations of Georgia and in the crowded tenements of Washington."—*The N.Y. Evening Post.*

$2.00

BONI & LIVERIGHT GOOD BOOKS 61 WEST 48TH STREET NEW YORK, N.Y.

(*In answering advertisements please mention* The Survey. *It helps us, it identifies you.*)

707

Figure 5. B&L advertisement. *Survey Graphic* (March 1925). *Courtesy of Trinity University Library.*

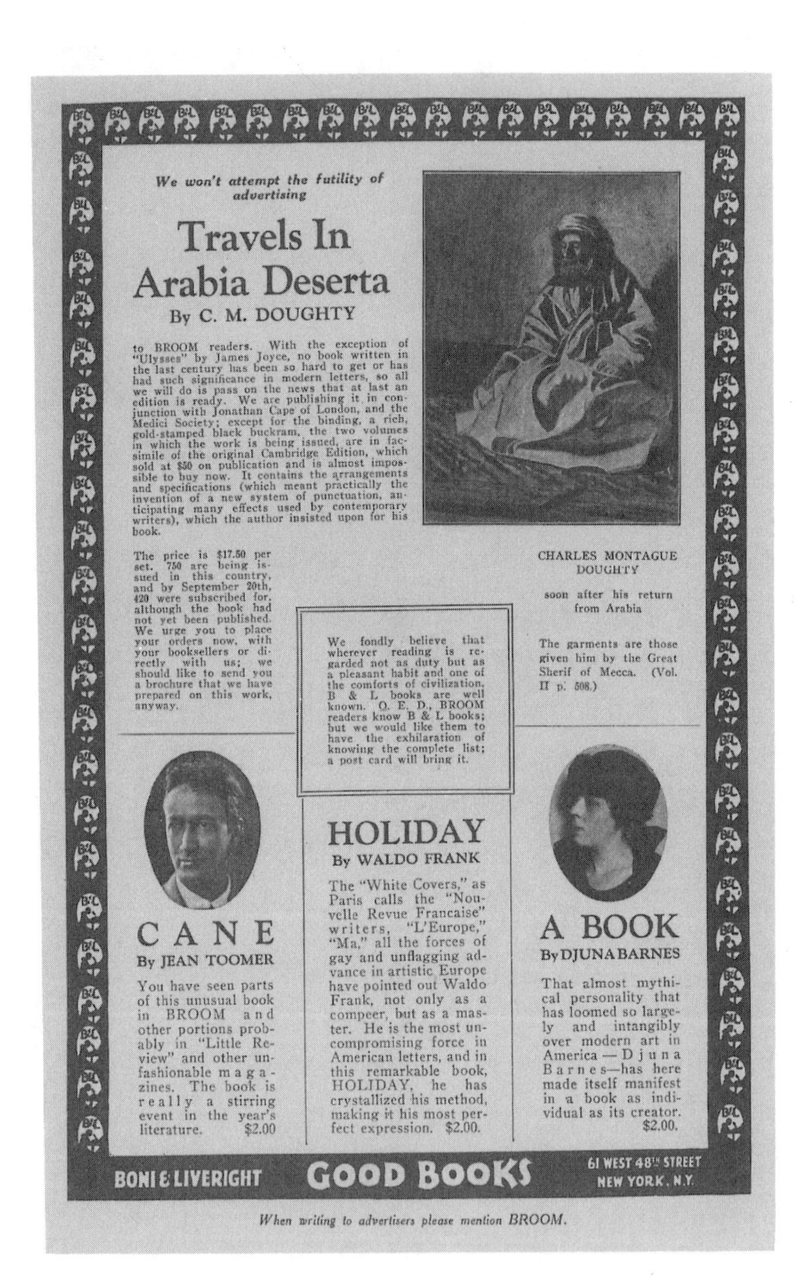

Figure 6. B&L advertisement. *Broom* (October 1923). *Courtesy of Harvard College Library.*

any of the firm's other unsuccessful titles. Liveright is remembered for spending equally extravagantly on bootleg liquor and on publicity,[42] and he continued to publicize *Cane* in spite of its commercial failings. Even when Toomer was not the center of attention, he found his way into B&L advertisements, and on his own race-neutral terms. In a half-page advertisement for Fauset's *There Is Confusion*, published in the April 1924 issue of *Crisis*, Toomer represents the heterogeneous literary tradition to which Fauset now belongs: "Theodore Dreiser, Eugene O'Neill, Franz Molnar, Hendrik Van Loon, Waldo Frank, Maxim Gorky, Jean Toomer, Konrad Bercovici—stars of the literary heavens—have been published by the firm that now proclaims the advent of a new constellation, Jessie Redmon Fauset."

Race was but one of many factors deployed by B&L in its sales pitch for *Cane;* that so much attention has been lavished on the subject perhaps says more about Jazz Age historiography than about Toomer or Liveright. It is understandable that Liveright would want the young writer to fill a specific role in a larger cultural drama, to be a Negro among Jews and Southerners and Irish Catholics. It is also understandable that Toomer would want the tag "one hundred percent American" (and not simply "Negro") applied to his life and work. As we know, such has not often been the case. Then as now, the culture industry sifts through all available categories for a winning formula, be it modernist, primitivist, or in between. When "taste" and "race" cross paths, as they do in the advertising campaign for *Cane*, it is hardly surprising that the Harlem Renaissance could once be viewed as both primitivist and a passing fad.

Notes

1. Hutchinson, *Black and White*, 342, 8.
2. Huggins, *Harlem Renaissance*, 128, 129.
3. Lears, *Fables*, 5.
4. Ibid., 1.
5. Marchand, *Advertising*, xx.
6. Toomer, *Wayward*, 114.
7. Jean Toomer, Papers, Yale Collection of American Literature, Beinecke Rare Book and Manuscript Library, box 3, folder 83 (hereafter cited as JTP, followed by box and folder numbers).
8. Charles Larson suggests that Frank may have entered into the friendship for mercenary reasons. At the time, Frank was looking for a Southern distributor for *City Block* (1922), which B&L refused to publish out of fear that the book would bring obscenity charges upon the publisher. Frank privately printed just over twelve hundred copies of *City Block*, some of which Toomer did in fact distribute in Washington. See Larson, *Darkness*, 19.
9. Toomer mentions the idea in letters to Frank (19 July 1922) and John McClure (22 July 1922).
10. In addition to the $150 advance, the terms of the contract were fairly standard:

on the book, priced at $2 per copy, Toomer was to receive a royalty of 10 percent on copies sold in the United States and a royalty of 5 percent on copies sold in Canada. (After 5,000 copies had been sold, the royalty would increase to 12 1/2 percent, and after 10,000 copies had been sold, it would increase to 15 percent.) B&L and Toomer were to share equally all serial, foreign, and motion picture rights, and B&L retained right of first refusal on Toomer's next two books. Toomer was also to receive 10 free copies of the book and a 40 percent discount on all additional copies purchased (JTP 1:16). Toomer never received any royalty payment from B&L because sales of *Cane* failed to cover the advance. According to the B&L royalty statement for the period ending 31 December 1923, *Cane* had sold 425 copies in the United States and 4 copies in Canada (for a total royalty of $85.20). Of these, 22 were purchased by Toomer, including copies shipped directly to Frank and Alain Locke (JTP 26:610).

11. Quoted in Larsen, *Darkness*, 21.
12. Dardis, *Firebrand*, 10–11, 14–17.
13. Toomer, *Cane*, 138–139.
14. Hughes, "Negro Artist," 692. Ironically, in the same essay Hughes describes *Cane* as a "truly racial" book.
15. Gilmer, *Liveright*, 10, 87, 89.
16. I examined a copy of the first edition available at the Yale Collection of American Literature, Beinecke Rare Book and Manuscript Library. It is autographed with the inscription: "For Carl Van Vechten greeting his own rich response."
17. North, *Dialect*, 168–169.
18. Unless otherwise noted, all reviews cited can be found in JTP 26:612.
19. Quoted in Durham, *Studies*, 34.
20. Toomer, *Selected Essays*, 14–15. Toomer sent "The South in Literature," which also reviews Frank's *Holiday*, to Liveright, who tried to place it for Toomer. Liveright wrote on 27 September 1923: "Your paper, The South in Literature, is a humdinger and I'm going to take it up with Mr. Messner, the head of our sales department just the best possible way of making use of it. We'll have a copy made of it and we'll send it to Ryan Walker of The Call who I know will be glad to print it. Of course, as you say, we'll have to sign it with a faked name" (JTP 1:16).
21. The advertisement also includes a large question mark where Samuel Ornitz's photograph should appear, since his *Haunch, Paunch and Jowl*—the "story of an immigrant boy who rose from gangster to judge of a high court. In the interim he was waiter, police court runner, lover, shyster lawyer, and strikebreaker"—was published anonymously.
22. Armstrong, "Real Negro," 26.
23. Review of *Cane*, by Jean Toomer, *Boston Transcript*, 15 December 1923, 8.
24. North, *Dialect*, 149.
25. Josephson, "Novels," 179–180.
26. Littell, review, 126.
27. McClure, review, 26.
28. Only one of Toomer's close associates at the time *Cane* was published—Gorham Munson in *Destinations* (1928), published after he introduced Toomer to the teachings of the Russian mystic George Ivanovich Gurdjieff (an earlier version appeared in *Opportunity* in 1925)—emphasized Toomer's "discriminating and analytical intellect" along with his "strong instincts, welling and deep and delicate emotions" in a published analysis of the book. See Munson, *Destinations*, 182.
29. Gregory, "Book Shelf," 374, 375.
30. Du Bois and Locke, "Literary Movement," 161, 162.
31. Cullen, *Caroling Dusk*, xi.

32. Frank, *Time Exposures*, 115–116.
33. Lears, "Courtship," 134. Marchand provides a more thorough analysis of the relationship between modernism, modernization, and advertising: "In a structural sense, the advertisers' claim to modernity rested on their role in pushing economic modernization further along its logical course of development. An economy organized for efficient production through economies of scale, rationalization of the working place, functional specialization, and a rapid and integrated flow of materials and communications also needed a high 'velocity of flow' in the purchase of goods by consumers. Ad creators were becoming highly specialized facilitators of that process" (Marchand, *Advertising*, 1–2).
34. Frank, *Time Exposures*, 111.
35. Quoted in Gilmer, *Liveright*, 91.
36. One early reviewer, Bruno Lasker, actually believed that "Jean Toomer" was one of Frank's pseudonyms. Referring to Lasker's review, several Southern newspapers (including the *Asheville Citizen*, the *Charlotte Observer*, the *Columbia Slate*, and the *Norfolk Virginian-Pilot*) carried an anonymous review on 18 November 1923 stating: "Boni and Liveright have two books dealing with the negro in the South—one, 'Holiday,' by Waldo Frank and the other 'Cane' by 'Jean Toomer.' A writer in the 'Survey,' we have not read the books ourselves, speaks of them as 'social studies' and suggests that, in reality, Jean Toomer is none other than Waldo Frank. Both books would seem to be in expressionist prose—a fact that means we never shall read them. There. That's prejudice for you!"
37. "I did see Liveright yesterday," Frank wrote Toomer in late 1923, "and he says he is going to enlist your help in reaching a possible Negro public for HOLIDAY" (JTP 3:84). *Our America* garnered a profit of just under $600. B&L lost money (over $2,500 by late 1927) on every other Frank title with the exception of *Virgin Spain* (1926). See Gilmer, *Liveright*, 242–243 n. 9.
38. In late 1923, *Broom* had roughly four thousand subscribers in Europe and the United States, a relatively sizeable number for an avant-garde journal; however, it never saw a profit, and when the final number (January 1924) was confiscated by U.S. postal censors, *Broom*'s editor, Matthew Josephson, pulled the plug on the little magazine. See Hoffman et al., *Little Magazine*, 105–106.
39. Although it is impossible to tell from Liveright's or Toomer's papers, particularly since many of the advertisements for *Cane* appear in tandem with other titles, according to my rough estimate, based on figures for titles with similar promotions and sales, the firm lost between $750 and $1,250 on Toomer.
40. I am very grateful to Frederik L. Rusch for sharing with me a Xerox copy of his personal copy of the dust jacket and title page of the 1927 reprint. He relates that "many years ago a friend of mine saw it in a barn sale or flea market in New England and bought it for me, for ten cents. Subsequently I informed Toomer's widow that I had it, and she denied it existed. She knew nothing about it" (letter to author, 4 June 1998). As far as I can tell, the 1927 reprint edition has disappeared from the literary historical landscape: it is not catalogued in any of the research libraries where one might expect to find it (including the Library of Congress, the Beinecke Library at Yale, the Moorland-Springarn Center at Howard, or the Schomburg Library in New York); nor is it listed in the *National Union Catalog*. This may be because Liveright was in the midst of changing the firm's name to Horace Liveright, Inc., and as usual B&L was flirting with financial collapse (which finally did occur in 1933). *Cane* is listed in the B&L trade list for 1927 (but not in 1926 or 1928); however, no mention is made of the fact that this is a reprint edition.
41. See West, *American Authors*, 28.

42. According to Gilmer (*Liveright*, 90), during the 1920s, B&L spent over one million dollars on advertisements in newspapers and magazines, not to mention billboards and radio. In 1925, one of the firm's best years, B&L sales approached one million dollars, but profits were less than ten thousand dollars. See Tebbel, *Golden Age*, 143.

References

Armstrong, John. "The Real Negro." 1923. Reprinted in *Studies in "Cane,"* ed. Frank Durham, 27–28. Columbus, Ohio: Charles E. Merrill, 1971.

Cullen, Countee, ed. *Caroling Dusk: An Anthology of Verse by Negro Poets*. New York: Harper, 1927.

Dardis, Tom. *Firebrand: The Life of Horace Liveright*. New York: Random House, 1995.

Du Bois, W.E.B., and Alain Locke. "The Younger Literary Movement." *Crisis* 27 (1924): 161–163.

Durham, Frank, ed. *The Merrill Studies in "Cane."* Columbus, Ohio: Charles E. Merrill, 1971.

Frank, Waldo [Search-Light, pseud.]. *Time Exposures*. New York: Boni and Liveright, 1926.

Gilmer, Walker. *Horace Liveright: Publisher of the Twenties*. New York: David Lewis, 1970.

Gregory, Montgomery. "Our Book Shelf." *Opportunity* 1 (1923): 374–375.

Hoffman, Frederick J., et al. *The Little Magazine: A History and a Bibliography*. Princeton, NJ: Princeton University Press, 1947.

Huggins, Nathan Irvin. *Harlem Renaissance*. New York: Oxford University Press, 1971.

Hughes, Langston. "The Negro Artist and the Racial Mountain." *The Nation* 122 (23 June 1926): 692–694.

Hutchinson, George. *The Harlem Renaissance in Black and White*. Cambridge, Mass.: Harvard University Press, 1996.

Josephson, Matthew. "Great American Novels." *Broom* 5 (1923): 178–180.

Larson, Charles R. *Invisible Darkness: Jean Toomer and Nella Larsen*. Iowa City: University of Iowa Press, 1993.

Lasker, Bruno. "Doors Opened Southward." 1923. Reprinted in *The Merrill Studies in "Cane,"* ed. Frank Durham, 29–30. Columbus, Ohio: Charles E. Merrill, 1971.

Lears, T. J. Jackson. *Fables of Abundance: A Cultural History of Advertising in America*. New York: Basic Books, 1994.

———. "Uneasy Courtship: Modern Art and Modern Advertising." *American Quarterly* 39 (1987): 133–154.

"Literary Vaudeville." Review of *Cane*, by Jean Toomer. *Springfield Republican*, December 1923. Quoted in *The Merrill Studies in "Cane,"* ed. Frank Durham, 34. Columbus, Ohio: Charles E. Merrill, 1971.

Littell, Robert. Review of *Cane*, by Jean Toomer. *New Republic* 37 (1923): 126.

Marchand, Roland. *Advertising the American Dream: Making Way for Modernity, 1920–1940*. Berkeley: University of California Press, 1985.

McClure, John. Review of *Cane*, by Jean Toomer. *Double Dealer* 6 (1924): 26–27.

Munson, Gorham. *Destinations: A Canvas of American Literature since 1900*. New York: J. H. Sears, 1928.

North, Michael. *The Dialect of Modernism: Race, Language, and Twentieth-Century Literature*. New York: Oxford University Press, 1994.

Review of *Cane*, by Jean Toomer. *Boston Transcript*, 15 December 1923, 8.

Rusch, Frederik L. Letter to author, 4 June 1998.

Tebbel, John. *The Golden Age Between Two Wars, 1920–1940*. Vol. 3 of *A History of Book Publishing in the United States*. New York: R. R. Bowker, 1978.

Toomer, Jean. *Cane*. Ed. Darwin T. Turner. 1923. Reprint New York: W. W. Norton, 1988.
———. Papers. Collection of American Literature, Yale University. Beinecke Rare Book and Manuscript Library, New Haven, Conn.
———. *Selected Essays in Literary Criticism*. Ed. Robert B. Jones. Knoxville: University of Tennessee Press, 1996.
———. *The Wayward and the Seeking: A Collection of Writings by Jean Toomer*. Ed. Darwin T. Turner. Washington, D. C.: Howard University Press, 1980.
West, James L. W. *American Authors and the Literary Marketplace since 1900*. Philadelphia: University of Pennsylvania Press, 1988.

Building the New Race

DIANA I. WILLIAMS

Jean Toomer's Eugenic Aesthetic

Let us do what we can to encourage the multiplication of the races best fitted to invent and conform to a high and generous civilization, and not, out of a mistaken instinct of giving support to the weak, prevent the incoming of strong and hearty individuals.

Francis Galton, *Hereditary Genius*

A country is like a huge stomach into which enters all kinds of materials, some unusable, some usable; and . . . it is nourished, it grows and develops by subjecting these materials to the processes of digestion and assimilation, rejecting unusable matters, incorporating usable materials into its structures and functions.

Jean Toomer, "The Americans"

JEAN TOOMER'S WRITINGS, particularly as they pertain to his racial identification, have sparked controversies among generations of critics. In these debates, understanding the man through his autobiographies, essays, personal and professional affiliations, family history, and the myriad ways he chose to live his life directly affects the critical consensus on his main work, *Cane*. Alice Walker summarized the problem Toomer posed to the African American literary tradition when she raised the issue of how to "keep [*Cane*'s] beauty, but let him go."[1] Recent criticism attempts to reclaim Toomer for the broader "American" literary canon by pointing out his overlapping personal and intellectual affiliations with both the Harlem Renaissance and the Lost Generation. This essay hopes to broaden the context even further by engaging in an analysis of Toomer and *Cane* in light of eugenics, the popular science of the day.

This investigation originated with my reading of George Hutchinson's article "Jean Toomer and American Racial Discourse," in which he reevaluates

Toomer in terms of what he calls his multiracial identity. Hutchinson criticizes recent scholars who have regarded Toomer's *Cane* as either a "*seminal* black text" (229) or as the escapist "response of one for whom black life . . . was too much to bear" (Gibson, "Denial," 179), arguing that such analyses spring from a "discourse that allows no room for a 'biracial' text . . . [or] identity" (Hutchinson, "Discourse," 228). Avoiding what he calls the "scapegoating" of "strange mixtures," he emphasizes Toomer's attempts to supplant traditional American racial ideology by utilizing an artist's rendering of the taboo "interracial subject" (227).

Hutchinson compellingly interprets *Cane* as a biracial text; that is, a work that attempts to formulate, through a focus on "mixed" characters, a racial consciousness beyond what he calls the "dualistic racial consciousness of 'white' and 'black' Americans" (231). Using Hutchinson's reading as a point of departure, I shall analyze Toomer's biraciality in terms of the constructed boundaries it affirms. I am particularly interested in investigating Hutchinson's claim that "Toomer dramatizes . . . another threshold of racial difference that he considers to be of a 'higher level' than the threshold between black and white . . . to give us a glimpse of what lies beyond" (228).

I think statements like this merit further scrutiny. Rather than viewing Toomer's work as progressive, I contend that his ideas about race have eugenic implications. There is a critical difference between terming the biracial character "neither black nor white" and labeling it "both black and white," a difference that is graphically demonstrated in *Cane*. Toomer's association, in his fiction, letters, and essays, of membership in the "new race" with superiority warrants analysis in terms of contemporary eugenic thought.

Toomer's rise to literary prominence coincided with the peak years of the Eugenics Movement. Francis Galton first coined the term "eugenics" in his 1869 work *Hereditary Genius*. Drawing on Darwin's theory of evolution, Galton suggested that "man might in part direct his own evolutionary future." His studies of the families of "eminent men" led to his belief in the practicality and advisability of "judicious marriages"—a form of artificial selection—as a means of producing "a highly gifted race."[2]

White supremacists and advocates of segregation in the United States incorporated Galton's theories, along with those of Social Darwinists such as Herbert Spencer, into their own racial ideology. Eugenicist reasoning reached its zenith in the 1920s with the 1922 formation of the Anglo-Saxon Clubs of America, whose goals were "the preservation and maintenance of Anglo-Saxon ideals and civilization in America . . . by the strengthening of Anglo-Saxon instincts, traditions and principles . . . by intelligent selection and exclusion of immigrants . . . [and] by the fundamental and final solutions of our racial problems in general, most especially of the Negro problem."[3]

American eugenicists' belief in the genetic heritability of traits such as criminality and feeblemindedness, which they associated with racialized others, immigrants, and the poor, led to their agitation for laws to protect the genetic constitutions of what they regarded as the "ruling race."[4] These measures, designed to protect the purity of Nordics, included the National Origins Quota Law of 1924; laws mandating involuntary sterilization; and such laws as the Virginia "Race Integrity Law" of 1924, which prohibited interracial marriage and required all Virginia residents to register their racial composition with the state (Kevles, 96–97; Smith, 4–5; 19–20).

The National Origins Quota Law, or Johnson-Reed Act, was primarily directed at curbing Eastern European immigration; it stemmed from a racialist view of these post-1840 immigrants that sharply distinguished them from "old-stock" or "Anglo-Saxon" whites. In this national movement (the Virginia example is somewhat unique), there was little emphasis on black race mixing because little was needed. Blacks did not constitute a major immigrant group, even though immigration from independent Western states (i.e., Latin America) remained unrestricted in 1924.[5] Moreover, blacks had been subject to legal segregation beginning in the 1890s; racial segregation was customary well before then.[6] Blackness was never far from the eugenicists' minds, however; one of the most outspoken eugenics advocates remarked that "we can assimilate only a small fraction of . . . other white races; and of the colored races practically none."[7]

Toomer's nonfiction writings bear startling affinities to the basic assumptions of eugenicist ideology—assumptions shared by diverse figures ranging from biologist Charles B. Davenport to Alexander Graham Bell, from birth control advocate Margaret Sanger to former president Theodore Roosevelt (Kevles, 44, 59, 94). Considering that some have read Toomer's work as rescuing the "mulatto" from notions of "degenerate mongrelization,"[8] my reading, which finds common ground between the Eugenics Movement and the author of *Cane*, may seem rather unorthodox. However, Toomer, like leading United States eugenicists, expressed great admiration for the writings of Herbert Spencer, calling him "one of my Gods."[9] He also went so far as to identify himself as a member of a group of people with superior qualities attributable to (or at least associated with) their genetic makeup. He differed from eugenicists in that he saw the keys to cultural superiority not in racial *purity* but in racial *mixture*.

When describing his own background, Toomer resisted the tendency prevailing in the United States to disparage race mixing. In a 1922 letter to

Claude McKay, he wrote that he was composed of "seven blood mixtures: French, Dutch, Welsh, Negro, German, Jewish, and Indian" (*Wayward,* 18 n). Toomer favored a conception of a "new race," a discrete entity: "We should not view it as part white, part black, and so on. . . . Water, though composed of two parts of hydrogen and one part of oxygen, is not hydrogen and oxygen; it is water, a new substance with a new form. . . . So the blendings of different racial strains . . . has given rise to a new race which is uniquely itself."[10] Having drawn this distinction between the "new race" and the "old" black and white races, Toomer suggested elsewhere that the other races, by their very "oldness," had no place in his unitary vision.

Toomer's complicated racial identity has been analyzed by a number of literary critics; it makes him difficult to fit neatly into the African American literary canon. Henry Louis Gates notes that "Toomer did not want so much to be white as most of us . . . would have it; rather he sought to be racially indeterminate."[11] Similarly, Toni Morrison writes that "race is unequivocally the overriding preoccupation of Jean Toomer's life: not Blackness or even being a Negro, but having (or having to have) a race at all."[12] Yet while *Cane* and Toomer's other writings suggest a yearning for racelessness, they also imply—and this is the main contention of this paper—that this raceless transcendence can only be attained by people of mixed racial descent.

Hutchinson shares the focus on Toomer's "mixed" identity; he suggests that Toomer was reacting specifically to the elimination of the "mulatto" category in the 1920 U.S. Census. Because this shift worked against the grain of Toomer's biracial aesthetic, he calls it the "greatest irony of Toomer's career." Hutchinson writes that "at the time modern racial discourse was taking its most definite shape, 'mulattoes'—because they threatened the racial bifurcation—'disappeared' as a group . . . while the 'one-drop rule' was defined in increasingly definite terms" (Hutchinson, "Discourse," 229).

One might dispute Hutchinson's periodization on the grounds that mulattoes as a group had been under attack for some time. For instance, the *Plessy v. Ferguson* case of 1896 indicated that a racially mixed background did not matter much where segregation law was concerned. Indeed, the 1893 death of Toomer's father's previous wife—a mixed-race woman of considerable wealth—has been attributed to hardships resulting from changes in segregation practices.[13] As a legal fiction, the "one drop rule" had stronger roots in slavery than in the Jim Crow era.

Nonetheless, transformations in race relations during the years leading up to the twenties did affect the "mulatto" category in general, and Toomer in particular. Barbara Foley has convincingly demonstrated that the increase in segregation of the black community in Washington, DC, affected the old, light-skinned elite to whom Toomer belonged.[14] In this sense, and for the reasons Hutchinson enumerates, it makes sense to examine both author and text for the ways they engage with this transformation.

Scholars such as Tim Brannan have remarked on the "strong feeling of regret throughout *Cane* for the disintegration of black culture and the black race in America,"[15] and Toomer himself cited such feelings as inspirations for his work. However, he wrote that *Cane* was "a song of an end": essentially an elegy.[16] Toomer regarded "black folk culture" as ephemeral, useful only as a museum piece. In his vision, the "new race" was predicated upon the destruction of the older races: "There must be death before there can be new life. . . . In America, the white race, the black race, the red race, the brown race must die before there can be a new race. They are dying. America is eating them . . . hypnotic labels and false beliefs . . . will die. They too must and will die."[17] In short, by identifying the "new race" with America's future, Toomer sought the engineering of a new society.

Critical attention to formal elements in *Cane* further undermines the argument that it celebrates a black aesthetic. Alice Walker's take on this issue was that *Cane* was Toomer's swan song "to the 'Negro' he felt dying in himself" as opposed to the swan song of traditional black oral culture (Walker, "Divided Life," 65). In a similar vein, Gates notes that in *Cane* Toomer presents "oral black culture as a counterpoint to the controlling consciousness of each discrete section of his carefully controlled book" (Gates, *Figures*, 211). Unlike Zora Neale Hurston's method of free indirect discourse, which allows the narrator to take on a black vernacular voice, Toomer's narrator/controlling consciousness is, depending on one's perspective, aracial, white, or mixed-race.[18] Hutchinson also finds that Toomer resisted writing in the black vernacular voice; he comments that Toomer followed Whitman's experiments with vernacular and thought of himself as "developing a 'classic American prose.' . . . Fascinated by the intercultural urban transformation of language, he resisted the romantic enshrinement of so-called authentic black folk speech."[19]

Given his belief that the old races could not endure, how did Toomer envision his "new race"? His autobiographies reveal some of its salient features. First, the idea of spiritual and interracial "fusion" is central. Toomer described his birth as an emergence "from a unitary world into the life of contrasts and opposites," contrasting the natural domain of the womb with the artificial constraints of the social world (*Wayward*, 16). Indeed, he characterized himself as an agent of unity, declaring that "I, together with all other I's, am the reconciler" of such opposites as white, black, night and day (54). Toomer seems to have viewed his mixed ancestry as a key element in this role as a reconciler and unifier of binary polarities.

Toomer's configuration of the members of the "new race" as privileged elites shaped another feature of his racial aesthetic. Speaking, for example, of his fellow high-school students in Washington, he wrote: "There was a flowering of a natural but transient aristocracy. . . . These people, whose racial strains were mixed and for the most part unknown, happened to find themselves in the colored group. They had a personal refinement, a certain inward culture and beauty . . . they were conscious that they were and had something in themselves. . . . They were my kind (85)."

Elsewhere, Toomer suggested that the new "aristocracy" transcended societal taboos, claiming that "a man of human aristocracy . . . knows that the taboos were made by his ancestors, men of his psychological class, not for him but for the herd" (47). His reading of Goethe's *Wilhelm Meister* influenced his conception of a natural aristocracy. His autobiography dates this reading as early 1920, only a few years before the publication of *Cane*, and suggests that it made a great impression on the mind of the young artist. He wrote that the text "seemed to gather together all the scattered parts of myself" and that it revealed his "real world . . . [of] the aristocrat of culture, of spirit and character, of ideas, of true nobility" (112). These passages reveal a great deal about Toomer's racial ideology. The hierarchy evoked by the word "aristocracy," coupled with his application of it to himself and other "mixed" persons, suggests that he viewed members of the "new race" as superior to members of "older races."

Toomer's attribution of aristocratic qualities to the "new race," along with his insistence on the "death" of the old race, strongly suggests the influence of contemporary eugenic thought. Yet although he wrote about the "races" in a biological sense, his work also focused on racial consciousness, which was shaped by—but not necessarily intrinsic to—a biologically "mixed" heritage. Hence, while he appreciated the color, economic class, and "mixed" status of his high-school peers, his main affinity to them lay in his perception of their awareness that "they were and had something in themselves." He reinforced this distinction in an unpublished essay, writing that "the real and main difference between this new American group and previous groups will be found, necessarily not in blood, but in consciousness."[20] Toomer distinguished himself from others not merely by saying that he was one of the first mixed-race persons in America or on earth; this was obviously untrue. Rather, he described himself as one of the "first conscious members" of the new race, "fashioned on no antecedent," and "a prototype for those to come" (16).[21]

In the United States context, it may be difficult to see an ideology of racial mixture as eugenic. Yet this is precisely the argument some have advanced regarding Latin American nationalist projects between 1920 and 1940. George Yúdice and Julie Taylor argue that Spencer's theory of Social Darwinism is "operative in many Latin American writings on *mestizaje*." Although conventional wisdom dictates that these new positive portrayals of the mestizo by Fernando Ortiz in Cuba, Gilberto Freyre in Brazil, and José Vasconcelos in Mexico represent progress, Yúdice and Taylor contend that the new concept of hybridization required "a principle of selection to limit it to those who have or can acquire 'superior faculties.' " In the works on which they focus, "*natural* selection gives way to *national* selection." Novelistic representations of *mestizaje* framed mixture as a norm, but one intended to maintain a (constantly whitening) racial "balance." Finally, according to Yúdice and Taylor, Social Darwinism continues to operate in these novels by "disqualifying certain characters as degenerate," even for being "failed attempts at transition or mixture."[22] As we shall see, this analysis closely parallels my reading of *Cane*.

An artist's work, particularly the work of a writer as accomplished as Jean Toomer, admittedly deserves more complex treatment than as a coded example of his or her ideological leanings. Toomer's modernist experiments with language result in a text that is far less transparent than its realist predecessors. He replaces explanation with juxtaposition of a number of symbols, and his characters struggle with how to deal with inarticulate experience. This ambiguity makes it difficult to present any particular reading as definitive. Gates writes that "it is *Cane*'s very ambiguity, of structure and of densely metaphorical lyricism, that continues to compel such a diversity of discursive responses" (Gates, *Figures*, 200).

Still, while recognizing the possibility of multiple readings of *Cane*, one finds overtones of eugenic struggle, particularly in light of Toomer's other writings and their resonance with contemporary racial thought. For instance, Toomer explicitly linked his racial ideology to his art in a passage in a letter to James Weldon Johnson: "In so far as general race or stock is concerned, they spring from the result of racial blendings here in America which have produced a new race or stock. We may call this stock the American stock or race. My main energies are devoted and directed towards the building of a life which will include all creative people of corresponding type."[23] This use of the word "building" is central to my argument that Toomer develops a eugenic aesthetic in *Cane*. The coming of the new race is not attained through a spiritual "birthing" or natural processes; rather, it is the product of deliberate engineering.

Toomer's efforts at the construction of the "new race" analogically manifest themselves as buildings in *Cane*. Toomer once thought of becoming an architect and described this desire as "the starting point of my interest in houses, churches, and cathedrals" (Toomer, *Wayward*, 49). In her commentary on the use of women's bodies as mediating forms in *Cane*, Janet Whyde notes that Becky's house, the building from which her mixed-race children emerge, "replaces her body."[24] Significantly, after the mixed-race children appear and leave the town, shouting, "Godam the white folks; godam the niggers," Becky's house/body collapses.[25] Having served its purpose in constructing the "new race," it can be discarded.

The analogy between buildings and women's bodies as mediators between the old and new races is central to *Cane* and is suggested through a network of figures that represent the collapse between buildings and birth. The exhortation of "Blood-Burning Moon," in which both the "white" and "black" protagonists are murdered, is to "come out that fact'ry door," which suggests the birth canal (Toomer, *Cane*, 37). Dorris of the "lemon-colored face" steps from the stage door in "Theater" (55). The "lemon-faced" Kabnis emerges from "the Hole" of the cellar. The "milk-white," racially mixed Esther appears to transcend the "hideous" world of the "clean-muscled, magnificent, black-skinned Negro," King Barlo, when she "steps out" of Nat Bowle's house (26–27). Paul of "Bona and Paul" is frequently compared to the moon in ways that alternately refer to his "dark blood" (74) or to his physical appearance, as when Bona says, "He is a harvest moon. He is an autumn leaf. He is a nigger" (72). The association of this "moon" image with the "new race" figure of Paul lends special significance to the "omen" of "the full moon in the great door" in "Blood-Burning Moon" (36). It, too, suggests the birth of a new race.

In a similar vein, Toomer uses buildings to signify a bygone mentality or prison. Rhobert, who refuses to commit the "sin" of drawing his head "out of live stuffing in [the] dead house," is weighed down and eventually drowns under its weight and pressure (42–43). In "Box Seat," the house operates as both the physical theater and the collective psyche of the "bolted masses" inside it (65). Rejected at the start of the story by Muriel, a woman with "hair like an Indian's" and cheeks of "flushed ginger," Dan, another racially ambiguous character, contemplates pulling down the building's girders (61).

Significantly, this evokes images of Samson, a biblical character of unusual strength. A Nazarite, Samson twice desired marriage with women of the Philistines, who were not, as his parents put it, "our people" (Judges 14: 2–3). Spurned by Delilah, the second object of his desire, and eventually captured and imprisoned by the Philistines, Samson's final act was to pull down the pillars of their temple (Judges 16: 27–31). Samson died destroying the Philistines, but Dan imagines that if he pulls down the house, "hid by the smoke and dust Dan Moore will arise" (Toomer, *Cane*, 68). Dan is not alone, however; mention of "the mutter of powerful underground races" at the beginning of the story suggests that more will follow (60).

Textual traces of eugenic struggle in *Cane* are not limited to the "building" trope. When Muriel asks him what he is killing, Dan replies, "What's weak in both of us" (63), supporting Alice Walker's comment that *Cane* was Toomer's "good-bye to the 'Negro' he felt dying in himself."[26] A similar image suggesting hybrid vigor is effected in "Bona and Paul" when Art talks about Paul's "dark blood": "Doesn't get anywhere unless you boost it. You've got to keep it going" (74).

The "immobile" character of Father John is described in "Kabnis" as a "bust in black walnut" (106–107); a living relic of slavery, he is left in the cellar below Halsey's shop by the newly awakened Kabnis. His "black" skin, in contrast to some of Toomer's more ambiguous phenotypic descriptions, bars him from any hope of becoming a member of the "new race" and hence any place in the future. Assuming that Father John's message of sin is directed at him, Kabnis cries angrily, "Th whole world is a conspiracy t sin, especially in America, an against me. I'm the victim of their sin. I'm what sin is. Does [Father John] look like me? Have you ever heard him say th things youve heard me say?" (116). Lewis views Father John not only as a "symbol" and "spirit," but "*flesh*" of the past (108; my emphasis). Driving this point home, Kabnis (with whom Toomer identified) says to Father John, "Youre dead already" (114).[27]

In contrast, Kabnis exhorts the "olive"-skinned Carrie to "come away" from the old man, arguing that she "shouldnt be down here" (116). Similarly, the narrator invites Avey to be part of a special group: "I talked, beautifully I thought, about an art that would be born, an art that would open the way for women the likes of her" (48). But Avey does not heed him, and he notices that "she did not have the gray crimson-splashed beauty of the dawn" (49).

In "Kabnis," as in "Blood-Burning Moon," Toomer symbolically jettisons both the "black" and the "white" past and present. Mr. Ramsay, a "shriveled, bony white man," serves the same oppressive function as Dan's or Rhobert's "house" (101). Around Ramsay, Kabnis "feels stifled . . . the whole white South weighs down upon him. The pressure is terrific" (102). A similar gesture occurs in "Esther" when Toomer writes that "white and black men loafing on the corner hold no interest for her" (22).

Indeed, "Kabnis" contains the clearest manifestations of the eugenic aesthetic. Lewis, the "copper-colored man" from the North, is "what a stronger Kabnis might have been, and in an odd faint way resembles him" (97). When Halsey quotes Lewis's talking "about a stream whats dammed has got t cut loose somewheres," it resonates on multiple levels, suggesting both a dammed stream ready to burst its banks and a stream of damned—or racially tainted—blood. Lewis, then, speaks for the "new race," which is characterized by a "stream" of mixed, and therefore (in Toomer's day) damned blood (91). Halsey, who is Carrie's brother and hence also racially mixed, finds Lewis's prophecy compelling, saying, "That sounds good. I know th feelin myself" (91). Carrie is similarly drawn to Lewis, who, like Kabnis, sees "new race" potential in her and "wants to take her North with him" (104). When she initially looks into his "Christ-eyes," she "fearlessly . . . loves into them." However, memories of the "sin-bogies of respectable southern colored folks" cause her to back away (103). Tied to the care of the old "black" man and rooted to the Southern soil, Carrie and Halsey can only experience transient flashes of "new race" consciousness.

Yet Kabnis, on the brink of awakening, is different. When Lewis's and Kabnis's eyes meet, they experience a fleeting moment of mutual recognition and desire: "[Lewis's] eyes turn to Kabnis. In the instant of their shifting, a vision of the life they are to meet. Kabnis, a promise of a soil-soaked beauty; uprooted, thinning out. Suspended a few feet above the soil whose touch would resurrect him. Arm's length removed from him whose will to help . . . There is a swift *intuitive interchange of consciousness*. Kabnis has a sudden need to rush into the arms of this man. His eyes call, 'Brother' " (98; my emphasis). This transcendent instance foreshadows Kabnis's eventual transformation into a member of the "new race." But I propose that Kabnis and Lewis's "brotherhood" comes at the expense of the violent rejection of malignant "others," those who, for reasons of phenotype or consciousness, are unable to participate in Lewis's racial plan.[28] In the final scene, when Kabnis ascends the cellar stairs, leaving Carrie and Father John behind, he is carrying a bucket of "dead coals," arguably symbols of the dead black people whose culture *Cane* attempted to eulogize.

Toomer's racial ideology displayed a striking resistance to the prevailing notion that "amalgamation" led to "degeneracy." However, his challenge to the ideology of "racial purity" movements of his age incorporated the basic tenets of eugenic thought.[29] Toomer's eugenicist tendencies lay in his association of a racially ambiguous or visibly racially mixed status—combined with a consciousness of racial transcendence—with survival in *Cane* and with an aristocractic elite in his nonfiction writing. It should not be surprising, then, that in 1929 he published, in a volume entitled *Problems of Civilization*, an essay advocating a eugenic solution entitled "Race Problems and Modern Society."[30] He concluded the essay with the following remarks:

> No description of the situation in America is faithful to the entire scene, which fails to notice and consider the positive possibilities contained in the emergence of a large number of the type of people

> who cannot be classified as separatist and racial. These people are *synthetic* and truly human. . . . There is enough knowledge of biology and genetics to enable us to make a . . . start at solving the organic problems of race. . . . Stripped to its essentials, the positive aspect of the race problem can be expressed thus: how to bring about a *selective fusion* of the racial and cultural factors of America, in order that the best possible stock and culture may be produced. This implies the need and desirability of breeding on the basis of biological fitness. . . . It means that the process of racial and cultural amalgamation should be guided by these standards.[31]

Although the word "mulatto" was expunged from the census after 1920, neither "mulattoes" nor the racial mixing they symbolized "disappeared" immediately from the national racial discourse, as George Hutchinson claims. Hutchinson's analysis is predicated on the assumption that both in the society of the 1920s and among modern literary critics the "biracial character" and the sex that produced it are repressed and silenced; to Hutchinson, Toomer's *Cane* represents the transgression of that silence. He contends: "Beyond all tragedies of the South lies the repression of 'natural' desires, repression of life itself by conventions governing all human relations. . . . When desire is freed (as segregation is dismantled), it will cross racial boundaries without violence, embarrassment, or perversion" (Hutchinson, "Discourse," 232, 234). While stopping short of invalidating Hutchinson's provocative comments on the maintenance of racial boundaries in the United States, this paper takes a different approach to the question of interracial sex and the mulatto complex. Michel Foucault writes that "rather than assuming a generally acknowledged repression," students of sexuality should begin by investigating the "positive" and expressive mechanisms that "produce knowledge, multiply discourse, induce pleasure and generate power."[32] Jean Toomer began his writing career at the height of the Eugenics Movement, during years that witnessed what Foucault calls "a proliferation of discourses concerned with sex" and in which mainstream intellectuals shared many of the assumptions of career eugenicists (Foucault, *Sexuality*, 18; Jacobson, *Whiteness*, 87–88). I submit that his writing participated in the movement's basic premises about the importance of racial exclusion more than it challenged them.

In Hutchinson's interpretation, Toomer's life and writing display resistance to the powerful repression of the dominant racial discourse. However, as Foucault writes, "Where there is power, there is resistance, and yet, or rather consequently, this resistance is never in a position of exteriority in relation to power" (Foucault, *Sexuality*, 95). Acknowledging that occasional "radical ruptures" occur, Foucault maintains: "But more often one is dealing with mobile and transitory points of resistance, producing cleavages in a society that shift about, fracturing unities and effecting regroupings, furrowing across individuals themselves, cutting them up and remolding them, marking off irreducible regions in them, in their bodies and minds" (96). Instead of freeing desire from the repression of social convention, Toomer sought to generate it to different ends. His resistance proved just as controlling as the ideology of those he appeared to challenge. In Toomer's ideology, sexuality is not represented in terms of liberation, the converse of repression; rather, it is deployed and administered for what Toomer believed was the benefit of America: the creation and legitimation of a "new race."

Notes

1. Alice Walker, "The Divided Life of Jean Toomer," in *In Search of Our Mothers' Gardens* (New York: Harcourt Brace Jovanovich, 1983), 65.
2. Kevles, *Eugenics*, 3–4, 12.
3. Smith, *Eugenic Assault*, 1–5, 13, 17.
4. Jacobson, *Whiteness*, 78–85.
5. Christopher Mitchell, "Immigration and U.S. Foreign Policy toward the Caribbean, Central America, and Mexico," in *Western Hemisphere Immigration and United States Foreign Policy*, ed. Christopher Mitchell (University Park: Pennsylvania State University Press, 1992), 11.
6. See C. Vann Woodward, *The Strange Career of Jim Crow* (New York: Oxford University Press, 1974). Woodward notes that segregation laws became widespread after 1890.
7. Harry Laughlin, cited in Jacobson, *Whiteness*, 84.
8. Bradley, "Looking," 689.
9. Toomer, *Wayward*, 102.
10. Toomer, "Americans," 108.
11. Gates Jr., *Figures*, 208.
12. Toni Morrison, cited in Gates, *Figures*, 221–222.
13. Kent Anderson Leslie, *Woman of Color, Daughter of Privilege: Amanda America Dickson, 1849–1893* (Athens: University of Georgia Press, 1995), 120–132.
14. Foley, "Toomer's Washington," 289–321.
15. Brannan, "Interpretations," 167.
16. "I realized with deep regret, that the spirituals . . . would be certain to die out. . . . The folk-spirit was walking in to die on the modern desert. That spirit was so beautiful. Its death was so tragic. . . . *Cane* was a swan-song" (Toomer, *Wayward*, 123).
17. Toomer, "Americans," 107.
18. Gates Jr., *Monkey*, 194.
19. Hutchinson, "Whitman," 210.
20. Toomer, "Americans," 109–110.
21. This bears comparison to Galton's notion of "sports": "In these, a new character suddenly makes its appearance in a particular individual, causing him to differ distinctly from his parents and from others of his race. . . . Here . . . a new point of departure has somehow come into existence . . . and consequently a real step forward has been made in the course of evolution" (Galton, *Genius*, xix).
22. Julie Taylor and George Yúdice, "Mourning and *Mestizaje:* Working Through Loss

in Transculturation" (paper presented at Center for Literary and Cultural Studies, Harvard University, Cambridge, Mass., February 18, 1998).
23. Jean Toomer to James Weldon Johnson, July 11, 1930, Rusch, *Toomer Reader,* 106.
24. Whyde, "Mediating Forms," 45.
25. Toomer, *Cane*, 8–9.
26. Walker, "Divided Life," 65.
27. In a letter to Waldo Frank, Toomer wrote that "Kabnis is *me*" (Toomer, *Cane*, 151).
28. This is also Toomer's racial plan. Darwin Turner notes that "Lewis resembles the self-portrait Toomer sometimes created in his fiction and drama" (Toomer, *Cane*, 91 n. 7). Turner also contends that "Toomer uses Lewis as a touchstone—that is, the reader is expected to accept Lewis' response to each character as the correct assessment of that individual's merit" (97 n. 4). Significantly, he further suggests a comparison between Lewis's attitude toward Carrie and the narrator's attitude toward Fern, an inarticulate biracial character in an earlier sketch (104 n. 1). Toomer's explicit identification with Kabnis (see note 27) and his implicit identification with Lewis are compatible if one chooses to view both characters as figures for Toomer at different stages in his life.
29. For an example of the collaboration between American white supremacists and Marcus Garvey, see Smith, *Eugenic Assault*, 23–35. The phenomenon demonstrates that one needed not be white to buy into the racial purity vogue.
30. For a view similar to the one Toomer expressed in "Race Problems and Modern Society," see Lindberg, "Raising *Cane*," 69.
31. Toomer, "Race Problems," 103–111. *Problems in Civilization* also contains essays by Ellsworth Huntington, Whiting Williams, Charlotte Perkins Gilman, and Thomas D. Eliot—most of which are concerned with eugenics. "Race Problems" has been recently republished in Robert B. Jones, ed., *Jean Toomer: Selected Essays and Literary Criticism* (Knoxville: University of Tennessee Press, 1996).
32. Foucault, *Sexuality*, 73.

References

PRIMARY SOURCES

Galton, Francis. *Hereditary Genius: An Inquiry into Its Laws and Consequences*. 1869. Reprint, London: Macmillan, 1925.

Rusch, Frederik L., ed. *A Jean Toomer Reader: Selected Unpublished Writings*. New York: Oxford University Press, 1993.

Toomer, Jean. "The Americans." In *A Jean Toomer Reader: Selected Unpublished Writings*, ed. Frederik L. Rusch, 106–110. New York: Oxford University Press, 1993.

———. *Cane*. 1923. Reprint, ed. Darwin T.Turner. New York: Norton, 1988.

———. "Race Problems and Modern Society." In *Problems in Civilization: Man and His World*. Vol. 7, ed. Baker Brownell, 67–111. New York: Van Nostrand, 1929.

———. *The Wayward and the Seeking: A Collection of Writings by Jean Toomer*. Ed. Darwin T. Turner. Washington, D.C.: Howard University Press, 1980.

SECONDARY SOURCES

Bradley, David. "Looking Behind *Cane*." *Southern Review* 21, 3 (1985): 682–694.

Brannan, Tim. "Up From the Dusk: Interpretations of Jean Toomer's 'Blood-Burning Moon.' " *Pembroke Magazine* 8 (1977): 167–172.

Byrd, Rudolph P. Foreword to *Essentials*, by Jean Toomer. Athens: University of Georgia Press, 1991.

Foley, Barbara. "Jean Toomer's Washington and the Politics of Class: From 'Blue Veins' to Seventh-Street Rebels." *Modern Fiction Studies* 42, 2 (1996): 289–321.

Foucault, Michel. *The History of Sexuality: An Introduction*. Vol. 1. Trans. Robert Hurley. 1978. Reprint, New York: Vintage Books, 1990.
Gates, Henry Louis Jr. *Figures in Black: Words, Signs, and the "Racial" Self*. New York: Oxford University Press, 1987.
———. *The Signifying Monkey: A Theory of African-American Literary Criticism*. New York: Oxford University Press, 1988.
Gibson, Donald B. "Jean Toomer: The Politics of Denial." In *The Politics of Literary Expression: A Study of Major Black Writers*, ed. Donald B. Gibson. Westport, Conn.: Greenwood, 1981.
Hutchinson, George. "Jean Toomer and American Racial Discourse." *Texas Studies in Literature and Language* 35, 2 (1993): 226–250.
———. "The Whitman Legacy and the Harlem Renaissance." In *Walt Whitman: The Centennial Essays*, ed. Ed Folsom, 201–216. Iowa City: University of Iowa Press 1994.
Jacobson, Matthew Frye. *Whiteness of a Different Color: European Immigrants and the Alchemy of Race*. Cambridge, Mass.: Harvard University Press, 1998.
Kevles, Daniel J. *In the Name of Eugenics: Genetics and the Uses of Human Heredity*. New York: Alfred A. Knopf, 1985.
Lindberg, Kathryne V. "Raising *Cane* on the Theoretical Plane: Jean Toomer's Racial Personae." In *Cultural Difference and the Literary Text: Pluralism and the Limits of Authenticity in North American Literatures*, ed. Winfried Siemerling and Katrin Schwenk, 49–74. Iowa City: University of Iowa Press, 1996.
McKay, Nellie Y. *Jean Toomer, Artist: A Study of His Literary Life and Work, 1894–1936*. Chapel Hill: University of North Carolina Press, 1984.
Smith, J. David. *The Eugenic Assault on America: Scenes in Red, White, and Black*. Fairfax, Va.: George Mason University Press, 1993.
Whyde, Janet. "Mediating Forms: Narrating the Body in Jean Toomer's *Cane*." *Southern Literary Journal* 26, 1 (1993): 42–53.
Williamson, Joel. *New People: Miscegenation and Mulattoes in the United States*. 1980. Reprint, New York: New York University Press, 1984.

The Reception of *Cane* in France

MICHEL FABRE

OF FRENCH ANCESTRY on his mother's side, Jean Toomer occasionally recalled his French connections with a degree of pride, as when he wrote to Mrs. Beardsley in 1930: "I am of French and English descent . . . ," but he continued, even more proudly, "I have been associated in New York and Paris with some of the men who have been trying to bring about a renaissance in American art and life."[1] His primary concern was with modernity and avant-garde experimentation rather than with inquiry into his multiracial heritage. Yet when the author of *Cane* first sailed for France in July 1924, he did not go there to meet the literary avant-garde at the Closerie des Lilas or the Lost Generation at Sylvia Beach's bookshop, Shakespeare & Company. He specifically intended to stay at the Institute for the Harmonious Development of Man, which Gurdjieff had recently opened at the former priory of Avon, on the outskirts of Fontainebleau. He remained in France from mid-July to September 1924 but, apparently, hardly left the priory. Only Claude McKay mentioned that he had met Toomer for five minutes in Montparnasse and "could not like him in that awful atmosphere at the Dome."[2]

The first mention of Toomer ever printed in France can be found in an article entitled "La jeune poésie africo-américaine" in *Les Continents* of September 1, 1924. It was provided by Alain Locke to the Martinican writer René Maran, who coedited the newspaper and published a translation of Locke's presentation of the New Negro movement under that title. The offerings of recent African American poets were only exemplified by Countee Cullen's "The Dance of Love," but McKay, Toomer, and Hughes were mentioned. In December 1925, an article by Maran, "Le mouvement négro-littéraire aux

Etats-Unis," came out in the better-known magazine *Vient de paraître*, but did not mention Toomer.[3] In March 1926, a brief mention of James Weldon Johnson's *The Book of American Spirituals* appeared in *Le Mercure de France*.[4] In October 1927, Harold Salemson mentioned *The Autobiography of an Ex-Colored Man* most favorably.[5] But there still was no word about *Cane*.

During his second stay in France, from May 29 to October 16, 1926, Toomer was less exclusively preoccupied with Gurdjieff, more willing to meet people and see places. This was also the case when he returned to sojourn in France from mid-May to mid-July 1927. This time he visited Paris frequently enough and probably appeared at Shakespeare & Company, where *Cane* was among the books for sale and lending.

In 1928, the Alsacian Eugène Jolas, editor of *Transition*, the review of the "Lost Generation," prepared an *Anthologie de la nouvelle poésie américaine* for Editions Kra. Cullen, Hughes, McKay, and Toomer were represented in the anthology, each by one poem preceded by a brief introduction. Toomer's notice specified that he was born in the South and was "probably the most gifted poet of his race. The publication of *Cane*, a collection of stories or prose poems reveal[ed] his great originality and imagination." He live[d] in utter solitude away from literary circles.[6] "Harvest Song" was the poem selected by Jolas.

A few French academics who occasionally lectured in the United States helped discover the New Negro writers. Professor Régis Michaud provided only a limited, yet interesting, view of the movement in his *Littérature américaine*: America was the home of the blues, jazz, and spirituals, characterized as "the revenge of the blacks in poetry and art." At the dawn of the American poetic renaissance, Negro poetry brimmed over with rhythm and color: Paul Laurence Dunbar, W.E.B. Du Bois, William S. Braithwaite, and James Weldon Johnson made up the established generation. Countee Cullen, Langston Hughes, the "errant bard" Claude McKay, Jean Toomer, Joseph Cotter, Jessie Fauset, Gwendolyn Bennett, Jeffrey Hays, and Lewis Alexander, among others of the new generation, expressed the grudges and hopes of their race. They were rather indiscriminately stereotyped as primitive, somewhat pagan, imaginative, and musical "natural" talents:

> They are spontaneous singers whose primitive strain has not been drained by the white man's culture. Ironical and throbbing, those black bards tell the regrets, rancors, and aspirations of their race (so pathetically encapsulated by Eugene O'Neill in *Emperor Jones*). They celebrate their past greatness: Egypt, Ethiopia, Abyssinia. . . . They worship the black Venus unabashedly. They smile a wide smile at suffering and the ugliness of the whites. A strange fragrance of

> paganism hovers over their baptism into Christianity; and what luxuriant imagery, what lively rhythms![7]

The critic may have alluded to the mixture of paganism and Christianity exemplified by "Georgia Dusk." Yet he more probably followed suit with the primitivism in vogue at the time, and he did not know of Toomer's existential dilemma, his quest for a synthesis, his interest in the effects of urbanization upon African Americans.

It was Professor Franck Louis Schoell who really introduced Toomer's work to the Paris readers of *Les Nouvelles littéraires*. An erstwhile teacher in U.S. colleges, who had witnessed the Red Summer of 1919 in Chicago and knew W.E.B. Du Bois, Schoell had a firsthand knowledge of the situation of African Americans. Somewhat unexpectedly, Schoell described *Cane* as a novel. In his favorable, largely descriptive review of *Cane*, Schoell extolled Toomer's artistry and delicate handling of language by contrasting him with other black writers (possibly Claude McKay) who, he claimed, were characterized by "primitive impetuosity" and exaggeration. Only in the case of Toomer was "the novelist the true essence, and the black man the accident."[8]

This characterization also served as an introduction to Toomer's story "Lune embrasée, Lune de sang" (a translation of "Blood-Burning Moon"), which had been recommended by Schoell. The emphasis could now be placed on Toomer as an experimental writer in prose, not a spokesman for his race, although his story was restricted to the Southern setting. But the French readers, eager for documents on Negro life, were unaware of Toomer's modernistic experiments. They apparently remained blind to his transposition of the antiphonal nature of the Southern black idiom. This contrast between an individual voice and a collective expression, which acts as a refrain, confers a musical quality to the interplay of the folk tradition of communal wisdom and the voice of the solitary modernist in the constitution of meaning. In "Blood-Burning Moon," the first paragraph hints at the moon as an omen against which women improvise a song, and the song turns out to be prophetic. This is no mere juxtaposition; the relationship is complementary. The modernist narrative thus appears as an explicitation of the folk expression. But no French critic addressed this aspect of Toomer's writing at the time.

Franck L. Schoell then published "La Renaissance nègre aux USA" in *La Revue de Paris* (January 1, 1929). This detailed study examined topics familiar to Toomer: the situation of African Americans after World War I, their urbanization and the growth of a middle class, the development of the black press, and the vogue of Negro art. The initial section dealt with the vogue of African art and American jazz. The second focused on literature about, as well as by, the Negro, represented notably by Hughes, McKay, and Cullen, who were quoted. Toomer's *Cane,* this time, was characterized as "a most curious . . . collection of tales."[9] This essay was included in Schoell's *U.S.A: Du côté des blancs et du côté des noirs*, published that same year by Honoré Champion in Paris. It reached a much wider audience.

But whatever interest there was in Toomer was soon superseded by the greater exposure of Langston Hughes and Claude McKay. Schoell himself sent "Un poète nègre: Langston Hughes" to the *Revue politique et littéraire*. A rather inaccurate biographical notice preceded the translations of six poems: "Cabaret," "Jeune Danseuse," "Lamentation pour les hommes au teint foncé," "La peur," "Moi aussi," and "Une mère à son fils." It was hoped that Hughes would not confine himself to racial themes, "the source of which would soon become dry."[10]

Probably as a consequence of having met French avant-garde writers or due to the recommendation of Waldo Frank, Toomer contributed a "Letter from America" to the first issue of the French surrealist/modernist review *Bifur* in May 1929. He did not deal with race. He reflected on the election of Herbert Hoover and the spreading prevalence of business over the American government. Soon America would be synonymous with business, whether it be in literature, art, professions, or any form of culture. He enjoyed the creativity of America and the vitality of Chicago, where tendency of Americans to discard objects quickly, not to become attached to what they built, was manifest. But he regretted it: "This is our vice: we do not feel attached to the things we build. . . . We throw more and more things into the trash can. . . . We tend to respect ourselves and others less and less."[11] Thus, the factual, "hard boiled" realists did not believe in anything except the feeling of power and pleasure provided by the earning and spending of money.[12] In literature, this "factualism" subjugated the younger generation and produced the literal, so-called realistic type of novel. Toomer noted that Waldo Frank had attempted to counter this tendency by resorting to symbolism, but he felt that Frank's position would have been stronger if his presentation was more simple and direct. Indeed, in *Rediscovering America,* Frank's style blocked his message. Toomer concluded that there had been a time when America was the proud champion of social idealism, a country of independence, equality, and freedom. But it was now a land of business. Yet he remarked:

> This change is no defeat of spirituality; among other things, it simply means that human values and the deep, moving and growing forces of life have definitively become a thing of the minority.[13]

Life itself was no longer the business of the masses but had become the concern of individuals (possibly an elite):

> I expect to see these very circumstances generate solidarity between individuals. I believe it will produce a greater and more efficient sense of personal responsibility. I expect to see the domination of business generate the spurt of a potent mode of life.[14]

The notice introducing Toomer, at the end of the issue, was probably borrowed from Eugène Jolas's anthology: once again he was hailed as "the most gifted poet of his race," reportedly living by himself in a New York luxury hotel or in the streets of Chicago. That he was not praised as an innovative modernist is somewhat surprising because the editor in chief of *Bifur*, Georges Ribemont-Dessaignes, was said to "expect anarchy in the midst of revolution"[15] and because the review boasted writers like William Carlos Williams, James Joyce, Ramon Gomez de la Serna, Bruno Barilli, and Gottfried Benn among its foreign advisers. Besides, Victor Llona, a specialist of American literature, had translated Toomer's piece. The board of *Bifur* should have been able to characterize Toomer's writing in terms of their own aesthetic concerns, but they probably did not know enough about him.

In June 1929, Toomer sailed for France again, but there is no information about his life there until his return in the fall of that year. The critic André Lévinson mentioned him in "Aframérique," an article in *Les Nouvelles littéraires*, but he mostly used Toomer as a foil to attack McKay's perspective in *Home to Harlem*. Lévinson tended to deny the Negro any great intelligence. Expressing surprise at the "perfect balance" achieved in *Porgy* by DuBose Heyward, whom he possibly believed to be black, he wrote: "The art of the primitive is intense, colorful, direct; it is also superficial, monotonous and short-winded." Jean Toomer, Eric Walrond, and Countee Cullen were merely mentioned in this article, which was largely devoted to Claude McKay's *Home to Harlem*, paternalistically reduced to a picture of the "debauchery of Harlem life."[16]

In "De Harlem à la Canebière," a rather adverse review of McKay's *Banjo*, which was then being published in the United States, André Lévinson again referred to Toomer as a model. Deprecating McKay's tone of revolt and "primitive racial vainglory," Lévinson contrasted Toomer's *Cane* as a literary embodiment of the "victory of spirit over instinct" with *Banjo*, which he termed "an apology for the abdication of the intellect."[17]

Meanwhile, one L. F. introduced Langston Hughes again in *Les Cahiers libres*. The author stressed the original, powerful talent of the young poet and his role as a representative of his race. "Spiritual power and the power to dream" were said to be "magnificently imprinted on the face and the poetry of Langston Hughes."[18]

According to all evidence, Toomer's *Cane* was really known only by a few

English-speaking individuals in France. Even Paulette Nardal, the racially committed Martinican student of English, did not grant Toomer any space in her *La Revue du monde noir*. In the first issue, in 1930, a description of a reading by Grace Walker mentioned her reciting poems by Cullen, McKay, Hughes, and Toomer, chosen in such a way as to highlight "the artistic temperament of these different Negro poets, distinctive in inspiration and style";[19] but the author did not indicate what these differences were, nor which poems were read. The following year, Nardal's own essay, "Eveil de la conscience de race," dealt with many topics: the African American slave narratives; the dialect poetry of Paul Laurence Dunbar; the influence of W. S. Braithwaite; the new pride embodied in the poetry of McKay and Hughes; and the theories of Marcus Garvey. She claimed that African American revolt was more explicit than that of black French people, as exemplified by the New Negro movement: "Though they are not of pure African origin either, the deliberate scorn with which they have always been treated by white Americans incited them to seek for social and cultural pride in their African past."[20] But no mention was made of Toomer.

Neither did Etienne Léro use Toomer as an example in his diatribe "Misère d'une poésie" in the one and only issue of *Légitime Défense* (1932). The Martinican iconoclast mentioned the poetry of Langston Hughes and Claude McKay very favorably. An excerpt from *Banjo* was used to criticize assimilated French West Indians, but Toomer, supposing that Léro knew about him (which is doubtful), could not serve as a mentor since he was not opposed to cultural assimilation.

During World War II, the Negritude poet Aimé Césaire provided a major essay on the New Negro movement in his "Introduction à la poésie nègre américaine" in the July 1941 issue of *Tropiques*, printed in Fort-de-France, Martinique. According to Césaire, African American poetry speaks in the name of millions of the "most wretched humans," which explains its closeness to original man, its ability to sympathize; it boasts no beautiful images but a deep, self-conscious drive toward art: frenzy and ancestral paganism reach for a form of mysticism but also for poetry as the escape of people who have been wounded for centuries. "Black lyricism remains short of grandeur"; it flows tempestuously like a torrent and remains devoid of artifice; its greatness lies in its ability to remain alive, "to open onto the whole of man."[21] Césaire paid tribute to Langston Hughes and to Sterling Brown (whose feeling for the folk he shared and on whose work he had written his master's thesis), but also to Jean Toomer and James Weldon Johnson: he stated that all of those poets had rehabilitated the everyday and commonplace Negro. Translations of Toomer's "Harvest Song" and of poems by James Weldon Johnson followed the essay.

One must wait until the Liberation of France to see Toomer's poetry receive close attention again, from the pen of the African poet, French *député*, and cofounder of the Négritude movement Léopold Sédar Senghor. In his brief introduction in *Poésie 45*, "Trois poètes négro-américains," Senghor begins with noting that Negro American poetry has been circulating all around the world where it has often been considered as a rejuvenating force by tired Westerners, yet one has not stressed sufficiently that it started essentially with the spirituals, the work songs, and the blues. Senghor posits as a principle that song and poetry are "the same thing for the Negro, whether he lives in Africa or in America." He finds proof of it in the fact that, in Negro African languages, the same word was used to designate "song" and "poem." But he is content with reiterating the affirmation that "it is no different with the American Negro," as shown in spiritual inspiration, "when the soul's strivings bring forth a fresh outburst of poetry."[22]

Senghor is not dealing here with folk poetry, although the "literati" often derive inspiration from it. Before Paul Laurence Dunbar, "learned" poetry was imitative of the Western literary tradition, and Senghor wants to consider only the New Negro poets, whose leader, Langston Hughes, explains that the Negro Renaissance is no longer a question of inferiority, superiority, or antagonism but of fruitful difference.

Senghor even paradoxically claims that, although the personality of the race took shape and asserted itself in the African past, slavery further enriched it by making it deeper. The question now is to express this personality authentically. And he quotes the well-known claim from Hughes in "The Negro Artist and the Racial Mountain" that Negro poets must express the personality of their race without shame or fear.

In his attempt to define the characteristics of this poetry, Senghor first mentions that, like its African counterpart, it is essentially devoid of artifice (Senghor uses the French word *non-sophistiqué* since *sophistiqué* does not mean "intelligent" but "overly complicated"). The second distinctive feature of Negro poetry is its aural/oral character and musicality: this poetry is made to be sung or recited, not to be read in silence. Hence the importance of "Negro rhythm, so despotic in spite of its apparent freedom." Hence the importance of its music that Senghor found so difficult to render in his translation of two poems by Jean Toomer. "Hence the characteristics of its images which, whether they are rare or abundant, adhere to the idea and feeling they express. Hence, in many cases, the limpidity of the text, because the words are rendered in their pristine purity and keep their paradisiacal power."[23]

For *Poésie 45*, Senghor selected two essential poems by Toomer: "Song of the Son" and "Georgia Dusk" (his translations follow the English original).

True to his intention of fully conveying the music in this verse, Senghor rendered the ending of "Song of the Son" thus:

> O Negro slaves, dark purple ripened plums,
> Squeezed, and bursting in the pinewood air,
> Passing, before they strip the old tree bare,
> One plum was saved for me, one seed becomes
> An everlasting song, a singing tree
> Caroling softly souls of slavery. . . .
>
> Esclaves noirs, prunes mûres de pourpre sombre,
> Chairs pressurées qui vous ouvrez à l'air parfumé de pins,
> Je passais avant qu'on eut dépouillé le vieil arbre,
> Une prune m'avait été sauvée, un seul noyau devient
> Un chant mémorial, un arbre qui chante,
> Modulant doucement des âmes d'esclaves. . . .[24]

Similarly, rhythm predominates over alliteration in Senghor's translation of the final stanza of "Georgia Dusk."

> The voices rise . . . the chorus of the cane
> Is caroling a vesper to the stars.
>
> O singers, resinous and soft, your songs
> Above the sacred whisper of the pines,
> Give virgin lips to cornfield concubines
> Bring dreams of Christ to dusky cane-lipped throngs.

Senghor translates these lines as:

> Leurs voix s'élèvent. . . . C'est le choeur de la canne
> Lançant suavement ses vêpres aux étoiles.
>
> O chanteurs, résineux et doux, vos chants
> Au-dessus du chuchotement sacré des pins
> Donnent des lèvres virginales aux concubines de la plantation,
> Font rêver du Christ des millions de noirs aux lèvres de canne.[25]

Senghor concludes that Negro poetry is "in one word, a poetry of flesh and earth, to speak like Hughes, a poetry of the peasant who has not severed ties with telluric forces."[26] Such a statement may surprise, considering the importance of the city and of the blues in the poetry of Langston Hughes, who was then extolled by the Left as the poet of the masses, i.e. mostly black industrial workers. But here Senghor selected "Our Land," "Earth Song," and "Minstrel Man" for translation, not Hughes's left-wing poems of the 1930s.

Therefore he could bring Hughes and Toomer closer together and claim that "this explains this cosmic rhythm, this music and imagery of rustling leaves, of scintillating stars"—which, in fact, are more characteristic of Toomer's *Cane*—although the quality of "deceptive limpidity" Senghor attributes to this poetry better applies to Hughes's verse. Here Senghor expresses, first of all, a notion that is dear to him and central to his conception of African Negritude: poetry is a "peasant/pagan" expression, and this is one of the many reasons why he thinks so highly of Toomer's two essentially rural pieces. Conversely, Senghor does not single out Countee Cullen's verse for any African American quality, and he is interested in translating "What Is Africa to Me?" for thematic rather than aesthetic reasons.

Not unexpectedly he concludes that the major offering of such poetry is not formal but spiritual. He calls it "a human poetry" and suggests that this is the reason why it deserves to be known. In this respect, he comes close to W.E.B. Du Bois's statement about the gift of the Negro in *The Souls of Black Folk*: the American Negro is a provider of soulfulness and the positive face of America. Finally, the Negro American is seen by Senghor as the representative of "black humanism" in a context similar to Claude McKay's or Langston Hughes's views: "America is not only a land of machines and records; it is also a land of youth and hope; and among its faces, her black face is one of the most thoroughly human."[27]

Thus in spite of Hughes's and Toomer's different poetic styles, social outlooks, and racial attitudes, both could bring grist to the mill of Negritude. Senghor pursued this argument in later essays and lectures. But, in his opinion, Langston Hughes (not Toomer) was the embodiment of the Harlem Renaissance. This movement comprised two trends—the poetry in dialect with James Weldon Johnson represented the epic and mystical trend; Sterling Brown and Hughes represented the elegiac and secular perspective. Yet both trends were close to the blues and spirituals.

In a 1950 lecture, Senghor used again much of his essay printed in *Poésie 45*. He saw McKay, Cullen, and Toomer as the best representatives of "learned poetry." The poems in which Negritude was proclaimed were not the "blackest" ones, since Negritude resided in style and emotion, not in skin color.

As a result of Senghor's translation of "Harvest Song," and especially "Song of the Son" and "Georgia Dusk," Toomer became slightly better known but somewhat limited to being a poet of the soil, the South, and the African heritage, whereas Toomer's own essay dealing with modernity had failed to call French attention to his modernism and his evocation of black city life.

When Marcel Beaufils published his book of poetry, *Christ noir*, he defined the bulk of black American poetry as an attempt to "sing one's pain in orphic chants, deep like the very stuff the world is made of."[28] He claimed that it could dig up gold from the Harlem underworld and testified to "a fateful and messianic loneliness exorcized by the jazz rhythms of Duke Ellington." On the title page, Beaufils's own poems were described as free adaptations of spirituals, blues, and poetry by Joseph Cotter, Countee Cullen, Georgia Douglas Johnson, Otto Leland Bohannan, Langston Hughes, Claude McKay, Jean Toomer, and Waring Cuney. The poem by Toomer that inspired him is "Harvest Song," somewhat misinterpreted, it appears, since Beaufils's adaptation restricts the aspirations of the black reaper to physical hunger. In 1948, Charles Cestre authored *Les poètes américains*, but only in the conclusion to his book does this professor in the English Department at the Sorbonne mention the names of a few black poets: "One would have to stop at the work of Negro poets, Paul Dunbar, James Weldon [*sic*], Fenton Johnson, Langston Hughes, Countée Cullen, Jean Toomer and Miss Weeden."[29]

Whereas *Sandy*, the translation of his novel *Not without Laughter*, was scantily reviewed in 1934, Langston Hughes benefited from a special treatment in France after the war and his reputation soon outshone Toomer's. But this was Hughes as a committed progressive rather than as a Harlem Renaissance poet. Reviews of his autobiography and his prewar novel stressed their value as testimonies to the depths of Negro life and the stereotypes about it, celebrating the scope of Hughes's illustration of black resilience. In 1948, in the newly launched *Présence africaine*, Pierre Minne claimed that "*The Big Sea* retraces, after Claude McKay and before Richard Wright, a quest for freedom which is being pursued from country to country, from continent to continent."[30] Hughes's writings were seen as the expression of mass conflicts as well as racial problems, and these would only be solved when economic justice was established. Hughes was routinely lauded in Communist publications, in opposition to the "renegade" Richard Wright. For instance, a 1949 issue of *Europe* provided an introduction to "the greatest black American poet" and printed the whole text of "La charrue de la liberté" ("Freedom's Plow").[31]

While new African American writers were hailed, one had to wait until the 1960s for Toomer's *Cane* to be (re)discovered in France, as it was in America, thanks to the Harper reprint prefaced by Arna Bontemps. The silence and seeming oblivion that followed the essays by Schoell and Senghor were largely due to the fact that *Cane* had never been translated and remained out of print until 1967. Jean Wagner had to buy a rare and expensive first edition when, in pre-Xerox times, he started work on his doctoral dissertation, which was published in 1963 as *Les poètes nègres des Etats-Unis: Le sentiment racial et religieux dans la poésie de P. L. Dunbar à Langston Hughes (1890–1940)*.[32]

A first-rate academic study of black American poetry, mostly of the New Negro movement, the work includes considerations on African American culture and the oral tradition, the minstrels, Dunbar and his contemporaries, the Harlem Renaissance ideology, and the roles of W.E.B. Du Bois and Marcus Garvey. The major chapters are detailed analyses of the themes and art of Hughes, McKay, Toomer, Cullen, J. W. Johnson, and Sterling Brown. They include detailed biographical sketches. In the some twenty-four pages devoted to Toomer, only his poetry is considered. Wagner remarks that *Cane* is almost entirely in prose, this probably being the reason why it has often been described as a novel. He further states that there is nothing of the novel genre in *Cane* and that the only genre to which it can be assigned is poetry. Yet, he never considers the pieces in poetic prose per se or analyzes them. The opening section, "The Destiny of Jean Toomer," takes into account Toomer's experience in Washington, D.C., and even his attempt at creating a synthesis transcending racial categories. The following section, "The Poetry of *Cane*, or, the Pilgrimage to the Origins," however, focuses exclusively on the rural South, although Wagner recognizes that Toomer had no intention of castigating the old South or of composing an apologia for his race. The works quoted and discussed are, once again, "Harvest Song," "Georgia Dusk," and "Song of the Sun," to which only one other poem, "Face," is added. Besides, possibly because Wagner considers only the verse in *Cane*—although he speaks of its prose as poetic—nothing is said of the short stories, whether set in rural Georgia or in the urban North, and Wagner at once moves from the verse in *Cane* on to considerations about Toomer's later career in his chapter entitled "Beyond Race: 'Blue Meridian.' "

In 1977, the U.S. Information Service African Book Bureau in Paris published a translation of *Cane* by Jean Wagner, entitled *Canne*, but, as was the case with all the volumes in the Nouveaux Horizons series, it was to be sold or distributed only in French-speaking African countries. As a result, one is still waiting for this fine French translation of Toomer's masterpiece to be made available, even though *Cane* enjoyed the "distinction" of being one of the three American literary works to be studied nationally for the competitive exam of *agrégation* for teachers of English during the school year 1997/1998.

Notes

Unless otherwise indicated, translations from the French are mine.

1. Jean Toomer to Mrs. Beardsley, November 1, 1930 (Toomer, Papers, Collection of American Literature, Yale University).
2. Claude McKay to Langston Hughes, August 8, 1925 (Collection of American Literature, Yale University).
3. René Maran, "Le mouvement négro-littéraire aux Etats-Unis," *Vient de paraître*,

no. 49 (December 1925): 645–646. White's novel appeared as *L'Etincelle* in the 1930s.

4. *Le Mercure de France*, no. 666 (March 15, 1926): 733. It was probably written by Jean Catel, who also contributed "Lettres anglo-américaines" to the December 1, 1927, issue of the *Mercure de France*. This included a presentation of *God's Trombones*, followed by excerpts from "The Creation."
5. Harold Salemson, "Quelques livres sur la question nègre aux Etats-Unis," *Le Monde*, October 1927.
6. Eugène Jolas, ed. *Anthologie de la nouvelle poésie américaine* (Paris: Editions Kra, 1928), 332.
7. "Ils sont des chanteurs spontanés en qui la culture du blanc n'a pas tari le jaillissement primitif. Ironiques et frémissants, ces bardes noirs disent les regrets, les rancunes, et les aspirations de leur race (si pathétiquement résumés par Eugene O'Neill dans *Emperor Jones*). Ils vantent leur grandeur passée: Egypte, Ethiopie, Abyssinie. . . . Ils adorent sans vergogne la Vénus noire. Ils rient de toutes leurs dents à la souffrance et à la laideur du blanc. Un étrange relent de paganisme flotte sur leur baptême chrétien; et quelle luxuriance d'images, quelle vivacité de rythmes!" (Jolas, *Anthologie*, 206–208.)
8. Franck Louis Schoell, "Un romancier noir américain: Jean Toomer," *Les Nouvelles littéraires*, no. 290 (May 5, 1928): 6.
9. Franck Louis Schoell, "La Renaissance nègre aux USA," *La Revue de Paris*, no. 1 (January 1, 1929): 124–165.
10. Franck Louis Schoell, "Un poète nègre: Langston Hughes," *Revue politique et littéraire*, no. 14 (June 20, 1929): 436–438.
11. "Voici notre vice: nous n'avons aucun attachement pour les choses que nous édifions. . . . Nous jetons de plus en plus à la poubelle. . . . Nous avons tendance à nous respecter de moins en moins, nous-mêmes et les autres" (Jean Toomer, "Lettre d'Amérique," *Bifur* [May 1, 1929]: 112).
12. " . . . la sensation de puissance et de plaisir que donne l'acte de gagner et de dépenser de l'argent" (Ibid., 114).
13. Ibid., 117.
14. "Je m'attends à voir cette circonstance même donner naissance à la solidarité entre individus. Je crois qu'elle produira un sens plus grand et plus efficace de responsabilité individuelle. Je m'attends à voir la domination des affaires produire le puissant jaillissement d'un mode nouveau de vie" (Ibid., 119).
15. "L'anarchie au sein de la révolution, voilà ce qu'il exige."
16. André Lévinson, "Aframérique," *Les Nouvelles littéraires* 7 (August 31, 1929): 6.
17. André Lévinson, "De Harlem à la Canebière," *Les Nouvelles littéraires* 7 (September 14, 1929): 7. This review was reprinted in *Figures américaines: Dix-huit études sur des écrivains de ce temps* (Paris: Victor Attinger, 1929), 177–195.
18. *Les Cahier libres*, n.s., 1, no. 6 (October 15, 1930): 353–354.
19. *La Revue du monde noir*, no. 1 (1930): 36–37.
20. Paulette Nardal, "Eveil de la conscience de race," *La Revue du monde noir*, no. 6 (1931): 25–31.
21. Aimé Césaire, "Introduction à la poésie nègre américaine," *Tropiques*, no. 2 (July 1941): 37–42.
22. "Quels sont les caractères de cette poésie? Elle est essentiellement non-sophistiquée, comme sa soeur l'africaine, elle reste près du chant. Elle est faite pour être chantée et dite, non pour être lue. D'où l'importance du rythme. Rythme nègre si despotique sous son aspect de liberté. D'où l'importance de la musique, si difficile à rendre dans la traduction d'un Toomer. D'où les caractères de l'image qui, rare ou pullulante, adhère étroitement à l'idée ou au sentiment. D'où souvent la limpidité

du texte, car les mots sont restitués à leur pureté première, conservant leur pouvoir paradisiaque. En un mot, poésie de chair et de terre . . . " (Léopold Sédar Senghor, "Trois poètes négro-américains," *Poésie 45*, no. 23 32).

23. Ibid., 33.
24. Ibid., 34.
25. Ibid., 35. See also "La poésie négro-américaine," in Senghor's *Liberté I: Négritude et humanisme* (Paris: Editions du Seuil, 1964), 119.
26. See note 25.
27. See note 25.
28. Marcel Beaufils, *Christ noir* (Lausanne: Abbaye du Livre, 1946), 7.
29. Charles Cestre, "Les poètes américains" (Paris: Presses Universitaires de France, 1948), 223.
30. Pierre Minne, "Langston Hughes, ou, 'Le train de la liberté,' " *Présence africaine*, no. 2 (January 1948): 340.
31. Renaud De Jouvenel, "D'une bibliothèque américaine," *Europe*, no. 39 (March 1949): 109. Also see E. Cary, "Trois cent trente ans d'esclavage," *Europe*, no. 50 (February 1950): 6–7.
32. Jean Wagner, *Les poètes nègres des Etats-Unis: Le sentiment racial et religieux dans la poésie de P. L. Dunbar à Langston Hughes (1890–1940)* (Paris: Librairie Istra, 1963).

Selected Bibliography

This is not an exhaustive bibliography. For further documentation one may consult the bibliographies that give a more complete listing of primary works (McKay, *African American Writers*, 439–440) or of critical essays (Reilly, "Annotated Checklist," and Jones, "Annotated Checklist").

Toomer's works are listed in two separate sections; critical works are listed in alphabetical order under the name of the author.

Jean Toomer

1. MAJOR WORKS AND COLLECTIONS

Cane. Introduction by Waldo Frank. New York: Boni and Liveright, 1923.

Reprint, 1927. Reprint, New York: University Place Press, 1967. Reprint, with an introduction by Arna Bontemps, New York: Harper and Row, 1969. "*Cane*": *An Authoritative Text, Background, and Criticism;* reprint, edited by and with an introduction by Darwin T. Turner, New York: Liveright, 1975. Critical edition, edited by Darwin T. Turner, New York: Norton, 1988.

A Jean Toomer Reader: Selected Unpublished Writings. Ed. Frederik L. Rusch. New York: Oxford University Press, 1993.

Essentials: Definitions and Aphorisms. 1931. 2d ed. Ed. Rudolph P. Byrd. Athens: University of Georgia Press, 1991.

The Wayward and the Seeking: A Collection of Writings by Jean Toomer. Ed. Darwin T. Turner. Washington, D.C.: Howard University Press, 1980.

The Collected Poems of Jean Toomer. Ed. Robert B. Jones and Margery Toomer Latimer. With an introduction by Robert B. Jones. Chapel Hill: University of North Carolina Press, 1988.

Jean Toomer: Selected Essays and Literary Criticism. Ed. Robert B. Jones. Knoxville: University of Tennessee Press, 1996.

The best collection is Turner, *Wayward*, compiled from earlier editions and from Toomer's manuscripts (see his introduction to each section).

2. OTHER WORKS (F: FICTION. P: POEMS. E: ESSAYS. D: DRAMA)

"An Open Letter to Gorham Munson." *S4N*, no. 25 (March–April 1923). (E)
"Gum." *Chapbook*, no. 36 (April 1923): 2. (P)
"Notations on *The Captain's Doll*." *Broom* 5 (August 1923): 47–48. (E)
"Waldo Frank's *Holiday*." *Dial* 75 (October 1923): 383–386. (E)
"Zona Gale's *Faint Perfume*." *Broom* 5 (October 1923): 180–181. (E)
"The South in Literature." In Jones, *Selected Essays*, 1996. (E)
"The Critic of Waldo Frank: Criticism, an Art Form." *S4N*, no. 30 (September 1923-January 1924). (E)
"Oxen Cart and Warfare." *Little Review* 10 (fall/winter 1924–1925): 44–48. (E)
"Easter." *Little Review* 11 (spring 1925): 3–7. (F)
Balo. In *Plays of Negro Life*, ed. Alain Locke and Montgomery Gregory, 269–286. New York: Harper and Brothers, 1927. (D)
"Reflections." *Dial* 86 (April 1929): 314. (P)
"Race Problems and Modern Society." In *Problems of Civilization*. Ed. Baker Brownell. Vol. 7 of *Man and His World*, ed. E. Huntington et al., 67–111. New York: Van Nostrand, 1929. (E)
"York Beach." In *New American Caravan*, ed. Alfred Kreymborg, Lewis Munford, and Paul Rosenfeld, 12–83. New York: Macaulay, 1929. (F)
"As the Eagle Soars." *Crisis* 41 (April 1932): 116. (P)
"Brown River Smile." *Pagany* 3 (winter 1932): 29–33. (P)
"The Hill." In *America and Alfred Stieglitz: A Collective Portrait*, ed. Waldo Frank et al., 295–303. New York: Doubleday, Doran, 1934. (E)
"A New Force for Cooperation." *Adelphi* 9 (October 1934): 25–31. (E)
"Of a Certain November." *Dubuque Dial* 4 (1 November 1935): 107–112. (F)
"For M. W." *Pembroke Magazine* 6 (January 1975): 68. (P)
"Glaciers of Dusk." *Pembroke Magazine* 6 (January 1975): 68. (P)
(Some of the essays are reprinted in Jones, "Annotated Checklist.")

Critical Works on Toomer and Related Issues

Abbot, Megan. " 'Dorris Dances . . . John Dreams': Free Indirect Discourse and Female Subjectivity in *Cane*." *Soundings* 80 (1997): 455–474.
Armstrong, John. "The Real Negro." 1923. Reprinted in *Studies in Cane*, ed. Frank Durham, 27–28. Columbus, OH: Charles E. Merrill, 1971.
Austin, John Langshaw, and J. O. Urmson, eds. *How to Do Things with Words*. Oxford: Clarendon Press, 1962.
Bachelard, Gaston. *L'air et les songes: Essai sur l'imagination du mouvement*. Paris: Jose Corti, 1914.
———. *The Poetics of Space*. Trans. Maria Jolas. Boston: Beacon Press, 1969.
Baker, Houston A., Jr. "Journey toward Black Art: Jean Toomer's *Cane*." In *Singers of Daybreak*, 53–80. Washington, DC: Howard University Press, 1974.
———. *Modernism and the Harlem Renaissance*. Chicago: University of Chicago Press, 1987.
Beardsley, Monroe C. "The Metaphorical Twist." *Philosophy and Phenomenological Research* 22 (March 1962): 300.
Bell, Bernard. "A Key to the Poems in Cane." In *Jean Toomer: A Critical Evaluation*, ed. Therman B. O'Daniel, 321–328. Washington, D. C.: Howard University Press, 1988.
Benson, Brian Joseph, and Mabel Mayle Dillard. *Jean Toomer*. Boston: Twayne, 1980.
Bone, Robert. "Jean Toomer." In *The Negro Novel in America*, ed. Robert Bone, 80–89. 1958. Reprint, New Haven, Conn.: Yale University Press, 1965.

———. "Jean Toomer." In *Down Home: A History of Afro-American Short Fiction from Its Beginnings to the End of the Harlem Renaissance*, part 2, ed. Robert Bone, 204–238, 301–303. New York: Putnam, 1975.

Bontemps, Arna. "The Negro Renaissance: Jean Toomer and the Harlem Writers of the 1920s." In *Anger and Beyond: The Negro Writer in the U.S.*, ed. Herbert Hill, 20–36. New York: Harper and Row, 1966.

Bourdieu, Pierre. *The Field of Cultural Production: Essays on Art and Literature*. Ed. Randal Johnson. London: Polity Press, 1993.

Bradley, David. "Looking behind *Cane*." *Southern Review* 21, 3 (1985): 682–694.

———. "Looking Behind *Cane*." In *Afro-American Writing Today*, ed. James Olney. Baton Rouge: Louisiana State University Press, 1985.

Brannan, Tim. "Up from the Dusk: Interpretations of Jean Toomer's 'Blood-Burning Moon.'" *Pembroke Magazine* 8 (1977): 167–172.

Bush, Ann Marie, and Louis D. Mitchell. "Jean Toomer: A Cubist Poet." *BALF* 17, 3 (1983): 106–108.

Byrd, Rudolph P. *Jean Toomer's Years with Gurdjieff: Portrait of an Artist, 1923–1936*. Athens: University of Georgia Press, 1990.

———. Foreword to *Essentials*, by Jean Toomer. Athens: University of Georgia Press, 1991.

Chase, Patricia. "The Women in *Cane*." *CLA Journal* 14, 3 (March 1971): 259–273.

Clark, Michael. "Frustrated Redemption: Jean Toomer's Women in *Cane*, Part One." *CLA Journal* 22, 4 (June 1979): 319–334.

Clary, F., and C. Julien, eds. *"Cane," Jean Toomer and the Harlem Renaissance*. Paris: Ellipses, 1997.

Cooper, Wayne F., ed. *The Dialect Poems of Claude McKay*. 2 vols. in 1. Plainview, N.Y.: Books for Librarians Press, 1972.

Cordesse, Gérard. "The Two Models in *Cane*." In *"Cane," Jean Toomer and the Harlem Renaissance*, ed. F. Clary and C. Julien, 22–42. Paris: Ellipses, 1997.

Cullen, Countee, ed. *Caroling Dusk: An Anthology of Verse by Negro Poets*. New York: Harper, 1927.

Dardis, Tom. *Firebrand: The Life of Horace Liveright*. New York: Random House, 1995.

Donohue, Charles Terrance. "The Making of a Black Poet: A Critical Biography of Claude McKay for the Years 1889–1922." Ph.D. diss., Temple University, 1972.

Douglass, Frederick. *Narrative of the Life of Frederick Douglass, an American Slave*. 1845. Reprint, New York: Penguin, 1986.

Du Bois, W.E.B. *The Souls of Black Folk*. 1903. Reprint, New York: Penguin, 1989.

Du Bois, W.E.B., and Alain Locke. "The Younger Literary Movement." *Crisis* 27 (1924): 161–163.

Durand, Gilbert. *L'imagination symbolique*. Paris: P.U.F., 1964.

Durham, Frank, ed. *The Merrill Studies in "Cane."* Columbus, Ohio: Charles E. Merrill, 1971.

Dutch, William L. "Three Enigmas: Karintha, Becky, and Carma." In *Jean Toomer: A Critical Evaluation*, ed. Therman O'Daniel, 265–268. Washington, D.C.: Howard University Press, 1988.

Eldredge, Charles C. *Georgia O'Keeffe*. New York: Harry N. Abrams, 1987.

Fabre, Michel. "Notes towards a Hypothetical Lesson on Jean Toomer's *Cane*." In *"Cane," Jean Toomer and the Harlem Renaissance*, ed. F. Clary and C. Julien, 11–21. Paris: Ellipses, 1997.

Faulkner, Howard. "The Buried Life: Jean Toomer's *Cane*." *Studies in Black Literature* 7, 1 (winter 1976): 1–5.

Foley, Barbara, "Jean Toomer's Sparta." *American Literature* 67 (1995): 747–775.

———. "Jean Toomer's Washington and the Politics of Class: From 'Blue Veins' to Seventh-Street Rebels." *Modern Fiction Studies* 42, 2 (1996): 289–321.

Foucault, Michel. *The History of Sexuality: An Introduction*. Vol. 1. Trans. Robert Hurley. 1978. Reprint, New York: Vintage Books, 1990.

Frank, Waldo. *Our America*. New York: Boni and Liveright, 1919.

———. [Search-Light, pseud.]. *Time Exposures*. New York: Boni and Liveright, 1926.

Fullinwider, S. P. "Jean Toomer: Lost Generation or Negro Renaissance?" *Phylon* 27, 4 (winter 1966): 396–403.

———. "The Renaissance in Literature." In *The Mind and Mood of Black America*, ed. S. P. Fullinwider, 123–171. Homewood, Ill.: Dorsey, 1969.

Galton, Francis. *Hereditary Genius: An Inquiry into Its Laws and Consequences*. 1869. Reprint, London: Macmillan, 1925.

Gates, Henry Louis. *Figures in Black: Words, Signs, and the "Racial" Self*. New York: Oxford University Press, 1987.

———. *The Signifying Monkey: A Theory of African-American Literary Criticism*. New York: Oxford University Press, 1988.

Gates, Henry Louis, and Nellie Y. McKay, eds. *The Norton Anthology of African American Literature*. New York: W. W. Norton, 1997.

Gilmer, Walker. *Horace Liveright: Publisher of the Twenties*. New York: David Lewis, 1970.

Green, Constance McLaughlin. *The Secret City: A History of Race Relations in the Nation's Capital*. Princeton, N.J.: Princeton University Press, 1967.

Gregory, Montgomery. "Our Book Shelf." *Opportunity* 1 (1923): 374–75.

Griffin, Farah J. *"Who Set You Flowin'?": The African-American Migration Narrative*. New York: Oxford University Press, 1994.

Griffin, John C. "Jean Toomer: A Bibliography." *South Carolina Review* 7, 2 (April 1975): 61–64.

Gurdjieff, G. I. *Récits de Belzébuth à son petit-fils*. Paris: Denoël, 1976.

Gysin, Fritz. *The Grotesque in American Negro Fiction: Jean Toomer, Richard Wright, and Ralph Ellison*. Bern, Switzerland: Francke Verlag, 1975.

Harris, Trudier. *Exorcising Blackness: Historical and Literary Lynching and Burning Rituals*. Bloomington: Indiana University Press, 1984.

Harris, Trudier, and Thadious M. Davis, eds. *Dictionary of Literary Biography*. Vol. 51, *Afro-American Writers from the Harlem Renaissance to 1940*. Detroit, Mich.: Gale Research, 1987.

Heidegger, Martin. *What Is Called Thinking*. Trans. F. D. Wieck and J. C. Grey. New York: Harper and Row, 1968.

Herschberger, Ruth. "The Structure of Metaphor." *Kenyon Review* 5 (1943): 434.

Hester, Marcus B. *The Meaning of Poetic Metaphor*. Mouton: The Hague, 1967.

Hicks, Onita. "Jean Toomer and the Politics and Poetics of National Identity." *Contributions to Black Studies* 7 (1985–1986): 22–44.

Hoffman, Frederick J., et al. *The Little Magazine: A History and a Bibliography*. Princeton, N.J.: Princeton University Press, 1947.

hooks, bell. *Yearning: Race, Gender and Cultural Politics*. London: Turnaround, 1991.

Huggins, Nathan Irvin. *Harlem Renaissance*. New York: Oxford University Press, 1971.

Hughes, Langston. "The Negro Artist and the Racial Mountain." *The Nation* 122 (23 June 1926): 692–694.

Husserl, Edmund. *Logical Investigations* I. Trans. J. N. Findley. London: Routledge and Kegan Paul, 1970.

Hutchinson, George B. "Jean Toomer and the 'New Negroes' of Washington." *American Literature* 63 (December 1991): 683–692.

———. "Jean Toomer and American Racial Discourse." *Texas Studies in Literature and Language* 35, 2 (1993): 226–250.

———. "The Whitman Legacy and the Harlem Renaissance." In *Walt Whitman: The Centennial Essays*, ed. Ed Folsom, 201–216. Iowa City: University of Iowa Press, 1994.

———. *The Harlem Renaissance in Black and White*. Cambridge, Mass.: Belknap Press of Harvard University Press, 1996.

Jacobson, Matthew Frye. *Whiteness of a Different Color: European Immigrants and the Alchemy of Race*. Cambridge, Mass.: Harvard University Press, 1998.

Jakobson, Roman. "Closing Statements: Linguistics Poetics." In *Style in Language*, ed. T. A. Sebeok. Cambridge, Mass.: MIT Press, 1960.

Johnson, James Weldon. *God's Trombones—Seven Negro Sermons in Verse*. 1927. Reprint, New York: Penguin Books, 1990.

Jones, Robert B. *Jean Toomer and the Prison House of Thought: A Phenomenology of the Spirit*. Amherst: University of Massachusetts Press, 1993.

———. "Jean Toomer: An Annotated Checklist of Criticism, 1923–1993." *Resources for American Literary Studies* 21, no. 1 (1995): 68–121.

———. *Critical Essays on Jean Toomer*. Forthcoming. Boston: G. K. Hall.

———, ed. Introduction to *Jean Toomer: Selected Essays and Literary Criticism*, ed. Robert B. Jones. Knoxville: University of Tennessee Press, 1996.

Jones, Robert B., and M. Toomer Latimer, eds. *The Collected Poems of Jean Toomer*. Chapel Hill: University of North Carolina Press, 1988.

Josephson, Matthew. "Great American Novels." *Broom* 5 (1923): 178–180.

Kanneh, Kadiatu. *African Identities*. London: Routledge, 1998.

Kerman, Cynthia Earl, and Richard Eldridge. *The Lives of Jean Toomer: A Hunger for Wholeness*. Baton Rouge: Louisiana State University Press, 1987.

Kevles, Daniel J. *In the Name of Eugenics: Genetics and the Uses of Human Heredity*. New York: Alfred A. Knopf, 1985.

Larson, Charles R. *Invisible Darkness: Jean Toomer and Nella Larsen*. Iowa City: University of Iowa Press, 1993.

Lasker, Bruno. "Doors Opened Southward." 1923. Reprinted in *Studies in "Cane,"* ed. Frank Durham, 29–30. Columbus, Ohio: Charles E. Merrill, 1971.

Lears, T. J. Jackson. "Uneasy Courtship: Modern Art and Modern Advertising." *American Quarterly* 39 (1987): 133–154.

———. *Fables of Abundance: A Cultural History of Advertising in America*. New York: Basic Books, 1994.

Lewis, David Levering. "Stars." In *When Harlem Was in Vogue*, 50–88. New York: Alfred A. Knopf, 1981.

Lindberg, Kathryne V. "Raising *Cane* on the Theoretical Plane: Jean Toomer's Racial Personae." In *Cultural Difference and the Literary Text: Pluralism and the Limits of Authenticity in North American Literatures*, ed. Winfried Siemerling and Katrin Schwenk. Iowa City: University of Iowa Press, 1996.

"Literary Vaudeville." Review of *Cane*, by Jean Toomer.1923. Reprinted in *Studies in "Cane,"* ed. Frank Durham, 34. Columbus, Ohio: Charles E. Merrill, 1971.

Littell, Robert. Review of *Cane*, by Jean Toomer. *New Republic* 37 (1923): 126.

Locke, Alain. Foreword to *The New Negro*, ed. Alain Locke. 1925. Reprint, New York: Atheneum, 1992.

———. "The New Negro." In *The New Negro*, ed. Alain Locke. New York: Atheneum, 1992.

Ludwig, Richard M., and Clifford A. Nault. *Annals of American Literature, 1602–1983*. New York: Oxford University Press, 1986.

Marchand, Roland. *Advertising the American Dream: Making Way for Modernity, 1920–1940*. Berkeley: University of California Press, 1985.

Massey, Douglas S., and Nancy A. Denton, *American Apartheid: Segregation in the Making of the Underclass*. Cambridge, Mass.: Harvard University Press, 1993.
May, Henry F. *The End of American Innocence: A Study of the First Years of Our Own Time, 1912–1917*. London: Jonathan Cape, 1960.
McClure, John. Review of *Cane*, by Jean Toomer. *Double Dealer* 6 (1924): 26–27.
McKay, Claude. *Harlem Shadows*. New York: Harcourt Brace, 1922.
McKay, Nellie Y. *Jean Toomer, Artist: A Study of His Literary Life and Work, 1894–1936*. Chapel Hill: University of North Carolina Press, 1984.
McLaughlin, Constance G. *The Secret City: A History of Race Relations in the Nation's Capital*. Princeton, N.J.: Princeton University Press, 1967.
Michlin, Monica. *Jean Toomer, "Cane."* Paris: CNED, Didier Concours, 1997.
Morrison, Toni. *The Bluest Eye*. 1979. Reprint, London: Picador, 1990.
Munro, C. Lynn. "Jean Toomer: A Bibliography of Secondary Sources." *Black American Literature Forum* 21 (fall 1987): 275–287.
Munson, Gorham. "The Significance of Jean Toomer." In *Destinations: A Canvas of American Literature since 1900*, ed. Gorham Munson, 178–186. New York: J. H. Sears, 1928.
Nadell, Martha J. " 'Nor Can I Reduce This Experience to a Medium': Art, Literature, and Race in America, 1920s–1950s." Ph.D. diss., Harvard University. Forthcoming.
North, Michael. *The Dialect of Modernism: Race, Language, and Twentieth-Century Literature*. New York: Oxford University Press, 1994.
O'Daniel, Therman, ed. *Jean Toomer: A Critical Evaluation*. Washington, D.C.: Howard University Press, 1988.
Omi, Michael, and Howard Winant. *Racial Formation in the United States: From the 1960s to the 1980s*. New York: Routledge, 1986.
Ouspenski, P. D. *Tertium Organum: A Key to the Enigmas of the World*. New York: Vintage Books, 1970.
Perry, Margaret. *The Harlem Renaissance: An Annotated Bibliography and Commentary*. New York: Garland, 1982.
Posnock, Ross. *Color and Culture: Black Writing and the Making of the Modern Intellectual*. Cambridge, Mass.: Harvard University Press, 1998.
Rawick, George P., ed. *The American Slave: A Composite Autobiography*. Vol. 3, *South Carolina Narratives*. Pt. 4. Westport, Conn.: Greenwood Press, 1972.
Reilly, John M. "The Search for Black Redemption: Jean Toomer's *Cane*." *Studies in the Novel* 2 (fall 1970): 312–324.
———. "Jean Toomer: An Annotated Checklist of Criticism." *Resources for American Literary Study* 4 (spring 1974): 27–56.
Rice, Herbert W. "Repeated Images in Part One of *Cane*." *BALF* 17, 3 (1983): 100–104.
———. "An Incomplete Circle: Repeated Images in Part II of *Cane*." *CLA Journal* 29, 4 (1985–1986): 442–461.
Rosenfeld, Paul. "Jean Toomer." In *Men Seen: Twenty-Four Modern Authors*, New York: Dial, 1925.
Rusch, Frederik L. "The Blue Man: Jean Toomer's Solution to His Problems of Identity." *Obsidian* 6 (spring–summer 1980): 38–54.
———. "A Tale of the Country Round: Jean Toomer's Legend, 'Monrovia.' " *MELUS* 7 (summer 1980): 37–46.
———. "Jean Toomer's Early Identification: The Two Black Plays." *MELUS* 13 (spring/summer 1986): 115–124.
———. Letter to Michael Soto, 4 June 1998.

Schultz, Joachim. *Wild, Irre und Rein: Wörterbuch zum Primitivismus der literarischen Avantgarden in Deutschland und Frankreich zwischen 1900 und 1940*. Gießen, Germany: Anabas, 1995.

Scruggs, Charles W. "The Mark of Cain and the Redemption of Art: A Study in Theme and Structure of Jean Toomer's *Cane*." *American Literature* 44 (May 1972): 276–291.

———. "Jean Toomer: Fugitive." *American Literature* 47 (March 1975): 84–96.

———. " 'My Chosen World': Jean Toomer's Articles in the New York *Call*." *Arizona Quarterly* 52 (1995): 103–126.

Shelley, Mary. *Frankenstein*. London: Penguin Books, 1992.

Smith, J. David. *The Eugenic Assault on America: Scenes in Red, White, and Black*. Fairfax, Va.: George Mason University Press, 1993.

Solard, Alain. "Myth and Narrative Fiction in *Cane*: 'Blood-Burning Moon.' " In *"Cane," Jean Toomer and the Harlem Renaissance*, ed. F. Clary and C. Julien, 136–148. Paris: Ellipses, 1997.

Soto, Michael. "Literary History and the Age of Jazz: Generation, Renaissance, and American Literary Modernism." Ph.D. dissertation, Harvard University, 1999.

Tebbel, John. *The Golden Age between Two Wars, 1920–1940*. Vol. 3 of *A History of Book Publishing in the United States*. New York: R. R. Bowker, 1978.

Terris, Daniel. "Waldo Frank and the Rediscovery of America, 1889–1929." Ph.D. diss, Harvard University, 1992.

Thompson, Larry E. "Jean Toomer: As Modern Man." *The Harlem Renaissance Remembered*, ed. Arna Bontemps, 51–62, 279. New York: Dodd, Mead, 1972.

Tillery, Tyrone. *Claude McKay: A Black Poet's Struggle for Identity*. Amherst: University of Massachusetts Press, 1992.

Turner, Darwin T. "The Failure of the Playwright." *CLA Journal* 10 (June 1967): 308–318.

———. "Jean Toomer: Exile." In *In a Minor Chord: Three Afro-American Writers and Their Search for Identity*, ed. Darwin T. Turner, 1–59, 121–131, 140–143. Carbondale: Southern Illinois University Press, 1971.

———. Introduction to *Cane*, by Jean Toomer. New York: Liveright, 1975.

———, ed. *The Wayward and the Seeking: A Collection of Writings by Jean Toomer*. Washington, D.C.: Howard University Press, 1980.

———, ed. *Cane*, by Jean Toomer. New York: Norton, 1988.

Wagner, Jean. "Jean Toomer." In *Black Poets of the United States from Paul Lawrence Dunbar to Langston Hughes*, trans. Kenneth Douglas, 259–281, 531–532, 541–542. Urbana: University of Illinois Press, 1973.

Wall, Joseph S., and William M. Ross. *Sorghum Production and Utilization*. Westport, Conn.: Avi, 1970.

Washington D.C: A Guide to the Nation's Capital. Works Progress Administration. 1942. Reprint, New York: Hastings House, 1968.

West, James L. W. *American Authors and the Literary Marketplace since 1900*. Philadelphia: University of Pennsylvania Press, 1988.

White, Walter. *Rope and Faggot*. 1929. Reprint, New York: Arno Press, 1969.

Whyde, Janet. "Mediating Forms: Narrating the Body in Jean Toomer's *Cane*." *Southern Literary Journal* 26, 1 (1993): 42–53.

Wideman, John Edgar. *Fatheralong*. New York: Random House, 1994.

Williams, Diana I. "Jean Toomer's Art and Ideology: Echoes of Eugenics." *Harvard College Forum* 9 (spring 1995): 1–12.

Williamson, Joel. *New People: Miscegenation and Mulattoes in the United States*. 1980. Reprint, New York: New York University Press, 1984.

Wittgenstein, Ludwig. *Philosophical Investigations*. Ed. G.H.M Anscombe. 3d ed. Oxford: Basil Blackwell, 1968.

Papers

Toomer, Jean. Papers. Collection of American Literature, Yale University. Beinecke Rare Book and Manuscript Library, New Haven, Connecticut.

About the Contributors

FRANÇOISE CLARY is a professor of American studies and head of the African American studies program at Rouen University, France. A contributor to *American Literary Scholarship*, she is the author of *L'espoir de vivre*, a critical study of the African American novel from Chester Himes to Hal Bennett, of *Jean Toomer et la Renaissance de Harlem*, and of essays on African American authors, racial Christianity in America, ethnocentrism and acculturation, and Affirmative Action. She edited *Black American Stories* and coedited *"Cane," Jean Toomer and the Harlem Renaissance*.

CÉCILE COQUET is an associate professor in American studies at the University of Aix-Marseille, France. She earned her Ph.D. on the topic of African American folk preaching. She was a teaching assistant in Romance languages and literatures at Harvard University and taught American history and literature first at Paris 7. She intends to concentrate on cultural and religious studies from a transatlantic viewpoint. Previous publication: an article on Melville's *The Confidence-Man* (1993).

GENEVIÈVE FABRE is a professor at the University of Paris VII Denis Diderot, where she is the director of the Center for African American Research. The author of books on James Agee and on African American Theater, she has contributed to several collective volumes and encyclopedias. In addition to being the author of books on F. Scott Fitzgerald and on American minorities, she has edited or coedited several volumes, such as on Hispanic literatures, on Barrio culture in the United States, and on ethnicity; two volumes on

"Feasts and Celebrations among Ethnic Communities"; two volumes on Toni Morrison; and a volume on *History and Memory in African American Culture*. She is now coediting, with Michel Feith, a collection of essays on the Harlem Renaissance. A fellow at the Du Bois Institute, Harvard, the National Humanities Center, and the American Antiquarian Society, she is currently working on African American celebrative culture (1730–1880).

MICHEL FABRE is professor emeritus at the University of Paris III (Sorbonne Nouvelle) and president of the Cercle d'Etudes Africaines-Américaines. He is the author of *The Unifinished Quest of Richard Wright*. His recent books include *From Harlem to Paris: Black American Writers in France, 1840–1980* (1991), *The French Critical Reception of African-American Literature, An Annotated Bibliography* (1993), and *The Several Lives of Chester Himes*, with Edward Margolies (1997).

MICHEL FEITH is an associate professor at the University of Nantes, France. He has spent several years abroad; his experience of living in Australia, Japan, and the United States has sensitized him to the issues of multiculturalism. He wrote a doctoral thesis on "Myth and History in Chinese American and Chicano Literature" (1995), and his publications include articles on Maxine Hong Kingston, John Edgar Wideman, and the Harlem Renaissance.

YVES-CHARLES GRANDJEAT is a professor of North American literature at the University of Bordeaux III, France, where he is the codirector of the Cultures et Littératures d'Amérique du Nord (CLAN) research center. After specializing in Chicano and then U.S. Latino cultures and literatures, on which he has published two books and numerous articles, he has developed an interest in African American literature that has led him to contribute papers on slave narratives as well as the fiction of John Edgar Wideman, J. A. Williams, and Charles E. Johnson.

GEORGE HUTCHINSON is Tarkington Professor of Literary Studies at Indiana University, Bloomington. He is the author, most recently, of *The Harlem Renaissance in Black and White* and is currently writing a cultural biography of Nella Larsen.

WOLFGANG KARRER, is a professor of American Literature at the University of Osnabrück, Germany. He is the author of publications on African American fiction, intertextuality, modern poetry, popular culture, Chicano literature, and literary history.

MONICA MICHLIN teaches American literature and civilization at the University of Paris IV. She wrote her thesis on Toni Morrison, with an emphasis on the "forbidden voices" that committed contemporary authors (African American and others) place at the center of their work. In a similar perspective, she is working on the voice of the abused child in contemporary American writing. She has published a book on Jean Toomer, *Jean Toomer's "Cane"* (1997).

MARTHA JANE NADELL is a Ph.D. candidate in the History of American Civilization Program at Harvard University and is completing a dissertation entitled " 'Nor Can I Reduce This Experience to a Medium': Race, Art, and Literature in America, 1920s to 1950s."

WERNER SOLLORS teaches African American Studies and English at Harvard University. Most recently he published *Neither Black Nor White Yet Both: Thematic Explorations of Interracial Literature* (1999) and edited *Multilingual America: Transnationalism, Ethnicity, and the Languages of America* (1998), *Interracialism: Black-White Intermarriage in American History, Literature, and Law* (2000), *The Life Stories of Undistinguished Americans* (expanded edition, 2000), *The Multilingual Anthology of American Literature* (2000), and The Norton Critical Edition of *Olaudah Equiano* (2000).

MICHAEL SOTO is an assistant professor of English at Trinity University in San Antonio, Texas. He is currently completing a study of modernist literary movements in the United States, tentatively titled *The Modernist Nation: Generation, Renaissance, and Twentieth-Century American Literature*.

DIANA I. WILLIAMS is a Ph.D. candidate in the History of American Civilization Program at Harvard University. Her research focuses on ideologies of race and systems of racial classification in North America and the Caribbean in the nineteenth and twentieth centuries and on Afro-Latin communities in the United States. She is currently conducting research for a dissertation on the history of interracial sex and marriage in nineteenth-century Louisiana.

Index